Early Childhood Education Today

George S. Morrison

Edinboro State College

Charles E. Merrill Publishing Company
A Bell & Howell Company
Columbus, Ohio 43216

Published by
Charles E. Merrill Publishing Company
A Bell & Howell Company
Columbus, Ohio 43216

This book was set in Times Roman.
The Production Editor was Jan Hall.
The cover was designed by Will Chenoweth.

All photographs were taken by George S.
Morrison.

International Standard Book Number: 0–675–08619–1
Library of Congress Catalog Number: 75–40524

4 5 6 7 8 9—81 80 79

Printed in the United States of America

*This book is affectionately dedicated to B.J.,
a very able helpmate.*

Foreword

For many years professional care for children under public school age was available only to those who could afford private nursery school fees, or to those working mothers lucky enough to find a properly run day care center. America, compared with other industrialized nations, has shamefully neglected its preschool children. We castigate mothers on welfare rolls, but provide them with two alternatives: the Busy Bee Day Care Center run by a woman who tossed a coin to decide whether to "take care" of children or do housework; or the neighbor woman with whom children may be left for quite casual care. All too often that care consists of sitting the children before the television set for as long as possible, then playing rock recordings loud and clear to which the children can mill about shouting as they go, then settling them down, if possible, for coloring exercises, until the time when tired mothers pick up tired, over-stimulated, and often cross children.

Dr. Morrison has described in a thorough and professional fashion the various types of quality care for young children. He has done his homework well; students reading appropriate chapters will gain a first-rate knowledge of open education, Head Start, day care, Montessori nursery schools, Piagetian curricula, and special language development programs. Dr. Morrison not only provides factual information about staff, goals, financing, daily schedules, and parent involvement, but he also sets forth the strengths and weaknesses of each type of program. The reader who is acquainted with Head Start as a much maligned enterprise will be agreeably surprised with the author's evaluation of it. I share his faith in the program. More than any other form of preschool education Head Start insists upon parents and staff setting common goals for children. This task is not always easy; parents may insist, "I want my kid to learn to read, not play all day" or "I don't send my kid to school to be yelled at and slapped" when the philosophy of the staff is very different. As such differences are threshed out and common goals are set for children, healthy socialization can proceed. Hopefully, as Dr. Morrison urges, these goals will be humane in character, so that eventually the highly materialistic, competitive, individualistic and destructive strands in the American character will fade away.

I like Dr. Morrison's chapters on the historical figures in preschool education. Students *should* be literate in their field and acquainted with the theories of Luther, Comenius, Rousseau, Pestalozzi, Froebel, Dewey and Piaget. Dr. Morrison's discussion makes these theories very relevant to the problems of today; we see that some of the ideas we think of as contemporary actually date back several hundreds of years!

Early Childhood Education Today is not confined to preschool education, but deals with early childhood education for children through age eight. Open education, therefore, receives a thorough treatment. Dr. Morrison is practical as well as theoretical, so the student gets a clear picture of open classrooms in operation. The author is perhaps more sanguine than I about their future. There are too many hastily conceived and mistaken applications of theory to do the concept justice. Removing classroom walls to put 100 children together is hardly progress to those of us who have fought for small classes where teacher and children can get to know one another on a humane, face-to-face basis. And there *is* a limit as to how much children get out of macrame, working with "found" objects, seriating leaves or stones, measuring classrooms, and doing workbook exercises. Yes, workbook exercises. They reassure the teacher that his or her children are covering the "fundamentals."

With the number of schools devoted to the "basics" increasing each day, the pendulum may be swinging back toward the traditional, as it did after the progressive education era. However, each new liberalizing movement does leave a residue of more humane classroom procedures, with more room for children to acquire knowledge at their own rate. We hope that open education will leave exactly such a legacy. Meanwhile let us not take too literally claims which attribute only virtue to open education and only vice to the traditional. There are good and bad classrooms in both camps.

Perhaps the most controversial chapter in the book is the one on behavior modification. Dr. Morrison gives the reader a clear description of the principles and practices of behavior modification in classroom settings. His position is that teachers are already using reinforcers, and that they ought to use them knowledgeably. With this position I couldn't agree more, but I would add two important cautions. First, there are many researchers, including those in the behavior modification school, who argue against using any punishment because of its adverse effects; they would ignore the bad and redirect the child into constructive behaviors where positive reinforcement will ensue. Second, Levine and Fasnacht (*Amer. Psychol.* 29:816–820, 1974) and others point out that token rewards may lead to token learning. Their position is that token type programs, since they tend to decrease the *intrinsic* value of an activity, may actually do more harm than good. They are not implying that operant approaches are without value, but they do urge that, since tokens were not necessary for the acquisition of problem behaviors, "we search for the 'natural' reinforcers of problem behaviors as a significant point of intervention." We *do* need information about causes of behavior.

I am glad to have had the chance to write a foreword for a clear, readable, sensible and sound text on early childhood education.

Celia Stendler Lavatelli

Preface

Students need more information about teaching, a profession towards which they commit four years of education. In teaching and advising them in elementary and early childhood education, it is my experience that they have a desire for three kinds of information. First, they want to know more about the career they have chosen, for in many instances, they have made decisions without knowing much about the field. Some students have a romantic view of teaching which idealizes a teacher's life as being devoted to doing good, saving children from eternal ignorance, and having the answers to all questions. This view is a powerful motivating force for entering the profession. Other students have decided to teach young children because of the recommendation of friends or the pressure of parents who are anxious to see them economically secure (so they think) with a teaching degree.

Secondly, students want to know about particular areas of teaching. Many are not sure if they want to major in special education, a subject area, or early childhood education. In many schools of education, the decision to specialize has to be made at the end of the sophomore year. Consequently, students seeking information to help in the decision-making process often elect an introductory course in education. Such students need a broad picture of education in general and early childhood education in particular.

There is a third group of students who want to know specifically what to do with children in the classroom. They desire a "How to Do It" or "cookbook approach" to teaching. However, just as books on the methodology of golf cannot lower your golf score, books on education cannot teach you how to teach. It is my opinion that teaching skills come best in preservice experiences with the guidance of competent professional school and college personnel.

This book, then, is designed to help in understanding the "state of the art" of early childhood education, the forces shaping its future, and the broad strategies that are available for application to classrooms. It is hoped that preservice teachers will find it interesting and challenging. Perhaps the ideas presented here will aid teachers in making better decisions and as a result, will benefit the children they teach.

You are encouraged to write me how you feel about the issues in this book. I particularly invite your views about topics needing clarification and ways to improve future editions. After all, if people are willing to say how they feel about a shampoo, facial cream, or car, why not a textbook? I may be reached through the publisher.

It is impossible to achieve success without the help of colleagues and friends who are willing to provide invaluable feedback and ideas. Those who have aided in this process are: Sister Rosanne Hynes, Fred Fedorko, Paul Vicinanza, Joe DeVitis, Lou DiPlacido, Harry Wachs, Constance Kamii, and Warren Fruechtel. Pat Graham helped with many technical details. Pictures for the text were taken at St. Benedict's Day Care Center and Eastminster Head Start Center, Erie, Pennsylvania; the Miller Research Learning Center, Edinboro State College, Edinboro, Pennsylvania; and the Head Start Center in Springboro, Pennsylvania.

George S. Morrison

Contents

Interest and Issues
What's All the Fuss About?

Evidence of interest in early childhood is all around us. Popular magazines contain articles dealing with childrearing practices, the importance of the early years in education, and tips for helping children read at home. Newspaper advertisements proclaim the advantages of investing in a Montessori preschool franchise and inform parents of the opportunities available in educational programs designed specifically for young children. Toy manufacturers are also interested in education, specifically designing toys to encourage early learning and to help children grow up "smart." Groups of concerned citizens are increasingly aware of the content of children's television programs and are showing their concern for young children by lobbying for legislation to control the amount of time devoted to commercials. Family planning organizations and other groups concerned with children constantly raise questions concerning how many children are desirable in a family and how best to educate young children.

The federal government's involvement in programs for the poor and oppressed continues to create interest in the area of early childhood education. Programs such as Head Start and federally supported day care are designed specifically to meet the special needs of children and their parents and have been established in order that some children might have better care than has been afforded them in the past.

Terminology

In discussing early childhood, a problem frequently encountered is terminology. Because people don't always mean the same thing when they use a word, confusion can result. For purposes of our discussion throughout this text, *early childhood* refers to the child from conception to age eight. This is a standard and accepted definition by most professional educators, although it is also a term used to refer to children before they enter school. The lay public usually uses the term *early childhood* when referring to children in a school setting. If the meaning is not apparent from the context of the discussion, ask what meaning the user has in mind.

Early childhood education refers to any program designed for children from birth to age eight.[1] Quite often the terms *early childhood* and *early childhood education* are used synonymously.

Other terms that are frequently used when discussing the education of young children are *nursery school* and *preschool. Nursery school* is usually used to refer to an educational program for children 2½-5½ years old operated as a service by public schools, or for profit by other agencies and individuals. *Preschool* is generally used to refer to any educational program for children prior to their entrance into first grade. When a public school operates one program for 5½ year olds, and another for 4½ year olds, the term *kindergarten* is applied to the former and nursery school to the latter. Some school districts will refer to their kindergarten as preschools, while others will consider it part of their regular educational program. A detailed definition of Head Start and day care terms are found in chapters six and seven.

Factors Influencing Early Education

Historical Influences

While we have always been interested to a greater or lesser extent in children, the most rapid period of growth in early childhood education has occurred from about 1965 to the present. It is only logical, therefore, that

---

[1]You may think it strange that I did not use in this definition the phrase, conception to age eight. This of course depends on your point of view. If you believe children learn prenatally, then use this as part of your definition. Since the use of programs to teach prenatally is not currently widespread, I chose not to include it as part of the definition.

this is the period of time which has witnessed the greatest interest in young children in general and early childhood programs in particular.

The beginning of the current interest dates back to the 1950s and two events which have had far-reaching and long-lasting impact on all education. The first event was the focusing of public attention on the inadequacy of the methodology and lack of success on the part of the public schools in teaching reading and related skills. The second was the launching of Sputnik by the Soviet Union on October 4, 1957.

The public schools have traditionally been under attack for their inability to do an adequate job of teaching basic skills in general and reading in particular. This was evidenced by a host of articles and books detailing why Johnny, Susie, and Mary couldn't read. The attack was led by R. Flesch with the publication of *Why Johnny Can't Read,* in which he criticized the schools for the way in which reading was taught.[2] Critics and parents of school children began to question methodology and results of the teaching of reading and other basic skills. Parents, dissatisfied with the inability of their children to read, write, and compute, demanded schools and programs that would teach these skills. Many parents felt that traditional play-oriented preschools and public school curricula emphasizing "socialization" were not preparing their children for college entrance and earning a living. These public needs were met by schools whose curricula were academic and stressed "the three R's." Preschools with an emphasis on cognitive learning became popular with parents who wanted to give their children both an early start and a good foundation in learning.

An effort to catch up in technological processes and to be first in space resulted in an increased interest in education by the federal government, who passed the National Defense Education Act in 1958. This act was designed to improve educational programs in order to meet critical national needs, particularly in the sciences. One of the results of the renewed interest in our own education system was that Americans became more interested in other educational systems, including that of the Soviet Union. What made it possible for the Soviets to launch Sputnik? Examination of the Soviet educational system led to the conclusion that they "taught" their children by providing them with educational opportunities at an earlier age than was customary in United States public schools. Some educators began to wonder if we were waiting too long in educating our children and suggestions were made that we could have more intelligent adults by teaching children at a younger age. This thought sparked a controversy about the pros and cons of early education.

---

[2]Rudolf Flesch, *Why Johnny Can't Read—And What You Can Do About It.* (New York: Harper and Brothers, Publishers, 1955).

Research Influences

At the same time the Soviet influence was causing a reappraisal of our system of education, other factors in the form of research studies were also influencing our ideas about education and psychology. These studies led to a major shift in basic educational premises concerning what children would be able to achieve. This shift can be attributed in part to works by B. S. Bloom and J. McV. Hunt.

One of the conclusions reached by Bloom in his book *Stability and Change in Human Characteristics* was

> When a number of longitudinal studies are compared with each other and allowances are made for the reliability of the instruments and the variability of the samples, a single pattern clearly emerges . . . Both the correlational data and the absolute scale of intelligence development make it clear that intelligence is a developing function and that the stability of measured intelligence increases with age. Both types of data suggest that in terms of intelligence measured at age 17, about 50% of the development takes place between conception and age 4, about 30% between ages 4 and 8, and about 20% between ages 8 and 17.[3]

Hunt in his book, *Intelligence and Experience,* draws the following conclusions:

> In view of the conceptual developments and the evidence coming from animals learning to learn, from neuropsychology, from the programming of electronic computers to solve problems, and from the development of intelligence in children, it would appear that intelligence should be conceived as intellectual capacities based on central processes hierarchically arranged within the intrinsic portions of the cerebrum. These central processes are approximately analogous to the strategies for information processing and action with which electronic computers are programmed. With such a conception of intelligence, the assumptions that intelligence is fixed and that its development is predetermined by the genes are no longer tenable.
>
> In the light of these considerations, it appears that the counsel from experts on child-rearing during the third and much of the fourth decades of the twentieth century to let children be while they grow and to avoid excessive stimulation was highly unfortunate . . .
>
> Further in the light of these theoretical considerations and the evidence concerning the effects of early experience on adult problem-solving in

---

[3]Benjamin S. Bloom, *Stability and Change in Human Characteristics,* (New York: John Wiley and Sons, Inc., 1964), p. 88.

animals, it is no longer unreasonable to consider that it might be feasible to discover ways to govern the encounters that children have with their environments, especially during the early years of their development, to achieve a substantially faster rate of intellectual development and a substantially higher adult level of intellectual capacity.[4]

Four implications can be drawn from this research, and all of them are important for the educational process. First, the most rapid period of intellectual growth occurs before age eight. What children are to become intellectually, as based on those things upon which we measure intelligence and school achievement, are determined before many children see the inside of a school classroom. This would seem to imply that children need enriched home environments and/or earlier admittance to the educative process. Some educators believe both should occur simultaneously. However, there is by no means general agreement in this regard and it is quite doubtful that there ever will be.

Second, it has become increasingly evident that educators can no longer view the child as being born with a fixed intelligence. Morally, this out-dated concept fails to do justice to the tremendous capacity for learning and change that people possess and have demonstrated they are capable of achieving. In addition to this consideration, there is evidence supporting developmental intelligence. Everyone who is responsible for the development of children must think in terms of children having the potential for intellectual growth within a broad range. The extent to which the intelligence of an individual is developed will depend upon many variables such as experiences, social background, child-rearing practices, economic factors, nutrition, and the quality of the prenatal and postnatal environment. The inherited genetic characteristics of the child sets a broad framework within which intelligence will develop. Heredity sets the limits while environment determines the extent to which the limits will be achieved. For example, the genetic make-up of most children carries the capacity for language development. However, a child reared in an environment devoid of opportunities for interaction with adults who encourage conversation will not develop as linguistically competent as the child who has such opportunities.

Third, since children lacking opportunities to develop in an enriched environment also lag behind intellectually, Hunt's implications concerning the home environment are obvious. While questions have been raised about how well current school achievement indicates real life achievement and success, experience has shown that children who lack an environment

---

[4]J. McV. Hunt, *Intelligence and Experience.* (New York: The Ronald Press Company, Copyright © 1961), pp. 362–63.

which promotes learning opportunities will be handicapped throughout life. On the other hand, homes offering intellectual stimulation will tend to produce students who do well in school.

A fourth conclusion that can be implied from the above studies is this: If 80% of the intellectual development occurs by the time children are age eight, then the environment will have its greatest impact during these first eight years. Two examples, one involving nutrition and the other socioeconomic background, may help clarify this point. Nutrition is very important for brain development. It is particularly important during the prenatal stage and during the first two years of life when brain growth is at its maximum. A child who is deprived nutritionally during this crucial time for brain development will likely be permanently brain damaged. On the other hand, if the nutritional deprivation occurs after age two, there is less chance of permanent brain damage. Thus the impact of the environment is greatest during the period of maximum growth.

It is generally recognized that children from low socioeconomic backgrounds do not perform as well on standardized achievement tests as do children from high socioeconomic backgrounds. Environmental factors present in the high socioeconomic environment contribute to the high achievement measured on tests, and have their greatest effect on the child during the years from birth to age eight. If a child is to experience an enriched environment, it ought to be during this important developmental period.

If intelligence does develop at the rates and in the proportions that Bloom states, then the concepts, attitudes, and ways of looking at the world that children learn early in life are going to be the ones that essentially remain with them for life. The things that a child learns early in life, especially from his parents, are hard to change later on. A child reared in an environment of noncommunication will later experience difficulty in communicating. Enrichment of the young child's life, therefore, can be accomplished earlier than the traditional age of six, which is usually the age for admittance to school.

Modern Factors

Poverty. During the 1960s the United States literally rediscovered the poor and recognized that affluence was not a privilege everyone enjoyed. In 1973, twenty-five million persons in the United States were classified as poor. That year the U.S. Department of Labor classified a person as poor if he was a member of a nonfarm family of four with an annual income of less than $4,200, or a farm family of four with less than $3,575. An interpretation of figures such as these is that children of low-income families may

A young child's interest awakens before traditional school age.

not have available to them opportunities to do those things which result in experiences which promote and encourage maximum intellectual development. Therefore the federal government legislated the Economic Opportunity Act of 1964. The EOA was designed to wage a war on poverty. Head Start, one of the most popular and publicized provisions of the EOA, attempted to break intergenerational cycles of poverty by providing education and social opportunities for the children of poverty families. It made a commitment to children whose needs had not been met by private and public schools. In my opinion, Head Start has done more than any other single force in making the nation interested in the business of educating the young child. It has literally shocked educators out of their complacency toward the young and has forced them to reexamine philosophies, methodologies and practices that had previously been taken for granted.

Women's Liberation. The movement for the equality of women to achieve liberation and self-fulfillment maintains, in part, that the achievement of these goals depends upon women being unburdened from the constant care of children. The National Organization of Women is working towards the implementation of a federally funded, twenty-four-hour child care program. In addition, the women's liberation movement focuses attention on the need for *comprehensive* child care. Many parents have become increasingly aware that simply to care physically for children is not, in and of itself, adequate. The total development of the child includes the social, emotional and intellectual as well as the physical. Previously we made the classic supposition that because a woman and a man conceived children, they knew how to provide experiences which would promote intellectual, social, and emotional growth. Today more parents and future parents are seeking help and advice for becoming effective parents.

Day Care. Closely associated with the political advocacy for child care is the political reality of federal, state and local welfare reform programs that are associated with and often linked to day care. The federal government presently operates a program of job training as a means for helping and encouraging welfare recipients to find jobs. However, in order to train supporters of dependent children, it is necessary to provide care for these children. The federal government provides such people with money which can be used to purchase day care services. While many of these who receive this money use it to pay private babysitters, enough utilize center day care facilities to help accelerate a need for more programs. In addition, as parents leave their children in day care centers, they become increasingly sophisticated about the kind of care their children should receive. As a result, day care is being forced to reexamine its programmatic objectives to include the traditionally overlooked cognitive component in its program.

Cutting and pasting develop fine motor skills that are necessary for formal learning activities such as reading and writing.

Rising Incomes. It is almost ironic that while figures of poverty are cited as a force which generates interest in early childhood, it is also asserted that families with rising incomes are also causing interest in the area. Nevertheless, these statements are true. As more parents become college graduates, and with an increasing number of them likely to have degrees in teaching or related fields, they are sensitive to the importance of early education in the life of the young child. Since many of these families have middle-level incomes (usually twice as high as a noncollege graduate), they are willing to invest money in the education of their children. They look for nursery schools and preschool programs which offer the kind of educational program they feel will provide their children a good start in life. Consequently, many Montessori schools and franchised operations have benefited in the process. The Montessori system in the last several years has experienced a tremendous boom, both in individuals seeking Montessori teacher training and clients demanding this educational program for their children. Many parents of three- and four-year-olds are spending almost as much tuition by sending their children to good preschools as parents of eighteen-year-olds are spending in sending their children to state-supported universities.

Issues and Controversies

Wherever there is interest in any subject, there is generally accompanying controversy. Although there has been tremendous interest in educating the young child, there has also been a resistance on the part of the general American public and many members of the teaching profession to recognize the importance of the early years in a child's life.

Early Admittance

Parental Control. When to send children to school has been an issue as long as there have been schools. In the United States, local control of education and the inherent right of parents for the responsibility for the education of the child tends to encourage late admission to school. While some parents are willing to have children enter school at age five, they may feel that early admittance to school takes away from the authority of the home and parent, and strips away the inalienable right of the mother to provide the early and basic educational program for the child. Or they may believe that early education acts as a force against the love of mothers for their children. Some contend there is no person better suited for and capable of educating the young child than the natural mother. This argument may be true as long as the mother knows what to do, how to do it, and at the same time wants to do what is best for the child. However, there are some parents that are really hassled, confused, and confounded by the complexities of child rearing. It is neither valid nor safe to assume that natural parents always possess the knowledge and skills necessary for effectively raising children.

The opinions of educators on this matter are mixed. There is a group of educators who believe that early admittance combined with programs designed to meet individual needs can provide the basis necessary for effective learning and living. On the other hand, some educators view children as able to benefit best from the preplanned programs of the school when they have matured with age. Those who favor early admittance can find research to support their position, while those against can also find research to bolster their point of view. Given this situation, then, early school admission is not likely to gain national acceptance except for special programs for the disadvantaged.

Admittance Procedure. Age as a criterion for school admittance raises the issue of procedure for admittance. Is the customary annual fall entrance to school sufficient for today's children? Some educators think not and feel entrance to school should be similar to England's policy of admitting the child in a term following his birthday. Others, including your author, feel children should be admitted on their fifth birthday. The current popular practice which makes some children wait a rather long period of time following the fifth birthday for entering school needs to be examined in light of research related to early learning.

Indoctrination. A change frequently leveled in opposition to early education is that it is un-American. Critics argue that attempts at such education will result in the "Sovietization" of America's children by early indoctrination, culminating in obedience to a central government.

School Readiness. No issue generates as much heat as school readiness. Interestingly enough, resistance to the education of young children sometimes comes from that group of professionals dedicated to educating. Some school districts, at the urging of their teachers, are raising the entrance age for admittance to first grade. They require the child to be six years of age by the first of September in order to be admitted to first grade. The reason generally given for this action is that many children are "not ready" for first grade and therefore teachers experience difficulty in teaching them. Comments such as "I can't teach them a thing" and "All I end up doing is flunking them" are frequently heard from first-grade teachers. This attitude would seem to be the opposite of what it ought to be.

Most teachers and lay personnel interpret readiness to mean ability to do school work. When interpreted in this way, *school readiness* means a child's ability to accomplish predetermined learning tasks. Decisions to determine if children are "ready" to accomplish these tasks and begin school are based on their ability to speak, listen, follow directions, pay attention, sit quietly, get along with others and generally participate in the school program in a nondisruptive manner. Commercial tests such as the Metropolitan Reading Readiness Test are administered in many school districts to help in the decision-making process. Depending on the child's performance, he is admitted or denied admission to school. If a child is denied admission, his parents are usually told he is "immature" and "not ready for school."

Although the issue we have been discussing is known as *school readiness,* it would appear a more appropriate term should be *child readiness.* As it now stands, many public schools want children to be ready for them and their predetermined and preconceived programs. I am of the opinion that in this respect, schools have their priorities reversed. Schools should provide programs based upon the needs of children, not on preconceived notions of what children ought to be able to do. Teachers should provide whatever program is necessary in order for children to learn. Schools should get ready for children, not vice versa. Teachers who send children home to "get ready for school" or to become more mature may not always understand the kind of environment they are sending these children back to. Will a child who does not have a language-rich home life benefit by spending an additional year there? I think not. A child of five who comes to school never having experienced coloring, writing, or other children is not going to go home to that same environment and accomplish in one year all those things which he has not had an opportunity to do in the first five years of his life! The only salvation for many children is the public schools, or, as we are finding out, good Head Start centers. What is needed is a renewed recognition that schools are for children.

Who Should Be Educated?

Day care and Head Start programs, operated with federal monies, provide services for some children of low-income families. On the other hand, private day care and preschools provide services for children of wealthier parents who can afford the tuition to send their children to the programs. The forgotten child in early education appears to be the middle-class child who does not qualify for special programs yet whose parents cannot afford the tuition of private programs.

How to Educate

How best to educate children is an issue which has faced educators and parents as long as society has determined its best interests depend on an enlightened citizenry. The issue is compounded by the assumption that parents know what is best for their children and this "knowing what is best" includes how to educate. As in many fields, the experts are not those who are willing to propose and implement creative solutions.

An oversimplification of this whole issue is the juxtaposition that occurs by those who advocate educating children in a strict, authoritarian, teacher-dominated setting with a rigid, predetermined curriculum as opposed to those who favor educating in an open setting which is characterized by self-discipline, freedom and self-selection of activities. However in reality, it is an issue to which there is no solution. The most dangerous mistake we can make is to believe and act as though there were one best way or method of educating. Instead of seeking a promised land, teachers should use an eclectic approach that takes the best from all approaches and applies them to the needs of children, parents and community.

What to Teach

The issue of how best to educate is almost always discussed in the context of the analogous issue of what to teach children. Again, this issue unfortunately is viewed simply as the polarization of basic education on the one hand and progressive education on the other.

The basic education viewpoint is best summarized by saying there are certain basics that should receive priority in learning and teaching. These "basics" are generally considered to include reading, writing, arithmetic and cultural heritage. Those parents who support this point of view generally advocate a no-nonsense approach to education which includes among other elements, homework, tests, memorization of information and strict discipline. They view the school as a place where hard work and obedience to teacher authority are expected. The schools view their functions as imparters of factual knowledge, preservers of the cultural heritage, promoters of basic values such as hard work, and guardians of the status quo.

At the opposite end of the spectrum are the child-centered advocates who feel the curriculum of the school should be based on the "whole" child and should be developed out of his interests and abilities. This system of educating usually goes by the name progressive education. John Dewey is generally credited with being the father of this movement. This progressive education "curriculum" currently finds expression in the open education method. Many teachers, however, while paying lip service to the ideals of

*Tracing and drawing help to develop the child's ability to
write letters and words.*

progressive education, act as though they were members of the basic education movement.

It seems as though the historical pendulum of education practice
swings alternately between basic education and other beliefs. The 1950s saw
a resurgence of basic education philosophy and it is likely that a renewed
emphasis will occur during the latter half of the 1970s and first part of the
1980s.

What Kind of Program. Historically and traditionally, programs designed for children prior to their entry into first grade have emphasized
social and emotional development in an ordered framework of free play
and large group activities emphasizing "getting ready" for first grade.
From this point of view, what are considered academic or cognitive activities
such as reading, writing and number computation are generally reserved for
first grade. While children would be read to and provided books to "read,"
they would not be introduced formally to reading, and writing is generally
confined to learning to print one's name. The main emphasis is placed on
those activities which promote socialization. It is thought that what children do specifically is not as important as their involvement in activities
with other children. Thus group activities which involve playing with materials and classmates are considered of utmost importance. The concept of
socialization in which children have opportunities to play with other children, learn to share, pay attention to the teacher, follow directions and
generally become acclimated to the process of schooling is generally congruent with the public's view of the purpose of preschool programs. When

mothers of young children are asked for their reasons why they want to send their children to kindergarten programs, they generally respond, "So my child can learn to get along with other children."

Figures 1 and 2 show hypothetical kindergarten schedules, one with a socialization emphasis and another with a cognitive emphasis. I would like to emphasize, however, that it is possible to find all sorts of combinations of activities and approaches. Kindergarten programs have a tendency to be very eclectic, with teachers choosing those activities which they think are best for children and themselves. A kindergarten program can have both a social emphasis and a cognitive emphasis. While the social and cognitive emphases should not be viewed as dichotomous, they oftentimes are in the sense that individual teachers tend to emphasize one or the other.

Also in Figures 1 and 2 I have placed rather rigid time frames on both kindergarten programs. While this kind of time scheduling is rather typical, it is not meant to imply that all programs are operated in such a manner or that they need to be. The more open kindergarten classrooms have a tendency to operate on a rather flexible schedule in that activities can occur over varying periods of time. On the other hand, many early educators feel that a time frame that is structured and consistent from day to day is necessary to give children a sense of security and belonging.

8:30 – 9:00 Arrival—free time during which children select an activity such as: block building, riding tricycles, climbing on a jungle gym, or using a dress-up corner.

9:00 – 9:30 Opening exercise—conversation, show and tell, activities related to the calendar.

9:30 – 10:00 Free time—selection of a wide range of activities such as art materials, games, puzzles, etc. Also doll corner, carpentry, water play, sand play.

10:00 – 11:00 Rest—snack time. Children are encouraged to rest on mats. This is followed by a snack of cookies and milk, juice and crackers, or something similar.

11:00 – 11:30 Storytime. Usually read to by the teacher—can occur by records, T.V., etc.

11:30 – 11:45 Dismissal.

Figure 1 *A Kindergarten with a Socialization Emphasis*

8:30 –   9:00 Arrival—free time—Children select an activity from a group of prearranged or selected teacher activities such as puzzles, games, books, records, etc.

9:00 –   9:15 Circle time—Conversation which emphasizes plans for day's activities. Can also include discussion of previous day's work.

9:15 –   9:45 Involvement with a language development program. Can be either teacher-designed or commercial such as Distar, Peabody Language Kits, Alphatime.

9:45 – 10:15 Storytime—The children are read stories, discussion occurs about them and children go to the school library to select books for taking home.

10:15 – 10:45 Activity Centers—Learning centers maintained by the teacher. Can deal with any topic, such as science, art, ecology, writing. All children participate in all the centers.

10:45 – 11:15 Free selection of games, puzzles, etc. selected by teacher for their ability to teach concepts such as size, shape, number, etc. This period can also be used for outdoor walks in which concepts being developed are extended.

11:15 – 11:45 Group discussion—Day's activities are reviewed and discussed. The next day's activities are anticipated. Dismissal.

Snack and rest opportunities may be provided for everyone or they can be provided on an "as needed" basis for each child.

Figure 2 *A Kindergarten with a Cognitive Emphasis*

In addition, the activities which I have included under each program should be considered descriptive rather than prescriptive. Many different activities could be included and the programs would still retain their distinctiveness as socially or cognitively oriented.

(2–1/2 Hours—3 Times a Week)

9:00 –   9:30 Outdoor play (depending on the weather), or gym activities (jungle gym, bicycles, sandtable, and carpenter benches).

9:30 –   9:40 Sharing, songs and fingerplays.

9:40 –   9:50 Language development programs—Peabody Language Development Kit or teacher activities such as a unit on family, pets, etc.

9:50 – 10:15 Juice time or rest time.

10:15 – 10:30 Rhythms (rhythm instruments, imitative actions, action songs, exercises, etc.).

10:30 – 11:15 Free play period—Interest centers including choice of easel painting, finger painting, screen or sponge printing, clay, scissors, plus all of the other games, toys, and educational equipment.
Art project—(during free playtime, is optional for children) involves cutting, pasting.

11:15 – 11:25 Storytime—Book or flannelboard story.

Figure 3 *A Nursery School Program for Four-Year-Old Children*

The programs in Figures 1 and 2 are also half-day programs, while some kindergartens operate on a whole-day schedule. Generally, when a school district operates a half-day program they operate a session in the morning and one in the afternoon so that one teacher will teach two kindergarten classes of about twenty-five students each. While most of the kindergartens are half-day programs, there is not general agreement that they should be so. Those who argue for the half-day session do so on the basis that this is all the schooling the 5½-year-old child is ready to experience and that it provides an ideal transition to the all-day first grade. Those in favor of the full day generally feel that not only is the child ready and capable for a program of this length; but it also can provide an opportunity for a much more comprehensive type of program.

Figure 3 represents a daily schedule that would be typical of many nursery school programs for four year olds operated by individuals for profit, by church groups, or by a group of parents. This daily program should be compared with the Head Start program. Figure 3 represents basically a socialization-oriented model and is designed as a three-day-a-week program. In such programs, parents have their choice of sending children any three days of the week. One problem, however, with this type schedule is that a working mother has to supplement the program with private child care services not only in the afternoon, but also on the days the child does not attend nursery school.

Play. One of the most nagging and persistent issues in early childhood education concerns play. To play or not to play is essentially an issue of what constitutes play and how it should be used in programs for young children. Following the launching of Sputnik, the traditional playschool curriculum of many preschools was questioned as being inappropriate for the children of a country which had made a commitment to be the first to put a man on the moon.

There has always been an intuitively held belief by parents and teachers that play is good for children and that time and facilities should be provided for children to play. When childhood is depicted, it is usually done through play of some kind. Many people feel that the right of children to play is one of the inalienable conditions of childhood. Any attempt to interfere with this process is viewed with suspicion and distrust. The question raised by the critics of this point of view, however, is whether or not any meaningful learning occurs from such playful activity. These people favor structuring, extending and utilizing play for the purpose of developing concepts at both the cognitive and affective levels. Thus, during block play, children may be encouraged to tell the difference between the size of the blocks that they are playing with and, after block play, put the blocks according to size in their appropriately marked shelves. Doll play may be utilized as an opportunity to teach body parts, care of the body (washing, etc.), and likenesses and differences between people.

Another group of educators view play as that which children engage in after they have completed prearranged teacher activities. While some prearranged teacher activities (games, puzzles, etc.) can also be called play, in a cognitive setting they are not since they have been selected by teachers to teach specific concepts such as shape discrimination. In this sense, there is a distinction (even though it may be artificial) between work (activities designed to teach concepts) and play (activities selected by children for the sake of playing).

It is unlikely that the issue concerning play will ever be adequately solved to everyone's satisfaction. This is particularly true as long as we insist on making a distinction between what constitutes work and what constitutes play. What we need to instill in both ourselves as teachers and children as learners is that learning can and should be a joyful, playful process. It is important also that all teachers know what they want children to learn and accomplish within the context of the learning environment and select the best means for achieving these goals, whatever one chooses to call them.

While the above points of interest and areas of concern are not all of the issues in early childhood education, they do represent some of the major ones that are frequently discussed. Others that could be added to the list are the nature-versus-nurture controversy, the effects and appropriateness of early stimulation on children, and the question of whether schooling really does do much to affect the lives of children. However, the topics that we have discussed have provided you with the background necessary to understand what all the fuss is about in early childhood education today.

BIBLIOGRAPHY

Bloom, Benjamin S. *Stability and Change in Human Characteristics.* New York: John Wiley and Sons, Inc., 1964.

Flesch, Rudolf. *Why Johnny Can't Read—And What You Can Do About It.* New York: Harper and Brothers, Publishers, 1955.

Hunt, J. McV. *Intelligence and Experience.* New York: The Ronald Press Company, 1961.

FOR FURTHER READING AND STUDY

Butler, Annie L. *Early Childhood Education: Planning and Administering Programs.* New York: D. Van Norstrand Company, 1974.

Deals with most of the issues presented in this chapter in a meaningful way. Easy to read with many good, practical suggestions.

Ebbeck, Frederick and Ebbeck, Marjory. *Now We Are Four—An Introduction to Early Childhood Education.* Columbus, Ohio: Charles E. Merrill Publishing Co., 1974.

Classroom practices for the preschool child based on creativity, concrete experiences and freedom to be individuals. Communicating with and understanding children is emphasized.

Fallon, Berlie J., ed. *40 Innovative Programs in Early Childhood Education.* Belmont, California: Lear Siegler, Inc./Fearon Publishers, 1973.

An excellent source of current early childhood education programs, including descriptions written by participating individuals.

Hymes, James L., Jr. *Teaching the Child under Six.* 2d ed. Columbus, Ohio: Charles E. Merrill Publishing Co., 1974.

A provocative look at the education of young children by an author who "tells it like it is." Deals with the curriculum of the preschool and ideas for coping with problems in education.

For Further Study and Involvement

1. Observe a young child. How are his mannerisms (speech and ways of doing things) similar to those of his parents? Which of these do you think will remain with him through life?

2. Give general definitions of the terms *heredity* and *environment.* Which of the two seems to you to pose the more immediate problem in educating children? Give reasons for your choice.

3. Interview people in education and other professions. How do they view the relationship between heredity and environment? What are their reasons? In what ways do you agree or disagree?

4. Would you consider sending your own child at age four to a nursery school? Why or why not?

5. Interview teachers, early childhood professors, psychologists, etc. to determine what they consider readiness or eligibility for first grade. What qualities, characteristics, and abilities do they consider in determining readiness? Compare their data with your classmates' ideas.

6. What are your opinions about *screening* children for eligibility for entry into kindergarten and first grade? Do you think tests which claim to measure school and reading readiness really do so?

7. What is the *legal* age for entrance into kindergarten and first grade in your state? local district? Do you agree or disagree with these age limits? Why?

8. List the pros and cons of early entrance into kindergarten and first grade.

9. Conduct a survey of parents and early childhood teachers. Ask the following:
   a. When should children begin school?
   b. What should be taught in first grade?

10. The question of what to teach children is a perennial problem. One way to deal with this issue is to determine what is worth knowing. In small groups, brainstorm this question; then combine the results from these groups into a what's-worth-knowing curriculum. How is your curriculum similar to or different from other early childhood education curricula?

11. Observe a kindergarten program. What were its goals and objectives? Do they agree or disagree with the ideas in your text? What are the areas of difference and agreement? How do you explain such differences?

Historical Influences
Who Are These Guys Anyway?

It is interesting that students of early childhood education generally have little desire to know very much about the historical background of their chosen profession. A suggestion that students read about Froebel, Comenius, Rousseau and Pestalozzi unfortunately seems to turn a class off. Sometimes a professor can turn this reluctance into resigned acceptance by some students and appreciation by others by informing them that questions related to the history of early childhood education will probably appear on some national examination, the scores of which may be necessary for placement on a school district's eligibility list for hiring.

Regardless of how you feel now about reading this chapter, the importance of knowing something about early educators (at least having heard their names) seems to be threefold. First, by reading of the hopes and ideas of people whom we have judged to be famous, we realize that our ideas today are not necessarily new ones. Topics such as individualizing instruction, open education, and behavior modification, for instance, have been talked about since earliest times. For example, Montessori is a modern precursor of open education. It is my opinion that we can more fully appreciate the basic premises of open education by at least having a rudimentary understanding of Montessori and the thinkers who influenced her, Pestalozzi and Froebel.

Second, many of the dreams of historical educators are still dreams, in spite of the advances we think modern schools have made. In this regard, we are the inheritors of a long line of questors and discoverers starting with Socrates and Plato. We acknowledge this inheritance and use it as a base upon which to build meaningful teaching careers. If these dreams are worthy of fulfillment, you are the ones who will have to make it happen.

Third, the ideas as expressed by these early educators will help us better understand how to implement our current teaching strategies. For instance, Rousseau, Froebel, and Montessori all believed children should be taught with dignity and respect. This attitude toward children is essential to an understanding of open education and often makes the difference between whether or not it "works" in more than name only.

Concepts Behind Formal Schooling

While it is possible to go back to earliest times and trace the path of early childhood education, it is not really necessary to do so. The education of the young child was never really a problem when humans were engaged in a basically uncomplicated way of life such as hunting, farming or herding. Whatever the child needed to know to prepare him for life in an agrarian economy was most often learned at the knee of the mother or father. If the daughter needed to sew and cook, she learned these from her mother. The son, on the other hand, learned to farm and hunt from his father. This form of education served well (and still does in underdeveloped countries) those economies and ways of life in which the skills needed for adult life can be learned from parents or surrogates through an apprentice system. However, once a society becomes "industrialized," this type of education no longer suffices to equip the child for later life. Because individual parents may lack the skills and resources needed to train their children for a technological society, formalized education is instituted.

The process of schooling is usually perceived as easy by those who have never tried to teach or by the romantic critics who would have us eliminate schools as we currently know them. The deceptive character of it has been experienced first-hand by some families who attempt to rear children in the communal settings which were popular several years ago. Frequently, the first problems that emerged in these attempts were the issues of what to teach children and how to teach them in the absence of schools. While a resistance to formal schooling may be maintained by certain subcultures such as the Amish on the grounds that schooling is unnecessary and inappropriate for their way of life, society in general benefits from this institution

Children need many opportunities to interact with a wide variety of materials prior to formal schooling.

and at the same time finds education by an institution easier to accomplish than through and within a family context.

Some critics believe institutions of schooling fail to teach basic skills and impart moral values. Because the process of education in our current society is too complex and time-consuming to be accomplished well by most families, there is little alternative to institutions. What is necessary, however, is a constant demand for accountability from those whom we charge and trust with this responsibility. We need to understand what the educational process involves as articulated by those who devoted their lives to influencing its growth and development.

European Educators

Martin Luther (1483–1546)

It was not until the sixteenth century that the issue of formalized schooling to teach reading was raised by Martin Luther. Simply stated, Luther replaced the authority of the Catholic hierarchy with the authority of the Bible. Since each man was free to work out his own salvation, this meant that people had to be taught to read the Bible. To this end the Protestant Reformation under the impetus of Luther encouraged and supported popular universal education. Throughout his life Luther remained a champion of education. He wrote letters and treatises and preached sermons on the subject. His best known letter on education is the *Letter to the Mayors and Aldermen of All the Cities of Germany in Behalf of Christian Schools,* written in 1524. In this letter, Luther argues for public support of education.

Therefore it will be the duty of the mayors and council to exercise the greatest care over the young. For since the happiness, honor, and life of the city are committed to their hands, they would be held recreant before God and the world, if they did not, day and night, with all their power, seek its welfare and improvement. Now the welfare of a city does not consist alone in great treasures, firm walls, beautiful houses, and munitions of war; indeed, where all these are found, and reckless fools come into power, the city sustains the greatest injury. But the highest welfare, safety, and power of a city consists in able, learned, wise, upright, cultivated citizens, who can secure, preserve, and utilize every treasure and advantage.[1]

In addition to arguing for the public support of education, Luther was also an advocate of coeducation.

Even if there were no soul, (as I have already said) and men did not need schools and the languages for the sake of Christianity and the Scriptures, still, for the establishment of the best schools everywhere, both for boys and girls, this consideration is of itself sufficient, namely, that society, for the maintenance of civil order and the proper regulation of the household, needs accomplished and well-trained men and women. Now such men are to come from boys, and such women from girls; hence it is necessary that boys and girls be properly taught and brought up.[2]

Luther advocated a system of compulsory education, necessary for the good of individuals and society, that was supported by the public. He felt that the curriculum of the existing schools should be broadened to include music and physical education and that young women should be encouraged to teach.

The modern interest in education for everyone began with Luther. While his contributions to early childhood education are not always obvious, he was, nevertheless, the catalyst for concern about the education of children in general. As a result of that attention, educational practices applicable to young children were formulated.

John Amos Comenius (1592–1670)

Comenius was born in Moravia, a former province of Czechoslovakia. He became a minister of the Moravian faith and spent his life serving as bishop of his Church, teaching school and writing educational textbooks. Of his

---

[1]From *Luther on Education* by F. V. N. Painter, © 1928 by Concordia Publishing House. Used by permission. Pp. 180–81.

[2]*Ibid.,* p. 196.

many writings, the ones that have received the most modern attention are *The Great Didactic* and the *Orbis Pictus* (*The World in Pictures*), which is considered the first picture book for children.

One of his fundamental beliefs was that the essential nature of man was good as opposed to the popular view of natural depravity, i.e., the essential tendency to do things judged to be bad. He viewed education, therefore, as a positive learning experience which included freedom, joy and pleasure. This is sharply contrasted to the concept of education as discipline, consisting partly of a rigid, authoritarian atmosphere designed to control the child's natural inclination to do bad things. In modern terms, the argument is, do children learn better in an authoritarian setting characterized by traditional classrooms, or in an open setting which encourages self autonomy and self regulation.

Another basic belief of Comenius was that education should follow the natural order of nature. This natural order implied a timetable and set order to growth and learning. One must observe this pattern in order to prevent forcing learning before the child is capable, or before the necessary steps to that learning had been taught. This concept is also reflected in Montessori's sensitive periods, Piaget's stages of development, and the perennial issue of readiness for school and learning.

Comenius thought that learning is achieved best when the senses are involved, and that sensory education formed the basis for all learning.

> Those things, therefore, that are placed before the intelligence of the young, must be real things and not the shadows of things. I repeat, they must be *things;* and by the term I mean determinate, real, and useful things that can make an impression on the senses and on the imagination. But they can only make this impression when brought sufficiently near.
>
> From this a golden rule for teachers may be derived. Everything should, as far as is possible, be placed before the senses. Everything visible should be brought before the organs of sight, everything audible before that of hearing. Odours should be placed before the sense of smell, and things that are tastable and tangible before the sense of taste and of touch respectively. If an object can make an impression on several senses at once, it should be brought into contact with several . . . [3]

We see an extension and refinement of this principle in the works of Montessori, Piaget and other contemporary programs that stress learning situations that involve the manipulation of concrete objects.

---

[3]Comenius, John Amos. *The Great Didactic of John Amos Comenius,* Ed. and Trans. M. W. Keatinge [1896, 1910] (New York: Russell and Russell, 1967), pp. 184–85.

In addition, Comenius believed that education should begin in the early years.

> It is the nature of everything that comes into being, that while tender it is easily bent and formed, but that, when it has grown hard, it is not easy to alter. Wax, when soft, can be easily fashioned and shaped; when hard it cracks readily. A young plant can be planted, transplanted, pruned, and bent this way or that. When it has become a tree these processes are impossible.[4]

Comenius's recognition of the significance of the early years is reflected today in the growth of programs, such as the National Home Start, which involve early stimulation and emphasize the parental role in the educational process.

A broad view of Comenius's total concept of education can be gained by an examination of some of his principles of teaching:

> Following in the footsteps of nature we find that the process of education will be easy
>
>   (i) If it begins early, before the mind is corrupted.
> (ii) If the mind be duly prepared to receive it.
> (iii) If it proceed from the general to the particular.
> (iv) And from what is easy to what is more difficult.
> (v) If the pupil be not overburdened by too many subjects.
> (vi) And if progress be slow in every case.
> (vii) If the intellect be forced to nothing to which its natural bent does not incline it, in accordance with its age and with the right method.
> (viii) If everything be taught through the medium of the senses.
> (ix) And if the use of everything taught be continually kept in view.
> (x) If everything be taught according to one and the same method.
>
> These, I say, are the principles to be adopted if education is to be easy and pleasant.[5]

There is a decided trend in education today to make learning, as Comenius suggested, more easy and pleasant. Efforts are being made by many teachers to instill joy in the learning process. While there are those individuals who would compare education to the bitter pill that must be swallowed, others feel that it can be humanized and personalized.

Today, probably the two most significant contributions of Comenius are textbooks with illustrations and the persistent emphasis in most early

---

[4]*Ibid.,* p. 58.
[5]*Ibid.,* p. 127.

childhood programs on training of the senses. We take the former for granted and naturally assume that the latter is necessary as a basis for learning.

Jean Jacques Rousseau (1712–1778)

Rousseau was born in Geneva, Switzerland, but spent most of his life in France. He is best remembered by educators for his book *Emile* in which he raises a hypothetical child from birth to adolescence. In *Emile,* Rousseau states theories that were considered radical for his time. The opening lines of *Emile* not only set the tone for Rousseau's educational views but for many of his political ideas as well. "God makes all things good; man meddles with them and they become evil."[6]

According to Rousseau, natural education promotes and encourages qualities such as happiness, spontaneity and inquisitiveness generally associated with childhood. In his method, one allows children to develop according to their own natural abilities. One cannot interfere with their development by forcing education upon them or by protecting them from the corrupting influences of society.

Rousseau felt that the education of Emile occurred through three sources: nature, human beings, and things.

> All that we lack at birth and need when grown up is given us by education. This education comes to us from nature, from men, or from things. The internal development of our faculties and organs is the education of nature. . . . It is not enough merely to keep children alive. They should be fitted to take care of themselves when they grow up. They should learn to bear the blows of fortune; to meet either wealth or poverty, to live if need be in the frosts of Iceland or on the sweltering rock of Malta.[7]

According to Rousseau, however, while we have control over the education that comes from other people via social experiences and through things via sensory experiences, we have no control of the natural growth of children. In essence, this is the idea of "unfolding," in which the nature of the child—what she is to be—unfolds as a result of maturation according to her own natural timetable. We should observe the growth of the child to provide appropriate experiences. This approach to education has been

---

[6] *Emile; Or, Education,* by Jean Jacques Rousseau. Trans. Barbara Foxley, Every Man's Library Edition. (New York: Reprinted by permission of the publishers, E. P. Dutton and Co., Inc., 1933), p. 5.

[7] Jean Jacques Rousseau, *Emile,* trans. and ed. William Boyd (New York: Teachers College Press, by arrangement with William Heinemann Ltd., London, 1962), pp. 11–15.

interpreted by some educators as laissez-faire. The noninterference method has had a rather large influence on modern educational practice.

Rousseau further explains:

> In the natural order where all men are equal, manhood is the common vocation. One who is well educated for that will not do badly in the duties that pertain to it. The fact that my pupil is intended for the army, the church or the bar, does not greatly concern me. Before the vocation determined by his parents comes the call of nature to the life of human kind. Life is the business I would have him learn. When he leaves my hands, I admit he will not be a magistrate, or a soldier, or a priest. First and foremost, he will be a man. All that a man must be he will be when the need arises, as well as anyone else. Whatever the changes of fortune he will always be able to find a place for himself.[8]

Those who specialize in the history of education feel that it is possible to point to Rousseau as the dividing line between what we call the historical and the modern periods of education. Rousseau established a way of thinking about the young child that is reflected in innovators of educational practice such as Pestalozzi and Froebel. His natural unfolding concept echoes Comenius and can be found in current programs which stress readiness as a factor of learning. The developmental stages of Jean Piaget seem to reinforce Rousseau's thinking about the importance of natural development. Today, educational practices such as open education that provide an environment in which the child can be autonomous and self regulating have a basis in his philosophy.

John Heinrick Pestalozzi (1746–1827)

Pestalozzi was also born in Switzerland. The influence of Rousseau is most apparent in Pestalozzi's belief that education should follow the child's nature. His dedication to this concept is demonstrated by the rearing of his only son using *Emile* as a guide. His methods were based upon harmonizing nature and educational practices.

> And what is this method? It is a method which simply follows the path of Nature, or, in other words, which leads the child slowly, and by his own efforts, from sense-impressions to abstract ideas. Another advantage of this method is that it does not unduly exalt the master, inasmuch as he never appears as a superior being, but, like kindly Nature, lives and works

---

[8]Rousseau, *Emile,* ed. Boyd, pp. 14–15.

with the children, his equals, seeming rather to learn with them than to teach them with authority.[9]

Sensory impressions are an important key. Pestalozzi believed that all education was based upon such impressions, and that through the proper sensory experiences the natural potential of the child could be developed. This belief led to the development of his famous "object lessons." As the name implies, Pestalozzi felt that the best way to learn many concepts was through manipulative experiences involving processes such as counting, measuring, feeling, and touching.

While teachers often feel they must major or be certified in a particular area before they can teach children, Pestalozzi felt that the best teachers were those who taught children, not subjects. He also utilized the multi-age grouping idea, advocated today as having potential for the improvement of education. In addition, Pestalozzi anticipated by about 150 years the National Home Start Program funded by the federal government for the purpose of developing strategies and procedures for working with young children in the optimum educational setting—the home. He believed that mothers could best teach their children and wrote *How Gertrude Teaches Her Children* and *Book for Mothers*, which detail procedures for doing this. He felt that "The time is drawing near when methods of teaching will be so simplified that each mother will be able not only to teach her children without help, but continue her own education at the same time."[10]

Pestalozzi would feel very much at home in an elementary school utilizing a program of occupational awareness for he felt that the world of work could be combined with education.

Friedrich Wilhelm Froebel (1782–1852)

Froebel, a German, devoted his life to the development of a system for the education of young children. While his contemporary, Pestalozzi, with whom he studied and worked, advocated a system for teaching, Froebel actually developed one. In the process he earned for himself the distinction of being known as the "father of the kindergarten."

The basis for Froebel's educational theories is the concept of natural unfolding. This belief finds expression in his insistence on the recognition of the basic uniqueness of each child and the necessity to respect individuality by all who would call themselves teachers. Children unfold their uniqueness in contexts which provide for play.

[9]Roger DeGuimps, *Pestalozzi: His Life and Work*, (New York: D. Appleton and Company, 1890), p. 205.
[10]DeGuimps, *Pestalozzi: His Life and Work*, p. 169.

Play is the purest, most spiritual activity of man at this stage, and, at the same time, typical of human life as a whole—of the inner hidden natural life in man and all things. It gives, therefore, joy, freedom, contentment, inner and outer rest, peace with the world. It holds the sources of all that is good. A child that plays thoroughly, with self-active determination, perseveringly until physical fatigue forbids, will surely be a thorough, determined man, capable of self-sacrifice for the promotion of the welfare of himself and others. Is not the most beautiful expression of child-life at this time a playing child?—a child wholly absorbed in his play?—a child that has fallen asleep while so absorbed?

As already indicated, play at this time is not trivial, it is highly serious and of deep significance. Cultivate and foster it, O mother; protect and guard it, O father! To the calm, keen vision of one who truly knows human nature, the spontaneous play of the child discloses the future inner life of the man.

The plays of childhood are the germinal leaves of all later life; for the whole man is developed and shown in these, in his tenderest dispositions, in his innermost tendencies.[11]

However, according to Froebel the teacher was responsible for guidance and direction so that the child would become a creative, contributing member of society. In order to achieve this end Froebel developed a systematic, planned curriculum for the education of the young child. The basis for his curriculum were "gifts," "occupations," songs which he composed, and educational games. "Gifts" were objects given to children so that through handling and using them in accordance with the teacher's instructions they could learn shape, size, color, and concepts involved in counting, measuring, contrasting and comparison. The first "gift" was a set of six balls of yarn, each a different color, with six lengths of yarn the same colors as the balls. The purpose of this gift was partly to teach color recognition.

Froebel felt that the ball (meaning a round, spherical object) played an important role in education and consequently he placed a great deal of emphasis on its use. He also believed that the ball was a perfect symbol for man's unity with the divine, a concept that he felt was important but is difficult for us to understand. Froebel said of the ball:

Even the word ball, in our significant language, is full of expression and meaning, pointing out that the ball is, as it were, an image of the all; but the ball itself has such an extraordinary charm, such a constant attraction for early childhood, as well as for later youth, that it is beyond comparison the first as well as the most important plaything of childhood especially.[12]

---

[11]Friedrich Froebel, *The Education of Man,* trans. M. W. Hailman (New York: D. Appleton and Company, 1887), p. 55.

[12]Friedrich Froebel, *Pedagogics of the Kindergarten,* trans. Josephine Jarvis (New York: D. Appleton and Company, 1902), p. 32.

"Occupations" were materials designed for the development of various skills, primarily the psychomotor skills, through such activities as sewing with a sewing board, drawing pictures by following the dots, modeling with clay, cutting, bead stringing, weaving, drawing, pasting, and paper folding. Many of the games or plays developed by Froebel were based directly upon his gifts. For example, part of the directions for play involving the use of a ball on a string are:

> As soon as the ball, which has been swung by the child standing in the middle of the circle, has ceased to move, the general impulse of the children to move likewise is greeted by the following song:
>> We too can move lightly
>> Here and there, here and there.[13]

Froebel is not called the father of the kindergarten simply because he coined the name, but because he devoted his life to both the development of a program for the young child and a system of training for kindergarten teachers.

Many of the concepts and activities found in the "gifts" and "occupations" are similar to activities provided by many kindergarten programs.

Schools should be happy places.

---

[13] *Ibid.*, p. 270.

Froebel's recognition of the importance of learning through play is reinforced by modern-day teachers who intuitively structure their programs around play activities. Other features of Froebel's kindergarten which we find evidence of today are: the play circle where children arrange themselves in a circle for learning; and songs which are sung by the teacher and children to reinforce concepts taught with the "gifts" and "occupations."

Froebelian Method in the United States. The educational concepts and kindergarten program of Froebel were imported into the United States virtually intact by individuals who believed in his ideas and methods. This Froebelian influence on early childhood education remained a dominant theme in educational circles for almost half a century until challenged by John Dewey and his followers in the early 1900s.

The credit for establishing the first kindergarten in the United States is accorded to Mrs. Carl Schurz. After attending lectures on Froebelian principles in Germany, she returned to the United States and, in 1850, at Watertown, Wisconsin, opened her kindergarten. Mrs. Schurz's program was conducted in German as were many of the new kindergarten programs of the time since Froebel's ideas of education appealed to many bilingual parents. Mrs. Schurz's other major contribution was her influence on Elizabeth Peabody, the sister-in-law of Horace Mann. Elizabeth Peabody opened her kindergarten in Boston in 1860, but almost immediately realized that she was lacking in the necessary theory. She then went to Germany and visited kindergartens and in the process became more committed to Froebel's ideas. Following her return to the United States, she spent a great deal of time in popularizing Froebel's methods. Elizabeth Peabody is generally credited with being the main promoter of the kindergarten in the United States.

The first public school kindergarten was founded in St. Louis, Missouri in 1873 by Susan E. Blow with the cooperation of the St. Louis superintendent of schools, William T. Harris. This endorsement of the kindergarten program by the public schools did much to increase its popularity and spread the Froebelian influence on early childhood education. In addition, Harris, who later became the United States Commissioner of Education, encouraged support for Froebel's ideas and method while Susan Blow became a staunch defender of Froebel's principles against the attacks of John Dewey and his followers.

There were several factors which made the Froebel-oriented kindergarten movement vulnerable to attack by its critics. Basically, there was a tendency on the part of kindergarten teachers to formalize the methods of Froebel to the extent that they became in practice somewhat mechanical and rigid. Many teachers placed emphasis on implementing his procedures in a strict manner, therefore the kindergarten programs tended to become teacher-centered rather than child-centered. In contrast, Dewey felt that children needed to be involved in their learning.

American Educators

While the European influence on American education has been great and will probably continue to be expressed through the writings of educational reformers and the programs they advocate, it would be unfortunate for us to assume that our schools have benefited solely from Europe.

John Dewey (1859–1952)

John Dewey from Burlington, Vermont, represents a truly American influence on American education. Through his positions as professor of philosophy at the University of Chicago and Columbia University, his extensive writing, and the educational practices of his many followers, Dewey did more to profoundly alter and redirect the course of American education than any other person.

The spirit of Dewey's "progressivism" places emphasis on the child and his interests rather than merely concentrating on subject matter. It is from this emphasis that the terms *child centered curriculum* and *child centered schools* were coined. The progressive movement also maintains that the schools should be concerned with preparing the child for the realities of today rather than for some vague future time. As this is expressed by Dewey in his famous *My Pedagogical Creed,*[14] "education, therefore, is a process of living and not a preparation for future living."

What is included in Dewey's concept of children's interests? ". . . Not some one thing;" he explained, "it is a name for the fact that a course of action, an occupation, or pursuit absorbs the powers of an individual in a thorough-going way."[15] In a classroom based upon Dewey's ideas, the child is involved with physical activities, utilization of things, intellectual pursuits, and social interaction as opposed to passive attendance. Interest in physical activities is expressed through play in motor activities such as running, jumping, and other autonomous activities. In this phase the child begins the process of education and the development of the other interest areas. The growing child then learns to utilize tools and objects. Dewey felt that an ideal setting for the fulfillment of this interest was through daily living activities such as cooking and carpentry. In order to promote an interest in the intellectual—solving problems, discovering new things, and

---

[14]Reginald D. Archambault, ed., *John Dewey on Education—Selected Writings* (New York: Random House, Inc., 1964), p. 430.

[15]Henry Suzzallo, ed., *John Dewey's Interest and Effort in Education* (Boston, Massachusetts: Houghton, Mifflin Company, 1913), p. 65.

figuring out how things work—the child needs opportunities for inquiry and discovery. *Social interest* refers to interactions with persons that are necessary for society as a whole; Dewey viewed this interest as being encouraged in a democratically run classroom.

While the curriculum of the school should be built on the interests of children, Dewey felt it was the responsibility of the teacher to plan for and capitalize on the many opportunities to weave traditional subject matter through and around the fabric of these interests.

Dewey provides us with the following description of a school based on his ideas:

> All of the schools . . . as compared with traditional schools . . . [exhibit] a common emphasis upon respect for individuality and for increased freedom; a common disposition to build upon the nature and experience of the boys and girls that come to them, instead of imposing from without external subject-matter standards. They all display a certain atmosphere of informality, because experience has proved that formalization is hostile to genuine mental activity and to sincere emotional expression and growth. Emphasis upon activity as distinct from passivity is one of the common factors.[16]

His description is a precursor of what the open classroom should include. Teachers who correlate subjects, utilize the unit approach, and

Materials in early childhood settings should reflect the interests of children.

---

[16]Archambault, *Dewey—Selected Writings,* pp. 170–71.

encourage problem-solving activities are also philosophically indebted to Dewey.

Other ideas expressed by Dewey have had considerable impact upon current curricula and classroom practice since they often incorporate his five steps involved in reflective thinking.

> In between, as states of thinking, are (1) suggestions, in which the mind leaps forward to a possible solution; (2) an intellectualization of the difficulty or perplexity that has been felt (directly experienced) into a problem to be solved, a question for which the answer must be sought; (3) the use of one suggestion after another as a leading idea, or hypothesis, to initiate and guide observation and other operations in collection of factual material; (4) the mental elaboration of the idea or supposition as an idea or supposition (reasoning, in the sense in which reasoning is a part, not the whole, or inference); and (5) testing the hypothesis by overt or imaginative action. The five phases, terminals, or functions of thought that we have noted do not follow one another in a set order.[17]

There has been a great deal of misinterpretation and criticism of the progressive movement and Dewey's ideas, especially by those who favor a traditional approach to education that emphasizes the basic subjects and skills. Actually, Dewey was not opposed to basic skill learning or to subject matter. He did believe, however, that traditional educational strategies imposed knowledge on children, whereas the interests of children should be a springboard for involvement with skills and subject matter.

In the 1950s, criticism of the schools' inability to teach basics was largely aimed at the progressive movement. Although this criticism led to a renewed interest in early childhood education, it ironically has encouraged an adoption of educational practices such as the open classroom. The plea of Dewey for child activity is actually reinforced in Piaget and open education.

Modern Implications

To what extent are we influenced by the great educational thinkers of the past? While it is difficult to ascertain always in what areas and to what degree, it is obvious, I believe, from the foregoing analysis that we can find evidence of their thinking in current educational practices. Although much of the modern jargon of today's teaching would be alien to Froebel, many of the strategies would not. Terminology such as "open education" and "individualized prescribed instruction" are merely new names for vintage wine differently bottled.

---

[17]John Dewey, *How We Think,* (Boston: D.C. Heath and Company, 1933), p. 107.

It would also appear that historically there are certain ingredients common to good teaching regardless of time or place. Respecting children, attending to individual differences, and getting children interested and involved in their learning will continue to be the framework on which quality educational programs are designed. Reading about and examining the experiences of educational reformers can help keep this vision before us.

Historians are always anxious to remind us that history has the ability to show us past mistakes and how to avoid them in the future. Perhaps as a result of the above discussion and further reading, you will be able to determine what ideas were unsuccessful and why. This may be an asset in the development of your educational philosophy and goals. As George Santayana has said, "Those who ignore history may be condemned to repeat it."

BIBLIOGRAPHY

Archambault, Reginald D., ed. *John Dewey on Education—Selected Writings.* New York: Random House, Inc., 1964.

Comenius, John Amos. *The Great Didactic of John Amos Comenius.* Edited and translated by M. W. Keatinge. New York: Russell and Russell, 1967.

DeGuimps, Roger. *Pestalozzi: His Life and Work.* New York: D. Appleton and Company, 1890.

Dewey, John. *How We Think.* Boston: D.C. Heath and Co., 1933.

Froebel, Friedrich. *The Education of Man.* Translated by M. W. Hailmann. New York: D. Appleton and Company, 1890.

————. *Pedagogics of the Kindergarten.* Translated by Josephine Jarvis. New York: D. Appleton and Company, 1902.

Painter, F. V. N. *Luther on Education.* St. Louis, Missouri: Concordia Publishing House, 1928.

Rousseau, Jean Jacques. *Emile.* Edited and Translated by William Boyd. New York: Teachers College, Columbia University, 1962.

————. *Emile.* Barbara Foxley. New York: E. P. Dutton and Company, Inc., 1933.

Suzzallo, Henry, ed. *John Dewey's Interest and Effort in Education.* Boston: Houghton Mifflin Company, 1913.

FOR FURTHER READING AND STUDY

Auleta, Michael. *Foundations of Early Childhood Education: Readings.* New York: Random House, Inc., 1969.

Contains historical, social and psychological background for early childhood education as well as curricular programs and issues. A comprehensive selection that many undergraduates seem to enjoy.

Cole, Luella. *A History of Education: Socrates to Montessori.* New York: Rinehart and Co., 1950.
Provides a detailed account of the life histories and philosophies of individuals who have had a great influence on education. A reference most beneficial for the student who wants a detailed account of a historical figure.

Dewey, John. *Experience and Education.* New York: Collier Books, 1938.
An excellent source for comparison between traditional and progressive education. The reader will gain an insight into how Dewey's ideas are modern and relevant for today.

Rusk, Robert R. *Doctrines of the Great Educators.* 4th ed. New York: St. Martin's Press, 1969.
Provides glimpses into the doctrines of fourteen great educators, including Plato, Locke, Rousseau, Pestalozzi, Froebel, and Montessori. Selections from original writings provide a basis for contrast and comparison of theories.

Ulich, Robert, ed. *Three Thousand Years of Educational Wisdom.* Cambridge, Massachusetts: Harvard University Press, 1954.
A collection of educational writings from Plato to Dewey. Based on the idea that educational problems can be understood by learning about the past.

For Further Study and Involvement

1. Compare the classrooms you attended as a student with classrooms you are now visiting. What are the similarities? What are the *major* differences? How can these differences be explained?

2. Do you think most teachers are aware of historical influences on their teaching? Is it important to know?

3. Historically, teaching has been considered by some educational leaders as equal to the ministry. According to this view, teaching is a vocation to which one is "called." As a class activity, discuss this concept.

4. Many teachers of young children are probably more Froebelian in their approach to teaching than they realize. Can you find evidence to support this statement?

5. Some critics of education feel that the schools have assumed (or have been given) too much responsibility for teaching too many things. Do you feel there are certain subjects or topics that could be better taught through another institution or agency? If so, what topics? Why?

6. Reflect upon experiences you had as a student in early childhood. What experiences do you feel were and are the most meaningful? Why?

Maria Montessori
The Start of It All

If any one person has had a major role in sparking a revival in early childhood education it has been Maria Montessori. From day care centers to PTA meetings, it is usually possible to find someone anxious to discuss the pros and cons of her methodology.

Maria Montessori, an Italian, was born in 1870. Until her death in 1952, she devoted her life to the development of a system for educating young children. In 1970, the centennial of her birth was commemorated. Montessori, a precocious young woman, thought of entering mathematics or engineering. However, she was also interested in biology and consequently chose medicine as her career. In spite of the obstacles associated with entering a field traditionally closed to women, she persevered and became the first woman in Italy to earn the degree of doctor of medicine. Following this achievement, she was appointed as an assistant instructor in the psychiatric clinic of the University of Rome. Since it was customary not to distinguish between mentally retarded and insane, her work brought her into contact with the mentally retarded children committed to the asylums of Rome. Although Montessori's first intentions were to study children's diseases, she soon became interested in finding medical cures through educational principles for such problems as deafness, paralysis, and idiocy. At this time she says of herself, "I differed from my colleagues in that I instinctively felt that mental deficiency was more of an educational than medical problem."[1] At this time Montessori became interested in the work of Edward Seguin, a pioneer in the development of an educational system for mentally defective children. Another forerunner, the Frenchman Jean Itard, spent the majority of his life developing an educational system for deaf mutes. Montessori read the works of both Itard and Seguin, and credits them with providing the inspiration necessary to continue her studies with mentally retarded children. Of her initial efforts she says:

> I succeeded in teaching a number of the idiots from the asylums both to read and to write so well that I was able to present them at a public school for an examination together with normal children. And they passed the examination successfully.[2]

This was a remarkable achievement, which caused interest in both Montessori and in her methods. However, Montessori was already considering something else:

> While everyone else was admiring the progress made by my defective charges, I was trying to discover the reasons which could have reduced the healthy, happy pupils of the ordinary schools to such a low state that in the intelligence test they were on a level with my own unfortunate pupils.[3]

While continuing to study and prepare herself for the task of educating children, the opportunity to perfect her methods and implement them with normal school-age children occurred quite by chance. In 1906 she was invited by the Director General of the Roman Association for Good Building to organize schools for young children of families who occupied the tenement houses the association had constructed. In the first school, named the Casa dei Bambini or Children's House, she had the opportunity to test her ideas and to gain insights which led to the perfection of her system.

While studying and reading the works of Montessori, one must understand she was a profoundly religious person and a religious undertone is reflected throughout her work. She often quotes from the Bible, whose passages are used to lend support to many points of view. At the dedication ceremonies of the first Children's House she read from Isaiah 60:1–5, and ended by saying, "Perhaps, this Children's House can become a new Jerusa-

---

[1]Maria Montessori, *The Discovery of the Child,* trans. M. J. Costello (Notre Dame, Indiana: Fides Publishers, Inc., 1967), p. 22.

[2]Maria Montessori, *The Montessori Method,* trans. Anne E. George (Cambridge, Massachusetts: Robert Bentely, Inc., 1967), p. 38.

[3]Montessori, *The Discovery of the Child,* p. 28.

lem, which, if it is spread out among the abandoned people of the world, can bring a new light to education."[4] Her religious dedication to the fundamental sacredness and uniqueness of every child and subsequent grounding of educational processes in a religious conviction undoubtedly accounts for some of the remarkable achievements she made both as a person and as an educator. Thus her system functions well for those who are willing to dedicate themselves to teaching as if it were a religious vocation.

Principles of the Montessori Method

The following principles by no means constitute all of the principles Montessori stressed. However, they do reflect the salient ideas based upon my synthesis of the system following the reading of Montessori's writings, interaction with Montessori teachers, and observation in many Montessori settings.

Respect for the Child

This is undoubtedly the basic cornerstone on which all other Montessori principles rest. If this cornerstone were removed the whole system would collapse, and any further attempt to implement her additional ideas would surely constitute hypocrisy in terms of the teaching act. Of respect for children, Montessori says,

> As a rule, however, we do not respect children. We try to force them to follow us without regard to their special needs. We are overbearing with them, and above all, rude; and then we expect them to be submissive and well-behaved, knowing all the time how strong is their instinct of imitation and how touching their faith in and admiration of us. They will imitate us in any case. Let us treat them, therefore, with all the kindness which we would wish to help to develop in them. And by kindness is not meant caresses. Should we not call anyone who embraced us at the first time of meeting rude, vulgar and ill-bred? Kindness consists in interpreting the wishes of others, in conforming one's self to them, and sacrificing, if need be, one's own desire.[5]

Because children are unique individuals, education should be individualized for each child:

---

[4]*Ibid.*, p. 37.

[5]Maria Montessori, *Dr. Montessori's Own Handbook*, (New York: Schocken Books, Inc., 1965), p. 133.

The educator must be as one inspired by a deep *worship of life,* and must, through this reverence, respect, while he observes with human interest, the *development* of the child life. Now, child life is not an abstraction; *it is the life of individual children.* There exists only one real biological manifestation: the *living individual;* and toward single individuals, one by one observed, education must direct itself.[6]

Children are not miniature adults. She was firm in her belief that the child must be recognized as having a life separate and distinct from that of the adult. She believed that a great deal of the responsibility for hampering the education of the young child could be attributed directly to adults who impose their ideas, wishes and dreams on children, failing to distinguish between the child's life and their own lives.

In their dealings with children adults do not become egotistic but egocentric. They look upon everything pertaining to a child's soul from their own point of view and, consequently, their misapprehensions are constantly on the increase. Because of this egocentric view, adults look upon the child as *something empty* that is to be filled through their own efforts, as *something inert* and helpless for which they must do everything, as *something lacking an inner guide* and in constant need of direction. In conclusion we may say that the adult looks upon himself as the child's creator and judges the child's actions as good or bad from the viewpoint of his own relations to the child. The adult makes himself the touch stone of what is good and evil in the child. He is infallible, the model upon which the child must be molded. Any deviation on the child's part from adult ways is regarded as an evil which the adult hastens to correct.

An adult who acts in this way, even though he may be convinced that he is filled with zeal, love, and a spirit of sacrifice on behalf of his child, unconsciously suppresses the development of *the child's own personality.*[7]

Recently some of my students visited a day care center where a Montessori program was being conducted by a Benedictine sister. The sister, seated on the floor next to a new student had just asked the three year old to perform a particular task. The child's response to this request was to scream that she did not want to do anything at all and reinforced this with slapping. The sister calmly repeated the directions for the child and a few minutes later the child stopped screaming and slapping. The sister perceived that an alternative task would be equally appropriate and encouraged the child's involvement in it. The scene ended (or began) with the child mean-

---

[6]Montessori, *The Montessori Method,* p. 104.

[7]Maria Montessori, *The Secret of Childhood,* trans. M. Joseph Costelloe (Notre Dame, Indiana: Fides Publishers, Inc., 1966), p. 20.

ingfully participating in this new task. The respect in this incident can be compared to the actions one might expect from a "typical" teacher.

The Absorbent Mind

Montessori believed that no human being is educated by another person, rather he must *do it himself.* Montessori states, "It may be said that we acquire knowledge by using our minds; but the child absorbs knowledge directly into his psychic life. Simply by continuing to live, the child learns to speak his native tongue."[8] There are unconscious and conscious stages in the development of the absorbent mind. From birth to three years of age the *unconscious* absorbent mind develops the senses used for seeing, hearing, tasting, smelling and touching. The child absorbs everything. From three to six years the *conscious* absorbent mind selects consciously from the environment sensory impressions and further develops the senses. In this phase the child is selective in that he refines what he knows. For example, the child in the unconscious stage merely sees and absorbs an array of colors without making distinctions between them. However, from three on, he develops the ability to distinguish, match and grade colors. Montessori challenges the teacher to think through the concept of the absorbent mind:

> How does a child, starting with nothing, orient himself in this complicated world? How does he come to distinguish things, by what marvelous means does he come to learn a language in all its minute details without a teacher but merely by living simply, joyfully, and without fatigue, whereas an adult is in constant need of assistance to orient himself in a new environment to learn a new language, which he finds tedious and which he will never master with the same perfection with which a child acquires his own mother tongue?[9]

Montessori wants us to comprehend that children cannot help but learn. Simply by living, the child learns from his environment. Jerome Bruner expresses this same idea when he says that "learning is involuntary." The child learns because he is Homo sapiens, a thinking man. The specific "what" he learns is dependent to a great extent on the people in his environment, what they say and do, and how they react to him. In addition, environmental factors such as the experiences and materials available also help to determine the type and quality of learning—and thus the individual.

---

[8]From *The Absorbent Mind* by Maria Montessori. Trans. Claude A. Claremont. All rights reserved. (New York: Reprinted by permission of Holt, Rinehart and Winston, Publishers, 1967), p. 25.

[9]Montessori, *The Secret of Childhood,* p. 48.

Sensitive Periods

Montessori believed there were certain *sensitive periods* when children were more "susceptible" to certain behaviors and when specific skills could be learned more easily:

> A sensitive period refers to a special sensibility which a creature acquires in its infantile state, while it is still in a process of evolution. It is a transient disposition and limited to the acquisition of a particular trait. Once this trait or characteristic has been acquired, the special sensibility disappears.[10]
>
> A child learns to adjust himself and make acquisitions in his sensitive periods. These are like a beam that lights interiorly or a battery that furnishes energy. It is this sensibility which enables a child to come in contact with the external world in a particularly intense manner. At such a time everything is easy; all is life and enthusiasm. Every effort marks an increase in power. Only when the goal has been obtained does fatigue and the weight of indifference come on.
>
> When one of these psychic passions is exhausted, another area is enkindled. Childhood thus passes from conquest to conquest in a constant rhythm that constitutes its joy and happiness.[11]

The secret of sensitive periods is to recognize them when they occur, for while all children experience the same sensitive periods, i.e., a sensitive period for writing, the time at which a period occurs for each child is different. Therefore, it becomes the role of the directress (as Montessori teachers are often called) or the parent to detect these times of sensitivity and provide the child with a meaningful learning setting for the optimum fulfillment. Observation thus becomes crucial for teachers.

Additional implications associated with this concept can be determined by an analysis of the research discussed in chapter I and in other studies. The sensitive period for many learnings occurs early in life during the most rapid intellectual growth. The experiences necessary for optimum development must be provided at this time. Through observation and practice Montessori was convinced the sensitive period for the development of language in most children was a year or two earlier than had been originally thought.

Once the sensibility for learning a particular skill occurs, it will not occur again with the same intensity to facilitate learning. For example, children will never learn languages as well as when the special sensitivity

---

[10]Montessori, *Ibid.*, p. 46.
[11]*Ibid.*, p. 49.

for language learning occurs. Montessori says, "The child grows up speaking his parent's tongue, yet to grownups the learning of a language is a very great intellectual achievement."[12]

In brief summary, teachers must do these three things: recognize that sensitive periods exist; detect their presence through skilled observation; and capitalize on them by providing the optimum learning setting.

The Prepared Environment

Montessori arranged for the child a *prepared environment,* which includes any setting, be it classroom, room at home, nursery, or playground where the child can learn in the optimum manner. Its aim is to make the child independent of the adult. It is a place where he can *do things for himself.* Classrooms as she described them are really what educators advocate when they talk about open education; in many respects she was the precursor of the current open classroom movement. Following a teacher's introduction, children could come and go according to their desires and needs, deciding by themselves which materials to work with. She removed the typical school desks as we conceive of them and replaced them with tables and chairs. In a modern Montessori classroom, much of a child's work is done on the floor on a piece of carpeting. Montessori saw no reason for a teacher's desk since the teacher should be involved with the children where they are doing their work, which is usually on the floor. She also introduced child-sized furniture, lowered chalkboards, and conceived of outside areas where children could go at will and enter into gardening activities. Her concept of a classroom was a place in which children could do things for themselves; where they could interact with materials that had been placed there for specific purposes; and *where they could be free to educate themselves.* In response to these concepts she developed a classroom free of many of the inhibitions that we find in some classrooms today.

An essential characteristic of this environment is freedom. Since children are free within the environment to explore and to interact with materials of their own choosing, they absorb what they find there. At first thought it may seem to you that nothing but chaos will result. Many adults feel that if a child is given freedom he will abuse it through acts destructive to himself or others. When it is anticipated these acts will occur, a Montessori teacher will quickly divert the child away from the undesirable behavior towards materials or activities. Although the Montessori teacher believes in freedom for the child and in the ability of the child to exercise that freedom, this does

---

[12]Montessori, *The Absorbent Mind,* p. 6.

Involvement in cooking activities can help children achieve independence.

not mean the child is free to make unlimited choices. For example, knowledge of the correct use of the materials must precede the choice. Within the framework of choices provided by the teacher, the student is free to choose.

Self- or Auto-Education

Closely linked to the principles of the prepared environment and freedom is the concept that children have the capability for educating themselves. This concept Montessori refers to as auto-education:

> The commonest prejudice in ordinary education is that everything can be accomplished by talking (by appealing, that is, to the child's ear), or by holding one's self up as a model to be imitated (a kind of appeal to the eye), while the truth is that the personality can only develop by making use of its own powers.[13]

The child actively involved in a prepared environment and exercising freedom of choice literally educates himself. The role freedom plays in self education is crucial according to Montessori:

> And this freedom is not only an external sign of liberty, but a means of education. If by an awkward movement a child upsets a chair, which falls noisily to the floor, he will have an evident proof of his own incapacity; the same movement had it taken place amidst stationary benches would have passed unnoticed by him. Thus the child has some means by which

---

[13] *Ibid.,* p. 254.

he can correct himself, and having done so will have before him the actual proof of the power he has gained: the little tables and chairs remain firm and silent each in its own place. It is plainly seen that the *child has learned* to command his movements.[14]

Our universal perception of the teaching–learning act is that the teacher teaches and because of this the child learns. We have overlooked that everyone has learned a great deal through their own efforts. Through the principle of auto-education, Montessori focuses our attention on this human capability. The teaching act therefore includes preparing the environment so that children, through participation in it, educate themselves. Think for a moment, if you will, of those things which you learned by yourself and the conditions and circumstances under which you learned them. This reflection should reveal, among other things, the self-satisfaction that accompanies self-learning and the power it has to generate continued and further involvement. Obviously there are instances in which it is quicker, more efficient and more economical to be told or shown directly. What we should understand, however, is that auto-education ought to have a more dominant role than we have been willing to give it.

The Role of the Teacher

The individual who will accomplish implementation of the Montessori Principles must obviously have certain qualities combined to effect a particular role. Generally the public conceives of the ideal teacher as one who stands in front of a classroom and dispenses knowledge to children as though it were going out of style. In summary, if you desire to implement Montessori ideas, your role as a teacher will include:

1. Making the children the center of learning. As Montessori said, "The teacher's task is not to talk, but to prepare and arrange a series of motives for cultural activity in a special environment made for the child."[15]

2. Insuring that children utilize the freedom provided. According to Montessori, "It is necessary for the teacher to *guide* the child without letting him feel her presence too much, so that she may be always ready to supply the desired help, but may never be the obstacle between the child and his experience."[16]

3. Observing the children to best prepare the environment, recognize sensitive periods, and divert unacceptable behavior to meaningful

---

[14] *Ibid.*, p. 84.
[15] *Ibid.*, p. 8.
[16] Montessori, *Montessori's Handbook*, p. 131.

activities. A system of organized records of children's activities will enable you to plan for new involvement on the part of each child.

The Method

In a prepared environment there are materials and activities which provide for three basic areas of involvement on the part of the child: practical life or motor education, sensory materials for the training of the senses, and academic materials for the teaching of writing and reading. All these activities are taught according to a prescribed procedure.

Practical Life

Basic, everyday motor activities of locomotion including walking from place to place in an orderly manner and carrying objects such as trays and chairs are emphasized in this area. Other activities include exercises on how to greet a stranger, how to offer a chair to someone, walking on a line, and being silent. The new observer to a Montessori classroom is always fascinated by the "dressing frames" designed to perfect the motor skills involved with buttoning, zippering, lacing, buckling, and tying. The philosophy for activities such as these is to make the child independent of the adult and to develop concentration. Water activities play a large role in Montessori methods and children are taught to scrub, wash, and pour as a means of developing coordination. Practical life exercises also include

Following a practical life activity of slicing carrots, a child offers them as a snack to a classmate.

polishing mirrors and shoes, sweeping the floor, dusting furniture, and peeling vegetables.

As the child becomes absorbed in an activity, he gradually lengthens his span of concentration. As he follows a regular sequence of actions, he learns to pay attention to details. Montessorians believe that without concentration and attention by the senses, no learning takes place. Although most people assume that many practical life activities are learned incidently, a Montessori teacher shows children how to accomplish these activities via precise details and instructions with an emphasis on sensory materials. Verbal instructions are at a minimum level. The emphasis is placed on *showing how.*

Montessori also believed children's involvement and concentration in motor activities lengthened their attention span. In a Montessori classroom it is not uncommon to see a child of four or five polishing his shoes or scrubbing a table for twenty minutes at a time!

The practical life activities discussed above have four sets of exercises. *Care of the person* involves using the dressing frames, polishing shoes, and washing hands. *Care of the environment* includes dusting, polishing a table, and raking leaves. *Social relations* allows lessons in grace and courtesy. The fourth involves *the analysis and control of movement* and includes walking.

Sensory Materials

The following sensory materials are used in Montessori programs for the training and development of the senses. The materials have the following characteristics:

1. Control of error. The materials are designed so that a child can see if he makes a mistake; e.g., if he does not build the blocks of the pink tower in their proper order, he does not achieve a tower effect.

2. Isolation of a single quality. The materials are so designed that other variables of a material are held constant except that quality or qualities isolated. Therefore, all of the blocks of the pink tower are pink because size, not color, is the isolated quality.

3. Active involvement. All of the materials encourage the active involvement of the child. The child, therefore, is involved through *doing* rather than through the rather passive process of looking.

4. Attractiveness. The materials are attractive. They possess color and proportions that are appealing to children.

Examples of Sensory Materials.

1. Pink tower - introduces the child to visual discrimination of dimension. Ten cubes of the same shape and texture, all pink, the

largest of which is ten centimeters square. Each succeeding block is one centimeter smaller. The child builds a tower beginning with the largest block.

2. Brown stairs - introduces the child to visual discrimination of width and height. Ten blocks of wood, all brown, differing in height and width. The child arranges the blocks next to each other from largest to smallest so they resemble a staircase.

3. Red rods - introduces the child to visual discrimination of length. Ten rodshaped pieces of wood, all red, of identical size but differing in lengths from four inches to forty inches. The child arranges the blocks next to each other from largest to smallest.

4. Cylinder blocks - introduces the child to visual discrimination by use of three individual wood blocks with holes of various sizes. One block deals with depth, one with circumference and one with both of these variables. The child removes the cylinders in mixed order and then matches each cylinder to the correct hole.

5. Smelling jars - introduces the child to discrimination involving the olfactory sense. Two identical sets of jars made of white, opaque glass. There are removable tops through which the child cannot see but through which odors can pass. The teacher places various substances, such as herbs, in the jars and the child matches the jars according to smell.

6. Baric tablets - introduces the child to discrimination of weight. Rectangular pieces of wood which vary according to weight. There are three sets, light, medium, and heavy in weight, which the child matches according to weight.

7. Color tablets - introduces the child to discrimination of color and the education of the chromatic sense. Two identical sets of small, rectangular pieces of wood used for matching color or shading.

8. Sound boxes - introduces the child to the auditory sense. Two identical sets of cylinders are filled with various materials such as salt and rice. The child matches the cylinders according to sound.

9. Tonal bells - introduces the child to the sense of sound and pitch. Two sets of eight bells which are alike in shape and size but differ in color. One set is white, the other brown. The child matches the bells according to tone.

10. Cloth swatches - introduces the child to the sense of touch. The child identifies two identical swatches of cloth according to touch. This is first done without a blindfold, but is later accomplished while blindfolded.

11. Temperature jugs or thermic bottles - introduces the child to the thermic sense and involves the ability to distinguish between tem-

peratures. Small metal jugs are filled with water of varying temperatures. The child matches jugs of the same temperature.

Use of Sensory Materials. Because sensory materials provide observers opportunities to pick up and examine materials and because of the intense involvement of children with them, they receive a great deal of observer attention. These materials are often labeled didactic (meaning materials designed to instruct) as their purpose is to facilitate learning of certain concepts.

There are several basic purposes of Montessori sensory materials. The first is to train the senses of the child so his mind focuses on some obvious, particular quality of the sensory material. For example, with the red rods, the quality is length; with pink tower cubes, size; and with bells, musical pitch. Montessori felt it was necessary for children to be taught to distinguish from among the stimuli that are already constantly stimulating them. Accordingly, the sensory materials help make children more aware of the capacity of their bodies to receive, interpret and make use of the stimuli they receive.

Building the Pink Tower, one of the Montessori Sensory Materials. The piece of carpeting defines the work area.

Montessori also thought that perception and the ability to observe details was crucial to the reading process. Montessori believed children should sharpen their powers of observation and visual discrimination prior to the reading process. Teachers of beginning reading can profit from using Montessori ideas prior to the introduction of formalized reading.

A third purpose of the sensory materials is to increase the child's ability to think, a process dependent upon the ability to distinguish, classify and organize. Children are constantly faced with decisions concerning the materials: which block comes next, which color comes next, which shape goes where. These are not decisions which the teacher makes nor are they decisions the child arrives at by guessing, but are decisions made by the intelligent process of observation and selection based upon knowledge gathered through the senses.

Lastly, it should be understood that all of the sensorial activities are not ends unto themselves. The purpose of any of the activities is not merely to have the child perform them but to prepare the child for the time when the sensitive periods for writing and reading occur. In this sense, all activities are preliminary steps in the writing-reading process. In addition, these activities should not be performed in isolation from the real world. If examples of relation are not found within the classroom then the child will not benefit. If a child is asked to deal with color only when he is working with the color tablets, there is no assurance he will have a meaningful understanding of color. While he may be able to identify red, his understanding of redness may be limited. Examples should be found within the classroom to call the child's attention to color. Only as he uses color as a basis for more learning will it enrich the child's life.

Materials for Writing and Reading

The third area of Montessori materials are academic, specifically items for writing and reading. In the Montessori method, exercises are presented to children in a sequence that encourages involvement in writing before reading. Reading is therefore an outgrowth of the writing process. Both of these processes, however, are introduced so gradually that children are never really aware they are writing or reading until, suddenly, one day, they realize they are writing and reading. To describe this phenomenon, Montessori said that children "burst spontaneously" into writing and reading. Montessori believed many children, by the age of four, were ready for the writing process. Consequently a child who enters a Montessori system at age three has done most of the sensory exercises by the time he is four; it is not uncommon to see four- and five-year-old children in a Montessori classroom writing and reading.

Sample Materials for Writing and Reading.

1. Ten geometric insets and colored pencils introduce the child to the coordination necessary for writing. After selecting a geometric inset, the child traces it on paper and then fills in the outline with a colored pencil of his own choosing.
2. Sandpaper letters - each letter of the alphabet is outlined in sandpaper on an individual card—vowels in blue and consonants in red. The child participates through seeing the shape, feeling the shape, and hearing the sound of the letter, which the teacher repeats when introducing it.
3. Moveable alphabet - individual wooden letters of the alphabet. The child learns to put together words familiar to him.
4. Command cards - a set of red cards with a single action word printed on each card. The child reads the word on the card and does what the word tells him to do; e.g., run, jump, etc.

Sample Materials for Mathematics.

1. Number rods - a set of red and blue rods varying in length, representing the quantities from one through ten. With the help of the teacher, the child is introduced to counting.
2. Sandpaper numerals - each number from one to ten in sandpaper on an individual card. The child participates through seeing, touching and hearing the numbers. He eventually matches number rods and sandpaper numerals. The child is also given the opportunity to discover the mathematical facts.
3. Golden beads - A concrete material for the decimal system. The single bead represents one unit. A bar made up of ten units in a row represents a ten; ten of the ten bars form a square representing a hundred; and ten hundred squares form the cube representing a thousand.

Additional Features of the Montessori System

Other features of the Montessori system which need to be considered are mixed age grouping, and self pacing. A Montessori classroom always contains children of different ages, usually from 2½–6 years of age. This strategy is becoming more popular in many open classroom settings and certainly has been popular in the British Primary Schools. Advantages of having mixed age groups in one setting are many: children learn from one another; children help each other; a wide range of materials is available for all children; and older children become role-models for younger children.

By stressing individuality and freedom in a Montessori classroom, children are free to learn at their own speed and level of achievement. The child becomes the determiner of the activities in which he participates at his own pace. It should not be assumed that the child is allowed to dally forever at a particular task. Through observation, the teacher determines when a child has perfected a particular exercise and is ready to move on to a higher level exercise or a different exercise. If a child does not perform an activity correctly, the teacher provides additional help and instruction.

Criticisms of the Montessori Method

It should not be assumed that the Montessori system is without opponents. One criticism deals with the didactic nature of the materials and the program. Such critics see the system as teaching a narrow spectrum of activities involving the senses, in which the materials and ideas are learned in a prescribed manner, following prescribed methods, using a prescribed set of materials. These people would prefer to have the child more involved in a wider range of materials and activities. These critics claim the sensory materials are limited in their usefulness. They see the pink tower being used only to teach visual discrimination. This may or may not be true according to the particular Montessori setting.

Some critics also see in the Montessori classroom a tendency toward formality and authoritarianism. They claim that while the Montessori method advocates freedom, they practice prescribed use of materials in prescribed ways. While children are free to use materials, they can only be used after they have been presented to them by the teacher who shows how to use them. Individuals who would like to see the child in a more "social" setting criticize the system on this basis. They maintain the Montessori classroom is not sociable enough and therefore does not provide for the socialization of the child. They cite as examples lack of child involvement in group play, games, and other activities normally present in traditional kindergarten programs. A related criticism is that children do not have opportunities to participate in dramatics, make-believe and pretending. The absence of a dress-up corner and free-play area is frequently used as evidence. However, Montessori felt that children of 2½–6 years of age were not mature enough to handle the demands placed on them by a make-believe world. This explains why provisions for it are not found in her system. It does not, however, solve the question of the appropriateness of these activities for young children.

Frequently the charge is heard that Montessori schools represent an elitist or middle-class system. This claim very likely stems from the fact that most Montessori schools are private schools, operated by individuals for profit or by Catholic school systems. While this seems to be the case, there is evidence that Montessori applications are being made to Head Start and day care settings and some public school settings.

More Information

Frequently students are interested in knowing more about becoming a Montessori teacher. Information about the American program can be obtained by writing The American Montessori Society, 175 Fifth Avenue, New York, New York, 10010, or information about the international program by writing The Montessori Institute, 2119 S Street Northwest, Washington, D.C., 20008. Generally, Montessori training takes one year to complete and results in an international certificate. Once a certificate is obtained it can be used to teach in Montessori settings. However, it does not generally substitute for public school certification. While a bachelor's degree is not necessary for entrance to Montessori training centers, it is helpful.

BIBLIOGRAPHY

Montessori, Maria. *The Absorbent Mind.* Translated by Claude A. Claremont. New York: Holt, Rinehart and Winston Publishers, 1967.

————. *The Discovery of the Child.* Translated by M. Joseph Costelloe. Notre Dame, Indiana: Fides Publishers, Inc., 1967.

————. *Dr. Montessori's Own Handbook.* New York: Schocken Books, Inc., 1965.

————. *The Montessori Method.* Translated by Anne E. George. Cambridge, Massachusetts: Robert Bentely, Inc., 1967.

————. *The Secret of Childhood.* Translated by M. Joseph Costelloe. Notre Dame, Indiana: Fides Publishers, Inc., 1966.

FOR FURTHER READING AND STUDY

Cartwright, Carol A. and Cartwright, Philip G. *Developing Observation Skills.* New York: McGraw-Hill Book Company, 1974.
   Because observation of children is so important in the Montessori system, I have included this book. Since I feel observation should be used by all teachers,

the concepts discussed by the authors are applicable to all teaching. There are many practical and usable ideas relating to specific types of records for observation.

Lillard, Raula Polk. *Montessori, A Modern Approach.* New York: Schocken Books, Inc., 1972.

A good account of what happens in the Montessori classroom. Begins with the life of Montessori and concludes with a description of current practices.

Montessori, Maria. *Spontaneous Activity in Education.* New York: Schocken Books, Inc., 1965.

A continuation of ideas and methodologies begun in *The Montessori Method.* Deals with concepts of attention, intelligence, imagination, and moral development, and discusses provisions for them in a Montessori setting.

Orem, R. D. *Montessori Today.* New York: G. P. Putnam's Sons, 1971.

A survey of the philosophies and programs of practices of Montessori schools in the United States. Will help all who want to know more about the Montessori method through accounts contributed from actual programs.

Standing, E. M. *The Montessori Revolution in Education.* 6th ed. New York: Schocken Books, Inc., 1971.

An excellent reference for students wanting to know more about the Montessori method. An easy-to-read, understandable description of activities, accompanied by illustrations.

For Further Study and Involvement

1. Following the reading of the chapter on open education, compare Montessori concepts to those of open education. What are the similarities and differences?

2. Compare Montessori materials to those found in other kindergarten programs. Do you think it is possible for teachers to make Montessori materials? What advantages and/or disadvantages would there be in making and using these materials?

3. What features of the Montessori program do you like best? Why? What features do you like the least? Why? What features are best for children?

4. After visiting a Montessori classroom and talking with teachers, evaluate the criticisms of the system listed at the end of the chapter. Do you think the criticisms are valid? Are there any additional ones you would add? Why?

5. If a mother of a four year old asked your advice about sending her child to a Montessori school, what would you tell her?

4

Jean Piaget
A New Way of
Thinking about Thinking

In education and psychology there is probably no single person more frequently mentioned than Piaget. His name is constantly dropped by those who would assure their listeners they are in the educational know. While a few enterprising educators are involved in developing curricula based on Piaget's ideas, the majority would like to have some understanding of his theory, for his writings are, at best, difficult to comprehend. While Piaget is popular as a name, too few know about his theory of intelligence. On the other hand, well-meaning teachers confuse his classical methods for analyzing children's thinking with an early childhood curriculum and think that by using these methods they are consequently teaching children. I am under no delusion about the inherent danger involved in trying to discuss in a short chapter the magnitude and power of Piaget's ideas for future educators of young children. Hopefully several things will happen: you will have an honest idea of the underlying principles of his theory; you will be able to talk knowledgeably about these ideas; you will be stimulated to do more reading and discussion; and you will consider his ideas when developing your curriculum for teaching young children.

Personal Data

Piaget was born in Switzerland in 1896. A very precocious person, he published his first article about a sparrow at the age of ten; received his baccalaureate degree from college at eighteen; and earned his doctorate three years later. His doctoral thesis concerned mollusks, which he had been interested in from a very early age. His training in the field of biology was an influential factor in the development of his ideas about intelligence; the primary basis for his theory of intellectual growth is biological. Piaget also spent time studying in Paris and working with Theodore Simon at the Alfred Binet laboratory, standardizing tests of reasoning designed for use with children. (You will recall that Binet and Simon developed a scale for measuring intelligence.) This experience also provided the foundation for his clinical methodology of interviewing used in studying the intellectual development of children. As Piaget recalls, "Thus I engaged my subjects in conversations patterned after psychiatric questioning, with the aim of discovering something about the reasoning process underlying their right, but especially their wrong, answers."[1] The emphasis on this methodology helps explain why developers of a Piaget-based early childhood curriculum place an emphasis on the teacher's role of developing and utilizing various questioning procedures. Following his work with children in Paris, which established the direction of his life work, Piaget became associated with the Institute J. J. Rousseau in Geneva, Switzerland. It was here that he began his career of studying the intellectual development of children. In 1925 the first of his three children was born. They played a major role in his studies since many of his observations and consequent insights about how children think are based upon his observations and work with them. The research procedure of using only his own children as participants in some of his studies, however, has sometimes been used as a criticism of his findings. His theory, however, is based not only on this research, but also on literally hundreds of studies involving thousands of children.

Adaptation

Biological Emphasis

One of the basic concepts that must be comprehended about Piaget's work is that his early training as a biologist permeates and influences his theory

---

[1] Edwin G. Boring et al., eds., *A History of Psychology in Autobiography,* vol. IV (Worchester, Mass.: Clark University Press, 1952; reprinted New York: Russell & Russell, 1968), p. 244.

of intelligence. In this regard, he conceives of intelligence as having a biological base. This biological basis for intelligence refers essentially to the belief held by many educators and psychologists that all organisms, including humans, can adapt to their environment. It is by this adaptive process that intelligence is *created*. Most people are familiar with the concept of physical adaptation whereby an organism or individual, when stimulated by environmental factors, reacts and adjusts in relation to that environment. This adjustment can often result in physical changes and alterations in ways of behaving. We think about adaptations to environmental factors involving, among other things, food and territory. Piaget has taken this concept of physical adaptation and applied it to the mental level. He thus conceptualizes people as adapting mentally to environmental experiences with other people, places and things. Interaction and adaptation to the physical environment on the part of an individual is much the same as that which occurs on the mental level. For example, as a college student you had to make many adaptations to the collegiate setting. You adapted to foods prepared in different ways, and to different standards of housing and privacy. At the mental level you had to adjust to a higher level of self-discipline and to the values and ideas of classmates and professors. Through the adaptive process, you were able to remain a student.

Intellectual Level of Adaptation

Piaget envisions the adaptive process as it operates at the physical level to be similar to that which occurs at the intellectual level. He sees the newborn child as lacking intelligence, except that intelligence expressed through reflexive motor actions such as sucking, grasping, head turning, swallowing, etc. It is through the process of interaction with and adaptation to the environment via these reflexive actions that the intelligence of the young child has its origin and is developed.

> *Adaptation* is for Piaget the essence of intellectual functioning, just as it is the essence of biological functioning. We have long been familiar with adaptation in the Darwinian sense of "survival of the fittest." But to Piaget the word means more than just survival; it means modifying the environment to our own ends. He believes that an essential part of our biological inheritance is a mode of intellectual functioning which remains constant throughout life. This functioning is characterized by the ability to organize the myriad sensations and experiences we encounter into some kind of order, and to adapt ourselves to our surroundings.[2]

[2]Mary Ann Spencer Pulaski, *Understanding Piaget* (New York: Harper and Row, 1971), p. 6.

It is through this process of interaction with the environment, resulting in adaptation, that the child "organizes" sensations and experiences. The resulting organization(s) and processes of interaction are what is called intelligence. It should be readily apparent, therefore, that the quality of the environment and the nature of the child's interaction with it will play perhaps the major role in the development of intelligence. For example, the child with various and differing objects available to grasp and suck and many opportunities for this behavior will develop differentiated sucking organizations (and therefore an intelligence) quite different from the child who has nothing to suck but a pacifier.

Processes of Adaption

Piaget believes that the adaptive process is comprised of two interrelated processes, *assimilation* and *accommodation.* Essentially, on the intellectual level assimilation is the taking in of data through sensory impulses via experiences and impressions and incorporating those data into the organizations or model of the world already created as a result of these experiences.

> Every experience we have, whether as infant, child or adult, is taken into the mind and made to fit into the experiences which already exist there. The new experience will need to be changed in some degree in order for it to fit in. Some experiences cannot be taken in because they do not fit. These are rejected. Thus the intellect assimilates new experiences into itself by transforming them to fit the structure which has been built up. This process of acting on the environment in order to build up a model of it in the mind, Piaget calls assimilation.[3]

Accommodation, on the other hand, is when the individual changes his way of thinking, behaving, believing, etc., to come into accordance with reality as it is shown to be. For example, a child who is familiar with cats because she has several at home may, upon seeing a dog for the first time, call it a cat. She has assimilated dog into her organization or scheme of cat. However, she must change (accommodate) her model of what constitutes "catness" to exclude dogs. She does this by starting to construct or build a scheme for dog and thus what "dogness" represents.

> Now with each new experience, the structures which have already been built up will need to modify themselves to accept that new experience, for, as each new experience is fitted in to the old, the structures will be slightly

---

[3]From *An Introduction to Piaget,* by P. G. Richmond, © 1970 bb P. G. Richmond, Basic Books, Inc. Publishers, New York, p. 68.

changed. This process by which the intellect continually adjusts its model of the world to fit in each new acquisition, Piaget calls accommodation.[4]

The twin processes of assimilation and accommodation, when viewed as an integrated, functioning whole, constitute adaptation.

Another term that Piaget uses in his theory of intelligence is *equilibrium*. Equilibrium is a balance between assimilation and accommodation. An individual cannot assimilate new data without changing to some degree his way of thinking or acting to fit those new data. People who always assimilate without much evidence of having changed are characterized as "flying in the face of reality." Yet on the other hand an individual cannot always accommodate to fit all the information he receives. If this were the case, no beliefs would ever be maintained. What is needed is a balance between the two. Diagrammed, the process would look something like that found in Figure 4.

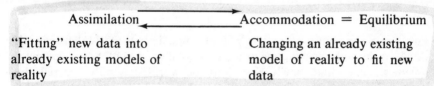

Assimilation	Accommodation = Equilibrium
"Fitting" new data into already existing models of reality	Changing an already existing model of reality to fit new data

Figure 4 *The Adaptation Process*

Upon receiving new sensory and experiential data, the child assimilates or "fits" these data into her already existing model (scheme) of reality and the world. If the new data can be immediately assimilated, then equilibrium occurs. If she is unable to assimilate the data, she tries to accommodate and change her way of thinking, acting, perceiving, etc., to account for the new data and restore equilibrium to the intellectual system. It may well be that she can neither assimilate nor accommodate the new data. If this occurs, she rejects the new data entirely.

Instances of rejection are common if what is trying to be assimilated and accommodated is radically different from past data and experiences. This would partially account for Piaget's insistence that all new experiences be planned so that the child has some connection or relationship to previous experiences. A further pedagogical implication of this idea for teachers would be an analysis through testing, observation, parent conferences, anecdotal records, student interviews, etc., of the experiential levels, both in quantity and quality, of their children. Present school experiences should be built on previous life experiences. Even more importantly, a teacher must

---

[4] *Ibid.*

try to assess the cognitive structures of all children and determine the suitability of school tasks in promoting cognitive growth. For example, prior to providing a child with activities in class inclusion, a teacher must first determine the level at which the child is functioning in relation to classification structures. A program such as the Lavatelli Materials can help determine such levels. It is also imperative that the teacher not assign (or demand, as is so frequently done) the child to do tasks for which she lacks the cognitive structure that precludes her completing the task. Undoubtedly some of the reasons for school failure can be attributed to teachers insisting that children engage in tasks for which they have no experiential background and consequently lack the necessary cognitive structure. For example, it is damaging to the mental health of the child to ask her to perform a task that requires her to discriminate between words when she cannot discriminate between the letters of the alphabet!

Schemes

Piaget uses the term *scheme* to refer to the model of the world that the child develops through the adaptive process. (In reality, the child develops many schemes.) The child, newly born into the world, has only her reflexive actions. It is by using reflexive actions such as sucking, grasping, etc., that the child comes to "know" the world and builds her concept and understanding of it. When the child is primarily utilizing reflexive actions to develop intellectually, she is in what Piaget calls the *sensorimotor stage.* This stage begins at birth and usually ends between eighteen months and two years. For example, using reflexive actions she constructs a mental scheme of what is suckable and what is not (what can fit into her mouth and what cannot), and what sensations (warm and cold) occur by sucking. She also uses her grasping reflex in much the same way to build schemes of what can and cannot be grasped.

In developing or building schemes of the world and reality you may well be wondering why it is that some children develop or create different schemes. Some of you have realized that this will depend to a great extent upon the *environment* in which the child is reared and the *quality* of the experiences which the child has in that environment. If the environment of the child and her interaction with that environment are going to establish parameters for the development of intelligence, then the child who is confined to a crib with no objects, with the possible exception of a pacifier, is at a definite disadvantage in building mental structures through the adaptive process utilizing sensorimotor responses. On the other hand, the child who has a variety of materials to interact with has more of an opportunity to develop alternative schemes. Children who have a variety of materials *and* a caring adult to help stimulate sensory responses will do even better. By the same token, as the child grows and matures she will have increased opportunity to develop intellectually in an environment that provides for interaction with people, processes, and things. You have probably come to the conclusion by now that the quality of the interaction is also important.

Two children become actively involved in learning with concrete materials.

In this interactive process of adaptation, Piaget ascribes primary importance to physical activity on the part of the child. Physical activity leads to mental stimulus which in turn leads to mental activity. Thus it is not possible to draw a clear line between physical activity and mental development in infancy and early childhood. Settings should be provided in which all children can explore their physical environment, and in this exploration have people and objects with which to interact. Consequently, the child who is confined to a playpen without opportunities for manipulating objects and for social interactions is limited in the adaptive opportunities available.

Everyone recognizes that children play. The recognition that all children should play is almost universal. However, we have not always recognized the importance of play in providing the context whereby the child builds mental schemes to form a basis for all other schemes. Play for Piaget becomes a very powerful process in intellectual development. Parents seem to sense this intuitively in wanting their children to play, particularly with other children. Many kindergarten and first-grade teachers have also had an intuitive insight into the importance of play by the inclusion of many opportunities for play in their curricula.

Maturation. An additional factor that Piaget believes has an influence on the intellectual development of the child is *maturation.* Maturation means the development of the child over a period of time. Factors which influence maturation are: (1) genetic characteristics peculiar to the child as an individual, (2) the unique characteristics of the child because he is a Homo sapiens, (3) environmental factors such as nutrition. Maturation accounts in part to help explain why the thinking of the child is not the same as the thinking of the adult and provides a rationale for why we should not expect the child to think the same as an adult. The child who has adults to interact with in a meaningful way, e.g., conversation which solicits and promotes the child's involvement, has the opportunity to develop schemes different from those of the child who lacks this opportunity.

Social transmission. Piaget feels social transmission is important because there are some information and modes of behavior which are transmitted best to the child by people rather than through other methods such as reading.[5] Examples of social transmission include behavior appropriate to certain situations such as not running in front of speeding cars and not blowing one's nose without benefit of a handkerchief.

Stages of Development

Figure 5 summarizes Piaget's developmental stages, and it may help the reader conceptualize stage-related characteristics. Piaget has identified these stages through which the child progresses. Piaget contends that the stages are the same for all children, including the atypical child, and that all children progress through each stage in the following order. However, the ages given are only approximate and should not be considered fixed. For all children, growth through the developmental stages is invariant while the ages at which this progression occurs are variant.

Sensorimotor Stage

This period begins at birth and continues until approximately eighteen months to two years. During this period the child utilizes her senses and motoric reflexes to begin building her model of the world. Consequently, she uses her eyes to view the world, her mouth to suck, and her hands to grasp. Through these innate sensory and reflexive actions the child continues to develop an increasingly complex, unique and individualized hierar-

---

[5]When discussing environmental influences, I included people as belonging to the environment. Piaget considers them to be a separate factor.

Stage	Age	Characteristics
Sensorimotor	Birth–18 months/2 years	Uses sensorimotor systems of sucking, grasping, and gross body activities to build schemes. Begins to develop object permanency. Dependent on concrete representations. The frame of reference is the world of here and now.
Preoperational	2–7 years	Language development accelerates. Internalizes events. Egocentric in thought and action. Thinks everything has a reason or purpose. Is perceptually bound. Makes judgments primarily on basis of how things look.
Concrete Operations	7–12 years	Capable of reversal of thought processes. Ability to conserve. Still dependent on how things look for decision making. Less egocentric. Structures time and space. Understanding of number. Beginning of logical thinking.
Formal Operations	12–15 years	Capable of dealing with verbal and hypothetical problems. Ability to reason scientifically and logically. No longer bound to the concrete. Can think with symbols.

Figure 5 *Piaget's Stages of Cognitive Development*

chy of schemes. What the child is to become both physically and intellectually is related to these sensorimotor functions and interactions. As Furth indicates, "An organism exists only insofar as it functions."[6] This extremely important concept stresses the importance of an enriched environment for children.

---

[6]Hans G. Furth, *Piaget for Teachers* (Englewood Cliffs, New Jersey: Prentice–Hall, Inc., 1970), p. 15.

Some of the major characteristics of children during the sensorimotor period include the following:

1. Dependency on and the use of innate reflexive actions.
2. Initial development of object permanency (the idea that objects can exist without being seen).
3. Egocentricity whereby the child sees herself as the center of the world and believes events are caused by her.
4. Dependence upon concrete representations (things) rather than symbols (words, pictures, etc.) for information.

By the end of the second year the child relies less on sensorimotor reflexive actions and begins to represent things that are not present.

Preoperational Stage

The preoperational stage begins at age two and ends at approximately seven years of age. The preoperational child is different from the sensorimotor child in the following ways:

(1) language development begins to accelerate rapidly;
(2) there is less dependence on sensorimotor reflexive action;
(3) there is an increased ability to internalize events, e.g., to think by utilizing representational symbols such as words in place of things.

The preoperational child continues to share common characteristics with the sensorimotor child such as egocentricity. At the preoperational level egocentricity is characterized by being perceptually bound. The outward manifestation of this occurs by making judgments, expressing ideas and basing perceptions mainly on an interpretation of how things are physically perceived by the senses. A preoccupation with how things look is in turn the foundation for several other stage-related characteristics. First, a child faced with an object or objects possessing multiple characteristics, such as a long, round, yellow pencil, will "see" whichever of those qualities first catches her eye or attention. Thus she may see yellow pencils but have difficulty understanding that they are also long and round. Secondly, the absence of operations makes it impossible for her to *conserve*, or determine that the quantity of an object or series of objects has not changed simply because some transformation has occurred in the physical appearance. For example, show a preoperational child two identical rows of matching blocks. Ask the child if there are the same number of blocks in each row. She should answer affirmatively. Next, spread the blocks out in one row and ask the child if the rows are still the same. She will respond negatively and insist that there are more blocks in one row "because it's longer." The child who does not have the logico-mathematical structure of number bases her judgment on what she can see, namely the spatial extension of one set beyond the frontiers of the other set. In addition to the above being an example of conservation, it is also an example of *reversibility*. In this case, the child is not capable of reversing thought or action which would have required that she mentally put the row back to its original length.

Yet another characteristic of the child during the preoperational stage is the use of *transductive reasoning*. Transductive reasoning is neither deductive reasoning (from the general to the specific) nor inductive reasoning (specific to the general), but reasoning from the specific to the specific. In reasoning transductively, there is no relationship between the two events or concepts under consideration. For example, the child may say that it isn't night because she hasn't gone to bed yet. It may be typical for her to say, "It's Saturday because we didn't have school today," when in fact it is Wednesday. Transductive reasoning is also characterized by the child's inability to "fill in" the parts of a process. She can usually deal with the first event and the last event in a process, but cannot account for any intervening steps. She can relate leaving for Grandmother's house and arriving there but will probably have difficulty specifying what was done in the process of traveling.

The preoperational child will act as though everything has a reason or a purpose. That is, she believes every act of her mother, her father, and her teacher or every event in nature happens for a specific purpose. This accounts for the child's constant and recurring questions about why things happen, how things work, and the corresponding exasperation of adults in trying to answer these questions.

Preoperational children also believe everyone thinks as they think and therefore act as they act for the same reasons. She is what is termed egocentric. Because the preoperational child is an egocentric child, she cannot put herself in the place of others. To ask her, therefore, to sympathize or to empathize with others is asking her to perform an operation beyond her developmental level. This egocentricity also makes it difficult if not impossible for her to participate in the act of sharing. Teachers of young children are often indignant by the child's wanting to play with all the blocks or her unwillingness to share candy, or anything else that she might have. The teacher's insistence that the child share in this stage is not only futile for the teacher but also incomprehensible for the child.

Concrete Operations Stage

The term *operation* for Piaget means activity and he defines it as follows: "First of all, an operation is an action that can be internalized; that is, it can be carried out in thought as well as executed materially. Second, it is a reversible action; that is, can take place in one direction or in the opposite direction."[7] Unlike the preoperational child, who performs in a motoric manner (using the body and sensory organs to act on materials), children in the concrete stage begin to utilize mental images and symbols during the thinking process. Although children are very much dependent on the perceptual level of how things look to them, during this stage the development of mental processes can be encouraged and facilitated through the use of concrete or real objects as opposed to hypothetical situations or places. Telling is not teaching. The obvious implication is to structure the learning setting so the child has experiences at his level with real objects, things, and people. Providing activities at the child's level cannot be overstressed. Teachers often provide activities that are too "easy" rather than providing activities that are too difficult. For example, in the block experiment the child should have practice utilizing objects in the practice of one-to-one correspondence.

A characteristic of the concrete operational child is the beginning of the ability to conserve. Unlike the preoperational child who thinks that because the physical appearance of an object changes it therefore follows that its quality or quantity changes, the concrete operational child begins to develop the ability to understand that change involving physical appearances does not necessarily change quality or quantity. She also begins to reverse thought processes, by going back over and "undoing" a mental action that she has just accomplished. At the physical level, this is related to conservation. In an example previously given, the child, when presented with two equal rows of blocks, one of which was spread out, indicated there were more blocks in the spread out row. The child who can reverse an operation can undo an operation by mentally going back to the beginning by reversing the blocks to their original position. She is then able to determine that there are not more blocks in the one row. The concrete operational child begins to manipulate mentally rather than being totally dependent on physical appearances or concrete objects. She can mentally return the blocks to their original position and determine that one-to-one correspondence exists. Whereas the preoperational child cannot "put back" the blocks mentally, the concrete operational child can.

---

[7]Jean Piaget, *Genetic Epistemology,* trans. Eleanor Duckworth (New York: Columbia University Press, 1970), p. 21.

Other mental operations which the child is capable of during this stage are:

1. Seriation, which begins with putting objects in order according to some criteria (small to large, short to tall)
2. transitivity
3. classification of objects, events and time according to certain characteristics
4. classification which involves multiple properties of objects
5. class inclusion operations
6. complementary classes

The child also structures time and space into logical, coherent, deductive systems. The development for this structuring begins in the sensorimotor period.

During the concrete operations stage, the child is less egocentric. She learns that other people have thoughts and feelings which can differ from her own. One of the more meaningful methods of helping the child develop beyond this innate egocentricism is through interaction with other individuals, especially peers.

It should not be assumed that this stage represents a period into which the child suddenly emerges, after having been a preoperational child. The process of development is not that of Athena stepping from the head of Zeus, but rather a gradual, continual process occurring over a period of time and resulting from maturation and experiences.

Formal Operations

The next stage of development represents the second part of operational intelligence and is called formal operations. It begins at about eleven years of age and extends to about fifteen years of age. During this period, the child becomes more capable of dealing with increasingly complex verbal problems and hypothetical problems, and less dependent upon the utilization of concrete objects to solve problems. She literally and mentally becomes free of the world of things as far as mental functioning is concerned. Thinking ranges over a wide time span including past, present, and future. The child in this stage develops the ability to reason scientifically and logically and can think with all of the processes and power of an adult. The way in which one will think is thus pretty well established by the age of fifteen. This should not be interpreted to mean that the child or adolescent will stop developing new schemes through assimilation and accommodation. However, the way she mentally handles the real world is determined, according to Piaget, by this age.

Educational Curricula Based on Piaget

It is interesting that nowhere in Piaget's writings does he make any suggestion for translating his theory of intellectual development into a curriculum for children. It cannot be stressed enough that Piaget's ideas are a theory of development and *not* a system for educating children. One of the educational problems with Piaget is that some teachers mistakenly apply his experiments directly to the classroom, thinking that these experiments constitute a Piaget curriculum. There have been some noteworthy attempts, however, to develop educational curricula based on Piaget's ideas.

The Kamii and DeVries Curriculum

Kamii and DeVries[8] have based their interpretation of Piaget's belief that the child's model of the world is "constructed" by activity and interaction with objects and people. They have emphasized children doing things for themselves and participating in self-initiated activities. The rationale for this approach is that the child's own initiative provides the motivation for involvement in activities. These activities in turn are the context for learning about the world. Knowledge necessary to know and to order the world comes through activities, not vice versa. This was Dewey's idea also, and we see this concept stressed in open education. Their curriculum, therefore, emphasizes the role of play in all preschool programs, since it is through play that the child manifests the initiative and interest that provide the motivation to become further involved. Using the context of play, the child can be encouraged to use her intelligence and to develop it further. Kamii and DeVries are critical of educators' attempts to provide artificial motivation for children in learning settings. They feel by following the interests of children, particularly as they express themselves through spontaneous play, that meaningful learnings can occur. Better yet, the motivation for learning is intrinsic since the child is interested and involved as a result of her own involvement.

Principles of Teaching. From an analysis of Piagets works, Kamii and DeVries have developed principles of teaching and objectives for the cogni-

---

[8]Constance Kamii and Rheta DeVries, "Piaget for Early Education," in *The Preschool in Action,* 2d ed., eds. M. C. Day and R. K. Parker (Boston, Massachusetts: Allyn and Bacon, in press).

tive and socio-emotional levels that provide a framework around which an early childhood curriculum can be formulated by the classroom teacher. In this regard, they do not prescribe a specific curriculum of procedures and activities. Rather, classroom teachers, utilizing these principles and objectives design their own curriculum utilizing three sources:

1. Activities associated with the daily lives of children
2. Curricula from already existing child development programs
3. Activities which can be inferred from Piaget's theories and ideas

The Kamii-DeVries principle of teaching for the socioemotional area are:

1. Promoting independence, curiosity, initiative, confidence, speaking with conviction and coping with fears and anxieties.
2. Encouraging interaction among children and helping them resolve their own conflicts.
3. Practicing cooperation and equality with children whenever and as much as possible.

Of course there would need to be a particular kind of classroom setting in order for these principles to be followed. It would be a place where the child is encouraged to act independently without fear of coercion by the teacher, and where right answers to problems are less important than the process of inventing problems and trying to figure them out. There should be an opportunity to quest for knowledge, raise questions, be curious and express feelings. Conflicts between children would be worked out through such processes as sharing and taking turns; through these methods children come to appreciate other people's point of view. Children should be treated as equal partners in the learning process by being shown that their feelings count and their views and ideas are respected.

Principles of teaching for the cognitive domain (the term *cognitive* refers to knowledge and knowing) are:

1. Using children's play as a means of developing concepts and insights. The play activities of children should be used as a basis for instruction because these activities are interesting to them and therefore children are intrinsically motivated to learn.
2. Respecting and accepting children's answers even though they may be "wrong." "Wrong" answers of children have to be ac-

cepted because their answers are based on the information they have, which is not the same information the adult possesses.

3. Adjusting the teaching style to account for the different levels of knowledge inherent in an activity such as physical knowledge, logical mathematical knowledge, and social knowledge.

4. Including both content and process in the learning environment through using activities that are interesting to children and that provide opportunities for dealing with content such as counting, ordering and classifying.

Kamii and DeVries see daily living activities as a rich source for providing meaningful learning opportunities for children. This is similar to Montessori's practical life activities for providing a learning context. The importance of daily living activities for Kamii and DeVries, however, is based on the child's opportunity to make decisions, raise questions, compare and contrast, make judgments, try out answers, and explore. All of these processes are viewed as crucial for developing intellectually. Kamii and DeVries believe that good teachers have always encouraged these processes "intuitively," through such activities as sand and water play, cooking, movement exploration, group activities, games, puzzles, stories, gardening, raising plants and animals, block building, and use of playground equipment. For the Piaget-based curriculum the importance of these traditional activities is that they contribute to the child's physical

Through involvement in water-play activities, these children are learning about the physical world.

knowledge of the world, and her structuring of space and time, as well as promote opportunities for language development. Other activities encouraging physical knowledge would include ball rolling and throwing; games which involve pushing, pulling, and swinging; and other natural phenomena of mechanics. Activities involving physical knowledge that would encourage reflective thinking would include observation of the environment and interaction with environmental objects through pouring water, water play, cooking, mixing paints, etc.

Kamii and DeVries also emphasize parental involvement, for unless parents are supportive of the objectives of a curriculum based on Piagetian theory, a dichotomy could exist between what is encouraged in school and what is practiced in the home.

In the Kamii-DeVries curriculum, language development is seen as a process that is developed by the individual's experience with people and objects. Representation for language occurs at the index, symbol, and sign levels. The index level refers to the representation of real objects by an attribute or portion of the object. For example, the ringing of a telephone would indicate the object *telephone.* The symbol level means representation of the object through pictures, models, sounds, make-believe or imitation. The sign level includes language.

While Kamii and DeVries are concerned with the growth of language in the child, they are not as concerned about it as are most early childhood educators. Whereas the majority of preschool and early elementary programs are concerned with the direct teaching of language through learning words for things, Kamii and DeVries believe that this method can result in the mere teaching of words without an understanding of concepts involved. They encourage a program whereby the child is involved with people and things; and from this active participation, language should develop.

Strengths and Weakness of the Kamii-DeVries Curriculum. The Kamii-DeVries curriculum appears to have several positive attributes. First, their understanding of Piaget's theory seems to be well conceptualized and refined after several applications in a number of different settings. They have a refreshing willingness to admit past mistakes and to change their philosophy, ideas and curriculum in accordance with their constant reappraisal of Piaget's theory. Second, their system does not involve purchase and utilization of special materials for implementation. All that the teacher needs is readily available in classroom or community. This is indeed a relief from many new curricula being currently developed which require a considerable outlay of money and understanding of the materials before utilization. Third, the curriculum does not confuse the teaching of Piaget's tasks with a Piaget-based curriculum. While they do recognize that certain Piaget tasks such as copying shapes with sticks can be used by children for structuring space and by teachers for diagnostic purposes, these experiments do not form the basis of their program.

There appears to be a shortcoming with the Kamii-DeVries curriculm which is actually a shortcoming with teaching in general. How does a teacher consciously implement a curriculum about which she knows very little? It has been my experience that theory comes last on the hierarchy of values held by many teachers. What teachers generally want to know first is how to implement a curriculum, and then, after the curriculum has been implemented, they are interested in knowing theory since the implementation has created a desire to know. This desire to know comes after involvement, not prior to it. A curriculum can be "packaged" in such a way that the teacher needs to know little of the theory behind it in order to implement it. While at first thought this may seem as a somewhat demeaning attitude toward teachers, it really is not. The best theoretical approach to teaching young children is really not of much value unless it is translated into actual practice. The major problem for all of education is *how* to translate theory into practice.

Kamii and DeVries indicate that some good teachers have always, by an intuitive means, conducted activities which have reflected Piagetian theory. Therefore, it would seem that Kamii and DeVries must find the means to illustrate to teachers the relationship between Piagetian theory and their everyday practice. They should package a training program, their curricular strategies, or both. By "packaging of the curriculum" I mean the development of a training program (perhaps consisting of audiotapes, videotapes, filmstrips), which can be "delivered" to preservice and inservice teachers for their consideration and implementation in classroom procedures.

Furth and Wachs—The School for Thinking

Framework. Furth and Wachs used Piaget's theory as a basis for conceptualizing what they call a School for Thinking.[9] The practical application of their ideas and concepts occurred at the Tyler Elementary School, Charleston, West Virginia (also known as the Tyler School for Thinking). From their own experiences and their understanding of Piaget's theory, they have abstracted seven concepts which they feel are of extreme importance. These form the conceptual framework for their School for Thinking.

---

[9]Hans G. Furth and Harry Wachs, *Thinking Goes to School: Piaget's Theory in Practice* (New York: Oxford University Press, 1974).

INTELLIGENCE VS. LEARNING

The first of these concepts is the difference between learning and development. Development can be considered synonymous with intelligence whereas learning is the acquisition of specific skills. In this sense, intelligence is seen as superseding learning. Intelligence includes theories and ideas and pertains to the development of knowledge of the world and reality. It is accomplished through the process of accommodation and assimilation, and requires active involvement with the environment and with people. Learning, on the other hand, is associated with the acquisition of facts, skills and information, which contribute to the development of intelligence but are not the primary sources of intelligence nor does their sum equal intelligence.

EQUILIBRATION

The second item of the Furth and Wachs theory is the idea of equilibration. It operates internally and is the regulatory mechanism of the processes of assimilation and accommodation. Thus, the child develops intelligence on his own through interaction in these processes; it can not be imposed from without. This idea is very similar to the Montessori's "spontaneous" activity of the intellect and her belief in auto-education. The equilibration concept stresses an active participation in activities, the manipulation of objects, and interaction with people. A telling and ordering educational setting is to be avoided. In this respect, the Kamii-DeVries and Furth-Wachs curricula have much in common.

LEVELS OF THINKING

The third idea of the School for Thinking is the distinction between high-level and low-level thinking. While low-level thinking is characterized by the learning of facts, high-level involves the abstraction of principles and concepts as a result of interaction with objects, people and things in the environment. An emphasis is placed on the latter kind of thinking.

LANGUAGE VS. THINKING

The fourth theoretical point is based on the premise that language and thinking are distinct and that thinking is not dependent upon language. Therefore the School for Thinking places emphasis on the mental manipulation of objects and symbols—mathematical, linguistic, and visual. There is no emphasis on the teaching of words, sentences and language per se. Language is used as a means for communication whereby thinking is encouraged. However, language cannot develop to its fullest unless the child has learned to think; it is only as the child learns to think and as his thinking matures that language can play a role in communication. These concepts are similar to the Kamii-DeVries curriculum.

EXTRINSIC VS. INTRINSIC MOTIVATION

The fifth theoretical concept is the distinction between extrinsic and intrinsic motivation. Intrinsic motivation is considered more important and plays the dominant role in intellectual development. Furth and Wachs believe the child does not develop through extrinsic motivation, e.g., motivation in the form of teacher or parent coercion, but that motivation for participation in an activity comes from within the child. Because the child is a Homo sapiens, a thinking animal, it is his nature to "know." For this reason, the child will, on his own, spontaneously participate in activities. It becomes the educator's job to create the environment within which the child can participate. Although this point of view is similar to Montessorian ideas of spontaneous activity of the intellect and the prepared environment, it does not appear to be as rigid. This concept also plays a key role in understanding the open classroom, where one of the critical features is the need to select activities based on the interests of children. In the School of Thinking, teachers present activities to the children and they are free to request a more or less complex activity. Furth and Wachs refer to this as *freedom within structure.*

INTELLIGENCE AS A COORDINATED WHOLE

The sixth concept views intelligence as a coordinated whole rather than as a subset of isolated constructs. While intelligence is sometimes thought to consist of the verbal, motoric, and spatial, Furth and Wachs interpret Piaget's theory to mean that intelligence is a coordinated whole, i.e., intelligence is the sum total of all behaviors. Thus the child demonstrates his intelligence through his actions, which include seeing, moving, listening, hearing, and communicating.

INTERPRETATION OF STAGES

The seventh point concerns their interpretation of Piaget's developmental stages. They view the child as acting in several developmental stages at one time; thus it would be possible for the child to give a preoperational answer on one task and concrete operational answer in another task. Undoubtedly, they would be critical of my use of the term *preoperational child.*

GOALS

Goals for the School of Thinking include:

1. creative, independent thinking
2. a positive self-image

3. social cooperation
4. moral responsibility
5. knowledge of the environment
6. the three R's

Activities designed to implement these long-range goals would:

1. demonstrate that thinking in and of itself is worthwhile
2. encourage intellectual development and individual freedom
3. be adjusted to the child's level of thinking
4. encourage children to be participants in the activity rather than passive observers
5. be performed with small groups in a cooperative manner
6. demonstrate that the teacher is a thinking person because she keeps activities challenging

Thinking Games. Furth and Wachs consider movement and thinking as two interdependent processes. They believe that muscle movement is the expression of the operational aspect of knowing. Consequently, movement can result only from the child's thinking, and schemes must be developed for movement as well as visual and auditory processes.

There are several areas in which games and activities are applicable as instruction for these processes. Within each area there are various types of control to be mastered. Following is a list of each area, the abilities which need to be developed, and some examples of instructive activities.

GENERAL MOVEMENT THINKING

These areas require cognitive schemes for large muscle control.

1. *Reflexive control.*
   To refine uncontrolled reflexive movements resulting in controlled activity. Developed by games which involve grasping and pushing.

2. *Mental map of the body.*
   To learn which body parts are related and how they function as a coordinated whole, resulting in mastery of the body. Developed by touching, walking, exploring things the body can do, and swimming in place.

3. *Coordination of the body's axes.*
   To learn how one's body functions from side to side, and top to bottom; to perform activities involving twisting and pivoting. De-

veloped by creeping, rolling, walking to rhythms, ball batting, making angels in the snow.

4. *Body balance.*
   To learn the relationship of gravity to an individual's body. Developed by walking on the balance beam and balance board, and using a trampoline.

5. *Coordinated action.*
   To refine the sequence and direction of movement. Developed by hopping, skipping, jumping rope, catching, kicking, and throwing.

DISCRIMINATIVE MOVEMENT THINKING

These areas require cognitive schemes for small muscle control and include particular manipulatory skills.

1. *Eye movement.*
   To maximize efficient and purposeful control of eye movement. Developed by focusing, tracking objects in space, jump fixation of the eyes from one object to another, and convergence.

2. *Digital movement.*
   To promote manual dexterity so that writing and other manipulation skills will be enhanced. Developed by paper tearing, paper folding, games played with string, working with clay, and finger painting.

3. *Lips and tongue movement.*
   To promote lip and tongue movement, which enhances articulation. Developed by asking the child to remove peanut butter placed on the teeth; point with the tongue; suck air through a straw held in the mouth; and making comic lip movements in front of a mirror.

VISUAL THINKING

To provide practice in detecting similarities and differences between visual configurations. Developed by design blocks, picture making, detecting similarities and differences between visual configurations, pegboard games, follow-the-number games, and sewing games.

AUDITORY THINKING

To enhance the ability to listen, resulting in the ability to follow directions. Developed through activities that involve distinguishing pitch, intensity, duration, pause; elements of sound, recall, location, identification, and the addition, subtraction, or substitution of sounds.

HAND THINKING

The processing of information through the hands to verify visual and auditory information. Developed by using a *tactile box* (also called a *tactile bag* or *feel and find box*) to identify objects.

GRAPHIC THINKING

To refine performance of graphic activities that involve arm-hand-finger-vision match. Developed through activities in which children draw forms with templates, construct dot pictures, trace, and duplicate previously drawn designs.

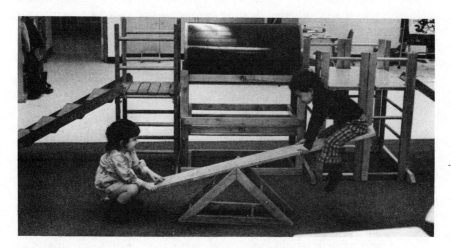

As these children enjoy self-initiated play, they also are learning. Teachers need to recognize and extend such opportunities.

LOGICAL THINKING[10]

The use of logical operations in the process of thinking developed by the following processes:

---

[10]Piaget's theory includes classification, seriation, cause-and-effect relationships, time relationships, and spatial relationships; most Piaget-based curricula emphasize activities involving these operations. While many math and science programs also utilize associated activities, they are not math and science activities per se as some curriculum developers would have you believe.

1. *Classification.*

   To develop the ability to classify according to criteria established by the child, teacher, or schemes based on qualities inherent in objects themselves. Also involves cross-classification, which utilizes sequential orders. Developed by working on matrix puzzles, matching activities, sorting.

2. *Ordering and Seriating.*

   To develop the ability to put things in sequence and order according to predetermined criteria. Activities to enhance this skill include pattern games, lining up games and seriating.

3. *Permutations.*

   To develop the concept that given a specified number of events, a certain fixed number of results will occur. Developed through such activities as figuring out combinations (for example, the number of different seating arrangements at a table with four chairs).

4. *Symbol-Picture Logic.*

   To develop in children the use of symbols in the thinking process. Enhanced by games that show symbols, such as $M \longrightarrow$, where the symbol M stands for the concept of man.

5. *Probability.*

   To develop an understanding of chance, greater and lesser likelihood, necessity, impossibility, and odds. Developed by throwing dice and using spinning devices to predict odds.

6. *Spatial Thinking.*

   To develop orientation of one's self in space in order to discover how things look when one is standing in front of, behind, or to the left. Activities would include having children arrange a table setting as it would look if they were seated at different places at a table.

SOCIAL THINKING

This area involves the affective domain of feelings and emotions and helps the child to explore her feelings, ideas, and opinions in relationship to others. With these activities, the child learns to "decenter" or "work out" of her egocentric point of view, and thus creates her own morality. Activities which help develop social thinking include:

1. *Drama.*

   To help children express feelings, ideas, and opinions about subjects. Developed by discussing teacher-initiated topics such as fighting, or student-initiated topics such as death.

2. *Photography.*
   Young children have not yet fully developed verbal techniques. Through this outlet, they may express themselves beyond the scope of their vocabulary range.

3. *Excursion.*
   To promote environmental knowledge by giving children an opportunity to know their environment by participating in it.

4. *Demonstrations.*
   To involve children in skills provided through adults brought into the classroom. Developed by participation activities such as cooking, painting, sewing, wood working, and other occupational areas as conducted by adults who possess these occupational skills.

While the emphasis in the School for Thinking would be on body, sense, logical, and social thinking, other areas of the curriculum would include reading, writing, arithematic, science, arts, crafts, music, and physical education.

Strengths and Weaknesses of the School for Thinking. As with the Kamii-DeVries curriculum, one of the strengths of the School for Thinking is its basis in a thorough understanding of Piagetian theory. Furth and Wachs seem to have made every effort to understand Piagetian theory and to translate that theory accurately into a sensible, workable curriculum for children. The program also has merit since it is implemented without a substantial investment in new equipment and material. Materials already used in good early childhood education classrooms can be modified, along with the addition of "found" items. A third strength of the curriculum is its utilization of children's interests and the active involvement in activities associated with these interests. In this regard, the curriculum fits well in nongraded and open classroom settings.

On the weakness side of the ledger, it would appear that teachers using the curriculum would need to have a thorough understanding of Piaget's theory and would need help with implementing the curriculum as suggested. A training program would be necessary to help in structuring the day-to-day activities. Teachers would also need feedback on their progress in achieving the goals of the program. The curriculum would need administrative support in the form of a knowledgeable principal who would be willing to help make the curriculum a success.

The Lavatelli Program

One noteworthy attempt at structuring a program which can be used both as a teacher training program and a curriculum for young children is explained in *Early Childhood Curriculum—A Piaget Program,* by Celia Stendler Lavatelli.[11] Lavatelli feels that since Piaget's theory provides a framework for knowing what the important cognitive developments are for children, it is possible to build a curriculum based upon them. The cognitive developments important in early childhood include classification, space and number, and seriation.

The program for developing these concepts consists of a detailed teacher's manual and materials to aid in the accomplishment of activities designed to involve the students through active participation. The manual lists the mental operations underlying each activity. An example of a classification activity is "Keeping in mind two or more properties at the same time in searching for an object to complete the set." Lavatelli believes that the teacher "holds" Piaget in her head as she understands what is supposed to be going on in a child's head to solve a task, and then she (the teacher) finds evidence of the mental operation or lack of it, in the child's behavior. The teacher is then in a better position to use the clinical method to find out about the child's reasoning, and to be alert to situations in other classroom activities where the same mental operation is called for. The manual also includes protocols of actual lessons conducted by individual teachers so that the novice can get the feel of how the program was carried out in other classrooms; the lessons are not intended as models to be followed. The goal of each lesson is not to "teach" a child to solve a particular task, but to present her with an interesting problem to solve at her own rate and in her own way. The teacher then asks questions in the clinical method to find out *where* the child is in her reasoning, and to see if disequilibrium can be produced so that the child assimilates previously neglected variables and begins to accommodate to the new ideas.

The training sessions are carried on in groups because Lavatelli believes strongly in Piaget's concept that a fundamental process of cognition is decentration. Egocentricism is challenged in the group, and the child moves toward an equilibrium between assimilation and accommodation.

In the classification area, the following concepts from the Inhelder and Piaget analysis include:

1. Simple sorting
2. Multiplicative classification
3. All-some relations
4. Class-inclusion relations
5. Discovering intension

[11]Celia Stendler Lavatelli, *Piaget's Theory Applied to an Early Childhood Curriculum* (Boston, Massachusetts: American Science and Engineering, Inc., 1970).

6. Combining objects to make up subclasses
7. Recognition of complementary classes
8. Extension of classes

In space and number, the following concepts are provided for:

1. Physical correspondence of objects on a one-to-one basis
2. One-to-one correspondence when physical correspondence is destroyed
3. Conserving the whole when the additive composition of its parts is varied
4. Conservation of area and transformation of perspective

Seriation includes:

1. Ordering objects in a series according to one property
2. Ordering objects in two series inversely related to one another
3. Seriation and visual representation
4. Transitivity

Lavatelli's program emphasizes the role of the teacher as a role-model for language usage in order to develop and establish grammatical structures in children's language. While Lavatelli agrees with Piaget that language is not necessary for intellectual operations and that logical thinking precedes the logical expression of ideas, she does believe that training for logical operations accompanied by training in syntactical structures may aid learning. In fulfilling the role of a language model, the teacher would:

1. Use many different kinds of sentences.
2. Provide and encourage teacher-pupil conversation.
3. Elicit from students the language structures being modeled.
4. Provide a warm, supportive atmosphere for language development.

The main goal of the Lavatelli curriculum is implemented through structured teaching sessions with small groups of children (four in a group) for short periods of time (anywhere from ten minutes upward depending on the attention span of the children). In the first set of lessons dealing with classification, the child is involved in identifying properties of objects and matching objects on the basis of a one-to-one correspondence of these properties. In the first activity of this lesson set, the child deals with color as a property by stringing beads. The second activity deals with shape and color and the third activity size, shape and color. During this lesson set, the role-model teacher uses language consisting of noun phrases, coordinate sentences involving the directions for multiple actions, and prepositions.

The Lavatelli program emphasizes having children find the solution to problems with each child using his own set of materials. The materials are pre-packaged as a time-saver for teachers, but many teachers whose classroom budgets do not permit purchase of materials, may carry out a number of activities with homemade materials. It is ideas which are important, not a particular set of materials. These materials are packaged in cardboard "chests" for easy use and storage. Some are three-dimensional and some pictorial. They are to be used in solving tasks which Lavatelli has gathered from a number of sources: Froebel, Binet, Piaget, Montessori, the Warsaw School of Mathematics, set theory, intersection of sets and Venn diagrams from nineteenth century mathematicians, and creative classroom teachers.

Teachers are urged to carry out the program in a supportive manner, keeping in mind that affective and cognitive development proceed together. Providing challenging activities for a child to solve at her own level will contribute to a positive self-image. Since the structured part of the program occupies only a small portion of the day, Lavatelli advocates that the rest of the day be organized in the fairly free, creative spirit we have come to associate with open education.

Her program represents a sequence approach to learning materials. For example, investigators who have done follow up work on the Piaget-Inhelder description of the acquisition of classification structures agree with the Geneva school that the more difficult operations are based upon the simpler. Thus the child develops the ability to recognize that an object can have more than one property before she acquires the concept that the same object can be classified in different ways. Learning continues in this manner until the complete classification structure is constructed in all its logico mathematical elegance.

Strengths and Weaknesses of the Lavatelli Program. There are several strengths of the Lavatelli program. First, Lavatelli not only explains Piagetian theory; she also shows how to use it in the classroom. While I have used the words *formal* and *structure* in describing her program, I do not mean to imply that the program needs to be taught to children in that manner. However, these terms provide the teacher with directions and plans, which is not always possible without some organizational framework.

A second strength of the program is that it provides teachers with theory and rationale for what they are doing while they are doing it. In essence, then, they are being trained while they are implementing the program. This blending of theory and practice is a step in the right direction.

There are also several points which are sometimes raised as criticisms of the Lavatelli program. Some individuals see her program as too prescriptive in terms of teacher role and student participation and response. For example, the manual which accompanies the program provides a list of the syntactical structures for the teacher to say to the child. If the child cannot put his thought into words, the teacher should model the expected student responses. This objection to structure is actually just a question of style on the part of the teacher. For those who need the structure, it is there.

Another frequent criticism of the program is that while the activities are derived from many sources, some of the activities in the program are similar to the experiments Piaget used with children in developing his theory. It is argued that using these activities to foster children's thinking processes does not really get at the objective of helping children think, but merely teaches them how to do particular tasks and activities. Lavatelli would agree that the concepts involved must be extended beyond the materials provided. Again, this seems to be a problem with how materials are used, which is not necessarily an inherent problem with the program itself. The goal of the program is not to solve Piagetian tasks, but, rather to foster the development of those mental operations defined by the Geneva School as essential for logical thinking. The materials are simply to encourage active problem solving by the child.

Themes Commonly Used in Suggested Curricula

In Piaget's theory, there seem to be four recurring themes that are accentuated by those who suggest curricula based upon his ideas. One of these themes is that the thinking of the child is substantially different from the thinking of the adult. This theme implies that adults must stop imposing their thoughts and manner of thinking on the child. Adults should provide a setting in which the child can think his own ideas and construct his own model of the world. Teacher behaviors would include tolerance, support, acceptance of "wrong" answers, and encouragement to make hypotheses.

A second recurring theme is that the child must be actively involved in learning. A setting in which the child is a passive recipient of information does not provide an opportunity for the child to develop her intelligence to its fullest.

A third theme is that learning should involve concrete objects and experiences with many adults. This is particularly true at the sensorimotor and preoperational stages. Too often, children are asked to deal with abstractions such as words and numbers at a time when they have not the slightest idea of the representation for these symbols.

The fourth theme pertains to the quality and relatedness of experiences. What the child is like at a particular stage in time is largely a function of past experiences. Nothing succeeds like good experiences. Good experiences lead to intellectual development. Since man is a thinking being—the only animal with this distinction—it behooves us to maximize in every way possible this uniqueness. Our job as teachers and parents is to maximize the quality of those experiences. In addition, the child's present comprehension of an event is largely dependent upon the proximity of the event in relation to the concepts involved. If the child has nothing to associate an experience to, then it is meaningless to him. Assimilation and accommodation cannot function unless experiences closely parallel each other.

Piaget—Issues

There are certain difficulties associated with Piaget and his theory of intelligence. First, his writings are hard to read and interpret. As a result, it takes a great deal of time, effort and energy to determine the implications for education. One is never sure about being correct when understanding Piaget. Individuals must be willing to change their thinking about their interpretation of Piaget's thinking! Difficulty is often used as an excuse for not trying at all. Unfortunately, some teachers are content to base their teaching on no theory rather than spend time and effort in developing a meaningful one.

A second danger is that Piaget's theory of intellectual development is not an educational theory. Educational implications have to be determined from reading and understanding. Many people mistakenly interpret Piagetian experiments for a Piagetian curriculum. It is inaccurate to teach these as a curriculum. It is unfortunate that a number of well-intentioned and well-meaning teachers believe by having students replicate Piaget experiments they are "teaching Piaget." These experiments do have merit as a diagnostic process for determining how the child is thinking. The results, however, should be used to develop meaningful experiences.

Another issue concerns the number of early childhood education curricula being developed around Piaget's ideas. Given this state of affairs, there is always the risk that there will be blind acceptance and adoption without a thorough knowledge and understanding of these curricula. The acceptance of a curriculum without an understanding of the inherent concepts could be just as bad as having a curriculum based on no theory. Since the name Piaget has a legitimate quality, teachers may, simply because his name is associated with a curriculum, adopt it as being worthwhile.

Just as a teacher must examine critically any curriculum before it is adopted, so too should it be with this chapter. It is hoped that the student will go on to read more of Piaget's ideas as well as other educators' interpretations of his ideas. Critically examine the information presented here. Then develop a meaningful program for your students.

BIBLIOGRAPHY

Boring, Edwin G., et al., eds. *A History of Psychology in Autiobiography,* Vol. IV. New York: Russell and Russell, 1952.

Furth, Hans G. *Piaget for Teachers.* Englewood Cliffs, N.J.: Prentice-Hall, Inc., 1970.

Furth, Hans G., and Wachs, Harry. *Thinking Goes to School: Piaget's Theory in Practice.* New York: Oxford University Press, 1974.

Kamii, Constance, and DeVries, Rheta. "Piaget for Early Education." In *The Preschool in Action.* 2d ed., edited by M. C. Day and R. K. Parker. Boston, Massachusetts: Allyn and Bacon, in press.

Lavatelli, Celia Stendler. *Piaget's Theory Applied to an Early Childhood Curriculum.* Boston, Massachusetts: American Science and Engineering, Inc., 1970.

Piaget, Jean. *Genetic Epistemology.* Translated by Eleanor Duckworth. New York: Columbia University Press, 1970.

Pulaski, Mary Ann Spencer. *Understanding Piaget.* New York: Harper and Row, 1971.

Richmond, P. G. *An Introduction to Piaget.* New York: Basic Books, Inc., 1970.

FOR FURTHER READING AND STUDY

To the person without a specialized interest in Piaget, reading his works can be somewhat difficult. The undergraduate student will probably have more success with understanding and enjoying Piaget if read with the help of one of the books listed below:

Brearley, Molly, and Hitchfield, Elizabeth. *A Guide to Reading Piaget.* New York: Schocken Books, 1966.
   The authors discuss *first* the processes of thought (number, measurement, perspective, space), and then these discussions are followed by relevant quota-

tions from Piaget's studies with children. A good way to be introduced to Piaget by two authors who seem perceptive of the difficulties involved.

Weikart, David P., et al. *The Cognitively Oriented Curriculum.* Urbana, Illinois: University of Illinois, 1971.

Although this was not one of the programs I chose to discuss in the text, it very well could have been included. I recommend it highly as an example of how Piaget can be applied to early childhood settings. Easy to read with many examples and schedules of activities.

For Further Study and Involvement

1. Observe three children at the ages of six months, two years, and four years. Note in each child's activities what you would consider typical behavior for his age. Can you find examples of behavior which correspond to one of Piaget's stages?

2. Observe children playing. What evidence can you find that learning occurs through play? Do you think most teachers are aware of the specific learnings that occur through play?

3. Observe a child between birth and eighteen months. Can you cite any concrete evidence, such as specific actions or incidents, to support the view that the child is developing schemes of the world with and through reflexive action?

4. Interview college professors to determine their impressions of how Piaget's theory should be applied to early childhood settings.

5. Compare Piaget's theory of intellectual development to another theory such as Montessori's. How are they similar and different?

5

Open Education
The Little Red
Schoolhouse Revisited

Open education is an attempt to restructure typical elementary classrooms by providing a setting which recognizes individuality, promotes independence, encourages freedom, and demonstrates respect for children. In this context, open education is a logical extension of many of the basic ideas of Montessori, Dewey, and Piaget.

Open education is a controversial topic that we can see all around us. Parents wonder if it will provide their children with a better education. Teachers debate its merits and shortcomings, while secretly wondering if they are the kind of teacher who can teach in an open classroom. We see textbooks published for enlightenment on open education. In the news, we can follow accounts of school board meetings called to discuss its implementation in the school district.

Everybody's talking about open education, but not too many people really understand what it is. In order to comprehend what open education and the open classroom are like, teachers and parents must actually become involved. One can also try to gain an understanding of the topic by reading. Hopefully what follows will provide the encouragement you need to say, "I can do it," and the help you want in order to avoid some problems others have encountered.

Historical Influences

The foundation for open education has been with us for a long time. Pestalozzi, Froebel, Montessori, and Dewey had ideas about what open education should be, although of course they did not use the terminology. Montessori was, in my opinion, the first modern open educator because her system of freedom within a prepared environment allows children to enjoy that freedom by exercising decision-making processes. She also encouraged individualized instruction and participation in a learning environment that is self-paced. Most important of all, however, she insisted on respect for all children, always required in open education.

Issues causing a renewed interest and redirection of early childhood education are also issues which have encouraged the current swing toward open education. In addition, during the 1960s many educators and critics of education called attention to ways in which schools were stifling student initiative, freedom and self-direction. Schools were pictured as institutions similar to prisons where students obeyed arbitrary rules autocratically enforced by the administration, and where teachers were viewed as "gods" who daily received pleasure and emotional reinforcement by playing the role. Critics saw students as sitting apathetically in straight rows, passively listening to robotlike teachers, with little or no real learning taking place. In short, classrooms and learning were portrayed as devoid of enthusiasm, joy, and self-direction.

Consequently, there occurred a national effort of school reform in order that students might experience schooling as though they were not in penal institutions. Educators and schools were challenged to adopt policies and procedures for educating which would involve students in their learning, create environments in which students could do things for themselves, and abolish policies and procedures which tended to be detrimental to the physical and mental health of students. In essence, schools were challenged to become happy places.

Concurrently, school reformers in the United States were being influenced by the "British Primary School," a comprehensive education program characterized, in part, by respect for children, responsiveness to children's needs, and learning through interests. The discovery of the "British Primary School" and the subsequent application of its main ideas caused a rapid acceleration toward open education.[1] Usually, *open education* is used to refer to teaching on the elementary level and, as used in the following discussion, will include the teaching of children ages three to twelve.

---

[1]It is not uncommon for the terms *open education, open classroom,* and *British Primary School* to be used interchangeably.

However, this should not be interpreted to mean open education cannot be successful with older students, including adults. There are many examples that demonstrate it works well with a wide range of students in a broad variety of settings.

Open Education—What Is It?

It is always somewhat risky to define a conceptual process such as open education because more often than not something is lost in the definition. Then, too, by the act of defining there is the chance that instead of viewing open education as a dynamic, ever-emerging process, it may become restricted to the defined meaning. Open education does not lend itself to a nice, neat definition. It is possible, however, for us to examine its essence through an operational definition of attributes inherent in the process.

Attitude

Open education is an attitude on the part of the teacher that encourages children to become involved in their own learning. Instead of constantly instructing or "snoopervising," the teacher allows the children to make choices about how and what they should learn. In my opinion, it is this attitude that makes the difference between success and failure in implementation.

Too often, we give one hundred and one reasons why something won't work so that we never get around to trying anything. Needless to say, this can lead to a closed mind. Open education exists in the mind; teachers should be able to conduct such a program regardless of the physical, social or financial setting of the school or community.

Freedom

Open education is an environment marked by limited freedom, where children are free from authoritarian adults and *arbitrary* rules. Contrary to popular misconception, children are not free to do anything they choose, such as wrecking the classroom or infringing on the rights of others. Since in most open classrooms the basic skills of reading, writing and computing are still emphasized, children are not free to choose to ignore these areas. It does mean that within certain broad guidelines or limitations (hopefully established through cooperative planning sessions of teachers, students and administrators) children are free to move about the room, interact with materials, carry on conversations, and enter into learning activities based on their interests.

Child Centered

Open education is child-centered learning, as opposed to learning totally directed by adults. Many adults do all the talking, decision making, organizing, and planning (you can continue to add to this list by remembering what your education was like), when it is the students who need to develop these skills, which are to be applied throughout their lives. Open education seeks to return the emphasis to the child, where it rightfully belongs. It recognizes that schools are not conveniences established for teachers and administrators, existing solely for providing employment opportunities; rather they are meant to be places of learning and joy.

Integration

Open education includes the integration of subject matter and student activities. There is a "breaking down" of subject matter distinctions so that subjects are no longer compartmentalized into nice, neat categories. The school day is no longer dominated by a series of lessons. Although the important skill areas of reading and mathematics are structured, attempts are made to apply the concepts involved to everyday life. The extent to which these skill areas are structured depends generally upon the attitude of the teacher, the philosophy of the school, and community needs. On the other hand, the areas of environmental education (science), creative arts and the social sciences are experienced or "taught" through activities. Thus, there is an integration of subjects into activities, with the activity becoming the vehicle for teaching the subject matter rather than imposing subjects on children. In some open education settings, mornings are structured to provide direct involvement in language, reading and math while the afternoon is devoted to general activities which involve students in the use and application of the basic skills. Insight into the activity approach may be gained from the following incident. While visiting open classrooms in England, I had an opportunity to discuss student involvement with the Head Master of the New Ash Green Primary School at Ash Green, Kent. Having just expressed my concern that students might not learn or write well unless they were directly taught, he replied, "Look here, you Yanks teach reading and then hope the youngsters will use it by getting interested in something to read. We get them interested in things and then use this interest as the natural motivation to read."

In the open system, there is no longer the necessity of an arbitrary time schedule for controlling the school day. Instead, students and teachers can participate in activities and follow their interests without undue consideration for time or for "covering" a specified amount of subject matter.

The term *integrated* often is used in a much broader sense than I have used it. The term has really been borrowed and adapted from the British Primary School movement where it is common for British educators to refer to the integrated school, the integrated day, and the integrated curriculum. In a most enjoyable and readable book, *The Integrated Day in the Primary School,* Mary Brown and Norman Precious give the term a number of other meanings:

1. The integration (relation) of the past experiences of children to their present needs and interests.
2. The integration of children and space in the sense that children are free, within limits, to go wherever they want to go.
3. The integration of the out-of-school environment (especially the community) with the environment of the school.
4. The integration of children's interests with subject matter.
5. The integration of children socially so that a mixed society exists.
6. The integration of schools so that children can experience a variation of age groups. In British schools, it is rather common to have mixed age grouping. Also, a school housing primary age children may be next to a school housing intermediate age children. Thus there would be opportunities for children to go from one school to the other for educational and social purposes.
7. The integration of the lives of teachers with each other and with the lives of children. By knowing each other better through social activities (faculty dinners, parties, etc.), teachers may be better able to teach. Teachers must also find out as much as they can about the children they teach by visiting homes, talking, and observing.
8. The integration of the home life of children with school life.[2]

While there are probably more meanings that can be applied to the term *integrated,* the above are sufficient, I believe, to provide a feeling of the spirit that should pervade open education in order to make it meaningful in the lives of children and parents. I do not mean to imply, however, that these underlying concepts are applicable only to open education contexts. They should apply to all education, wherever it occurs.

---

[2]Mary Brown and Norman Precious, *The Integrated Day in the Primary School* (New York: Agathon Press, Inc., 1968).

Teacher Role

Just as the basic principles of the Montessori system conceptualized a new role for the teacher, so also open education encourages a redefinition of teacher role. The individual who believes that open education is possible is well over one of the first obstacles that prevent many teachers from even trying it. An open education teacher must, in addition, respect children and believe they are capable of assuming responsibility for their own learning. Such a person views himself as a teacher of children, feeling free and confident to work with all students in all subject areas. Like the Montessori teacher, he is a keen observer of children, for many of the decisions regarding instruction and involvement in activities depend upon a thorough knowledge of what children have or have not accomplished. Adjectives used to describe the teacher's role include learner, guide, facilitator, catalyst, and director.

Open to Community

Open education should imply that schools are "opened up" to the real world of places, people and things. In such a setting, it becomes legitimate for the student to go to the playground and other areas to pursue appropriate activities. It means also that a group of students, under the direction of the teacher, might go into the countryside and parks to watch birds and/or talk to people who are involved in bird watching. This setting allows community members to come into the school to share their information, skills, and expertise with children. Open education breaks down school walls so that the world of learning in a very real sense is the whole world. The two-by-four concept in which all learning is conceived as confined to the two covers of a book and the four walls of a classroom is rejected. In its place is the idea that the whole world is a classroom, that the playground and the community are classrooms, and that students should be free to go into that world to learn and apply the concepts they have learned. In addition to preparation for life, schooling is viewed as *life*. Ideally, the ultimate school is no school at all but a place to shelter children while they develop strategies for going into the real world to learn.

Utilization of Space

In the United States, open education is frequently thought of as synonymous with open space. Large, open areas are provided for children to engage in activities. In these settings, marked by an absence of walls, children are supposed to get a sense of freedom, and learning is supposed to be enhanced. However, the necessity of an open space has been overemphasized, since an open space is not necessary for open education to occur. On the contrary, it is possible to have an open-space facility and have a rigid and traditional educational program. If, for example, there is a large, open space and the teacher is still authoritarian and does not encourage children to exercise options and make decisions, then open education will not be a reality. The most modern open classroom that is architecturally possible will fail in the absence of good teaching. One of the striking differences between open education as practiced in the United States and as practiced in England is that educators in the United States are more concerned with open architecture. This personal observation tends to reinforce the idea that open eduction is a state of mind. Because of economic considerations, teachers are realizing they probably will not have new, open schools in which to teach. Consequently, they are seeking ways to make increased and different uses of their present facilities. Thus they are utilizing halls, closets, passageways, corridors, and other spaces as learning areas. From my observation of schools in England, it is my opinion that open education is based on the utilization of all the available space. In American schools there is a tendency to have a great deal of space (such as hallways) which serves no instructional purpose. Every teacher should ask "Am I using all the space possible?" Some teachers have found it beneficial to solicit the help of their children in answering this question and then, as a group, redesign the learning setting.

A Day in an Open Classroom

Getting Started

One of the difficulties often expressed by many college students (and in-service teachers as well) is that they cannot visualize or understand how the open classroom process works. A frequently heard lament is, "I'd begin, but I don't know how or where." Certainly these feelings of anxiety can be sympathized with since there is a difference between conceptualizing and the reality of implementation. In addition, the image of what a classroom and teacher are supposed to be like (straight rows with the teacher standing in front teaching) are so ingrained in our minds that we have difficulty thinking that education by any other means would be possible. Guilt feelings also almost always accompany any attempt at change and these feelings may be strong enough to prevent change from occurring. The feelings of guilt which accompany a person's voyage into a new world are often a strong enough barrier to prevent the voyage. It is curious indeed that although teachers should educate for a changing world, they are surprisingly resistant to change.

It might be illuminating, therefore, for us to look in some detail at what could happen in an open classroom. It should be emphasized that what follows is not a prescription or a recounting of the "only true way" of operating within an open classroom. The ensuing is merely a description of one of many different options available.

The physical appearance of the open classroom is usually quite different from a traditional one.

Surroundings

The appearance of an open classroom is usually quite different from a traditional classroom. There are no straight rows of desks oriented to the front of the room. The "front" of most typical classrooms is determined by where the teacher's desk is located. If there is a teacher's desk, it is in a corner or some other out-of-the-way area. Desks and chairs are grouped according to the needs of children and the demands of the learning activities. The classroom arrangement is dynamic as opposed to the static kinds of arrangements we normally find. If the area is an open one, division between groups of children and activity areas is achieved by bookshelves, portable bulletin boards, furniture or movable storage facilities. What one is immediately impressed with on entering an open classroom is the freedom that space encourages. It is designed to encourage children to become involved in their learning. Whereas students usually keep their belongings in a desk, in an open setting a container similar to a plastic wash basin which stacks on or fits into shelving might serve the same purpose.

Sample Day

The way in which an open classroom begins its day is different for almost every setting. However, let us follow a hypothetical child, whom we will call Andy, through a day in the open classroom.

Andy, upon arriving in the morning, "finds out" what he will do for the first part of the day. This "finding out" can be accomplished in several ways. First, upon entering, he can be "told" directly by the teacher. He might find a message from the teacher written on the board which provides activities or tasks from which he can choose. Another way he can find out is by sitting down individually with his teacher and entering into a planning session. He could also engage in a planning session with an older student or a small group of children. Frequently—particularly in the British Primary School—the whole group of children enters into a planning session with the teacher during which the group decides what they will do, how they will do it, and how long it will take. Yet another alternative for Andy would be for him to provide his own plan of activities through self-direction. Based upon previous activities and events, or the activity in which he was last involved, he makes a plan for the morning's work. It is conceivable that the previous day's work will determine where he will begin. It needs to be understood that regardless of what strategy or combination of strategies is used, it must be tailored to the age and maturity of the child.

Andy might become involved in a number of activities. There may be a general understanding that everyone will be involved in communication. Andy could begin with creative writing by joining a group of his classmates in writing, producing, and acting in a play later on in the day. Andy could also write about himself, utilizing the poetic format of cinquain; do remedial work on pronouns; or work on handwriting involving certain skills he and his teacher feel need improvement. Other alternatives could be involvement in communication as editor of the school newspaper, or as a member of a group writing a series of interview questions which they will use when interviewing the president of the local birdwatching society. Communication can occur in many different ways in many different settings. Traditionally, involvement in communication has occurred by children reading stories, filling out worksheets or listening to the teacher. In open education, there is an emphasis on the involvement of children in activities which encourage a particular skill.

Communication activities can take anywhere from ten to forty-five minutes or longer. Also, Andy could participate in one activity for forty-five minutes, or engage in a series of two or three activities for forty-five minutes. The learning setting is controlled by the teacher through the limitation of subject matter. This should not be interpreted to mean that as children and teachers become accustomed to working in an open setting, Andy would not be allowed to read about mathematics. It simply means that, in the initial stages at least, this is the procedure or organization that some teachers have used. It should be obvious, however, that in the subject of communication there are very few activities that could not be justified.

The next broad area that Andy might experience is mathematics. As was previously indicated, mathematics and communication seem to be the two areas of most concern to teachers and parents. In order to satisfy this important concern, specific opportunities are given to work on math. Andy could be involed with calculators, measuring the playground with a measuring wheel, graphing the room, or measuring water with various size containers. On the other hand, he could be learning to count by counting the number of napkins that will be needed by his group during lunch time.

Before we continue, several points need clarification. First, there are a myriad of details associated with managing any kind of classroom. For example, attendance has to be taken. In an open classroom, however, it is not uncommon to find children accounting for their own attendance. This can be accomplished by Andy reporting his attendance to a parent or aide who is marking attendance in a book. There may be a chart on the wall which has student name tags on it and Andy, when he comes in in the morning, turns his name tag over. In this way, someone (usually one of the students) can merely look at the chart on the wall and see who is present or absent. Generally, the children are given the responsibility for seeing that many of these "housekeeping" chores are accomplished.

Many times, and in many ways, we underestimate the ability of children to do things. I recently had an opportunity to visit the classrooms of a group of teachers who had previously expressed to me their skepticism of the ability of young children to count their own lunch money. At my urging they designed methods for their children, ranging in ages from five to twelve, to do this. All of the teachers were surprised and delighted with the results.

During the morning, there is also opportunity for children to participate in certain special curricular areas if there is a need, and if it is thought appropriate by the local community. For example, Andy could go to remedial reading or to speech correction and therapy. If the school is structured so that there are specialists in physical education and music then Andy could also be experiencing these activities during various times throughout the morning.

In an open education setting, there is much less need for play time or recess periods as such. Since children are involved and participating at a much higher level than in a traditional classroom, they are expending energy through their involvement in learning. Consequently, there is less need to have them go outside "to run around the school four or five times to get rid of their excess energy."

Following the math involvement Andy would eat his meal in a manner similar to that of a family. In this arrangement, children of different ages eat in groups of eight or ten. The children are responsible for setting their table, bringing food to the table, serving themselves, and deciding the size of the portions they are going to eat. Of course conversation is encouraged during the meal, and eating is a happy, pleasurable time. Clean-up is handled by the children and, if necessary, they take responsibility for seeing the table is prepared for the group that follows.

After lunch, it is conceivable that a block of time, perhaps an hour or so, would be devoted to creative arts with children involved in "clean crafts" consisting of such activities as sewing, needlepoint, and woodworking. Drama would also be an alternative with children making costumes for the play they wrote earlier in the day. Designing and constructing scenery or practicing for their play would also be possibilities. Andy could be part of a group of students involved in the exploring of their environment through movement, while a group or individual children are listening to music, whether it be a current top hit or Beethoven.

An hour or so could be devoted to environmental studies. Children would be involved in cooking and baking activities or studying the quality of the water the community is drinking. Opportunities would also undoubtedly exist for involvement in "cleaning up" the community. This might include planting shrubbery around the school and flowers in local minigardens. Painting old buildings and graffiti-covered walls in the neighborhood offer other possibilities for involvement. Of course these activities provide many opportunities for decision making: Can we paint? How do we get permission to paint? What colors shall we use? Who will do the painting? Andy and his friends might become interested in writing a history of the school or knowing why the trolley cars no longer run through their neighborhood. Questions which students might raise as possibilities for other involvement are: What is a post office? What problems does it have? What is the bakery all about? Why does the baker have to get up at 4:00 A.M.?

At the end of the day a period of time is set aside for small-group or large-group discussion. This is when the day's activities are summarized; learnings and involvements are accounted for and evaluated. It would also provide an opportunity for the children to engage in record-keeping activities whereby they record what they have accomplished throughout the day. It is the responsibility of Andy and his classmates to maintain these record-keeping activities. The next day's activities can be anticipated at this time and plans be made for how to begin the next day. This does not mean changes cannot be made the next morning, for undoubtedly they will;

however, this period of time provides the opportunity, climate and encouragement for children to reflect on what they have accomplished.

We have been discussing a school day which, in terms of time and activities, might look like the one in Figure 6. As was indicated earlier, this "look" at an open classroom should be considered only as representative of what can occur. The innumerable ways the day can be organized are dependent upon the interests of children and teachers, the creative energies they bring to the learning setting, the kinds of schools in which they find themselves, the attitudes of administrators, and the desires of parents.

8:30 Enter School
↓
Plan
↓
Participate in
—communication
—math
↓
12:00 Family-Style Lunch
↓
Plan
—creative arts
—environmental studies
↓
Review/Recap/Plan
↓
3:30 Dismissal

Figure 6 *Time Schedule in an Open Classroom*

Role of the Teacher

Good Habits and Qualities to Develop

How do you know if you would be the kind of teacher who would be happy and effective in an open classroom? There are certain qualities and habits that constitute "musts" for the teacher if the classroom is to be successful.

Planning. Planning on the part of the staff, the individual teacher, and the teacher in cooperation with pupils is mandatory if open education is to be anything but an uncontrollable, drifting chaos. Generally, the cause of a directionless program can be laid directly at the door of poor planning. It has been my experience that the high mortality rate of good-intentioned beginnings toward open education is due to inadequate *time, thought, cooperation, effort, and creativity* spent on planning. Teachers not used to planning must acquire the habit. Planning must answer such questions as:

Where are my children now in skills and abilities? What do I want them to learn? What are my students interested in? What do my students want to learn? What direction do I want them to go? How are we going to achieve what we have planned? Included also are the myriad of other questions associated with good teaching.

It is rather easy to assume that in a curriculum which relies in part on following the interests of children there is no need for planning. On the contrary, quite the opposite is true. It takes a great deal more planning of a more difficult and creative type. It is not too difficult at all for an adult to plan for a classroom of children to do the same things in unison throughout the school day. But to plan for individuals and small groups based upon observation of what they are involved in and interested in requires a great deal of hard work. Just as a teacher cannot know exactly what thirty or more children are doing exactly every minute, so it is not possible to plan precisely and in detail for each child every day. However, it is possible to know generally what they are doing so that general plans can be made. It is also possible to plan specifically for a few children and groups each day. In this way, specific attention and guidance can be given as you plan with children and interact with them in the open classroom setting.

In some open settings, it is common to practice *teaming* whereby groups of teachers teach and plan together. Where this is the case, there is the advantage of planning as a group for instruction and activities. Many teachers have found that team teaching (not taking turns teaching) is a very worthwhile venture in implementing open education.

Record Keeping. Associated with planning is record keeping. If teachers are going to plan effective programs for children, they must assess their previous accomplishments. This assessment, which can occur through observation, interviews, and informal and standardized tests forms the basis for planning. In order to teach accountably and to report accurately to parents, planning strategies for children and keeping accurate records of their progress is necessary. A system of record keeping has to be developed which is simple and efficient. Ideally, this system ought to be one that is easy to work with, and at the same time have the built-in ability for utilization by children. Although some teachers feel that kindergarten children are not capable of keeping their own records, this is not necessarily so. Children must be involved in your record keeping and helped to keep their own.

Patience. A quality which teachers must possess if they and the children are going to be happy in an open setting is patience. Patience means allowing things to work, and not giving up too soon. For example, a teacher may have a child whom he thinks works too slow. His pace of learning is irregular from that of his classmates. In such a situation, the best approach may be to have the patience to allow the educative process to work. The teacher needs to be able to say, "Maybe the child will work this out on his own; perhaps I can get him involved in certain kinds of activities that will help him work out of the stage he is in; perhaps it is a case of needing more time than other children to do things." This should not be interpreted to mean teachers can rationalize their way out of children's learning problems, and do nothing. This latter kind of teacher behavior has been much too common. It is too easy to say, "He's a nonlearner; I won't worry about him."

In an open education setting, the kind of student behavior under discussion may be more apparent because children are not told constantly what to do. Therefore, teachers must have the patience necessary to deal effectively with this type of student behavior. They must also have patience when their aids do not always get immediate results. Perhaps their system of record keeping might not work as quickly or as well as they think it ought to. This means they must have the patience to stick with it, modify, reassess, and keep trying. Some open classrooms fail because teachers give up too quickly on certain ideas or features. A typical remark is: "Oh, it's too hard to keep records; I'm not going to do it anymore," and the teacher reverts to old behavior patterns.

Persistence. Associated with patience is the ability to stay with a method or procedure and say, "I'm going to keep trying it and changing bits and pieces of it and it will work out." This doesn't mean that the teacher becomes bullheaded about something and sticks with it in the face of all opposition and all problems. However, there needs to be a certain amount of persistence in order to see that the ideas that professionals and the literature say can be accomplished are given a chance to be successful.

Adaptability. Another quality which teachers must possess is adaptability. Adaptability is being able to look at alternative ways of doing things, examining different approaches, and adjusting teaching style to match open education concepts and student learning styles. Without this quality, they will have problems in the open classroom. The obvious area that always comes to mind is noise level. Teachers have to adapt to an increasing level of noise. This does not mean the teacher adapts to children tearing the classroom apart, or that children should be allowed to scream and yell at will. However, an open classroom will have a higher noise level than a traditional classroom and this requires teacher adjustment. In addition, teachers must adapt to different learning styles of children. In an open education setting, children will be involved in activities and procedures that differ from traditional education; memorizing and keeping quiet will not suffice.

From Subject Matter to Interests

Teaching from interests invariably poses problems for teachers who have never tried the procedure or who don't know what constitutes interests. It is very easy for teachers in the beginning stages of involvement to get "hung up" on subject matter. Teachers must be willing to learn along with children, and recognize that, if interests of children are followed, there will naturally be many areas with which they are not familiar. If teachers refuse to try teaching unfamiliar subjects, many important and interesting topics will be missed. This practice has lasted too long. A better teacher will say "If children are interested in a topic, this is how learning can take place. Therefore, it is legitimate to get involved and even though I don't know anything about it, I can learn with the children."

This open environment provides a setting for self-selection of activities and independent learning.

How are interests of children determined? By asking them! Other methods of determining student interests can be through interest inventories, observation, and by having students bring in hobbies from home. In psychological jargon, it is a matter of intrinsic motivation being more effective than extrinsic motivation. There are no guarantees that these efforts will motivate student interest in some topic, but the likelihood that he will become interested increases in this setting.

Figures 7 and 8 may help clarify the different emphasis that interest is accorded in traditional classroom settings and open education.

Respect for Children

It seems almost insulting to the teaching profession in general that a discussion of respect for children is necessary. After all, it is assumed that because

Environment

1. Difficult for students to become committed to learning task because of lack of interest.
2. Teacher spends much time and energy controlling behavior due to lack of interest.

Motivation

1. Limited opportunities to become interested in things.
2. Restriction of choices.
3. Students who are not already highly motivated have difficulty learning (especially disadvantaged).
4. Motivation basically extrinsic, i.e., grades.
5. Success mainly a function of how well school tasks are mastered.

Method

1. Learning occurs in same way for all students.
2. The same rate of learning is generally maintained for all students.
3. Generally all students learn same thing at same time.

Curricula

1. Predetermined curricula.
2. Material may or may not be interesting—student has no control over this.
3. What is studied is determined mainly by textbooks and/or teacher.
4. What is studied is generally not matched to students' previous achievement or experiences.
5. Most problems for work and study are posed by the teacher.

Figure 7 *Interest as a Factor in Learning—Traditional Classroom*

you are a teacher you respect children. Unfortunately, when people list their reasons for choosing teaching as a career, respect for children gets relegated to the bottom of the list or is not considered at all.

Respect for children as an indispensable quality for teachers in open education needs to be thought of in two ways. First, it means liking children; recognizing the basic humanity present in everyone and encouraging its fulfillment; and being able to accept them for what they are, including children who are not sweet, clean, mannerly, or well behaved.

Second, respect for children means being able to believe that all children have a sacred right to be different; that individuality and uniqueness is the normal state of man; and that these qualities should be encouraged by programs predicated on individual differences. Unless the uniqueness of

Environment

1. Teacher and students *viewed* as partners in learning.
2. Teacher provides a setting (prepares the environment) to encourage and promote interests.
3. Teacher has empathy for students.
4. Teacher spends less time controlling behavior.

Motivation

1. Child is encouraged to become interested in a wide range of topics.
2. Opportunities to make decisions and choices.
3. Motivation is basically *intrinsic,* i.e., the interests of the child provides the motivation.

Child in an Open Setting

Method

1. Learning tends to be individualized, based on interests.
2. Creativity is encouraged.
3. Student is responsible for his own learning.
4. Many opportunities for success in self-selected activities.

Curricula

1. Predetermined goals, i.e., reading may be required.
2. Student encouraged to select own goals based upon what he knows.
3. The "what" which is studied determined, in part, by interests of students.

Figure 8 *Interest as a Factor in Learning—Open Classroom*

each person is professed and implemented through educational programs, teaching becomes a masquerade with the teacher playing the role of charlatan.

Role of the Student

Good Habits and Qualities to Develop

The teacher is not the only person challenged to assume a new role in the open classroom. Students in open education must also exhibit a different set of behaviors if open education is to be a worthwhile endeavor. If children are to achieve their potential and if they are to be meaningfully involved and successful, the following qualities must constantly be developed and refined.

Responsibility. The child has to assume responsibility for several items: making decisions; becoming interested and involved with people, places and things; keeping records of what he has done and is doing; and for assuming social duties that are necessary while living and learning with a group of people. Of course Andy is not simply thrown into an open setting and told to be responsible, for this behavior only develops within the context of the setting and matures within the guidelines established by the teacher. The teacher has to help students by providing opportunities to be responsible. Obviously some students are much more ready than are other students. However, if a child is denied responsibility he can never become responsible. If Andy and his peers cannot be counted on, their teacher will have a hard time making open education work.

Making Decisions. Closely associated with the role of responsibility is that of decision making. It really is impossible to separate one from the other in terms of learning from day to day in an open classroom. If students are to have responsibility for their learning, they must exercise decision-making skills and decision-making processes. If students do not have these skills, part of the teacher's job is to help develop them. It may be that the child has never had an opportunity to make decisions, so he will have to be led gradually into the decision-making process. A very basic example of how decision making might begin with a five year old is by giving him the opportunity to decide whether or not he wants jelly on his crackers during snack time. You ask the child the question, "Would you like your cracker with or without jelly?" He starts to appreciate the idea that he can make decisions. This decision-making process could be further extended to the lunch time where he is free to say how big a serving he wants. This process is then extended to making decisions about what to get involved with and goes right up the line to decisions concerned with the self-evaluation of work accomplished.

Record Keeping. One of the reasons teachers often give for the abandonment of the open classroom for a more traditional program is problems with record keeping. How can students be involved? With kindergarten children a simple strategy might be to have the child's name on an individual folder in which he keeps work he has completed. A more sophisticated approach would be to have a twelve year old use graph paper to figure his progress in a particular area. Other alternatives for record keeping include the teacher's utilization of adult help in the classroom to share in the details of record keeping. Many parents are anxious and willing to help in classrooms on a volunteer basis. Regardless of the methods employed, students can and must participate in keeping their own records.

Three children of different ages participate in peer tutoring.

Peer Tutoring

If open education is going to provide students with the help they need regardless of the nature of the classroom setting, then Andy and other children must provide that help whenever possible. One of the features of the British Primary School is family grouping. This mixed age group can be any ages thought desirable; however, it is generally ages five to eight, and nine to twelve. In England, the parent is responsible for seeing that the child enters school in one of the terms (September—January—April) immediately following his fifth birthday. Therefore, five-year-old children are entering school three times a year and consequently there is a mixed age group. It is natural therefore that older children help younger children become acclimated to school and provide guidance in whatever ways they can. This idea of older children helping younger children is extended to include all children helping each other. Good students learn they are responsible for others who need help. It should be recognized, however, that most of the benefit in multi-age grouping accrues to the younger child. It is always necessary, therefore, to make sure the older children in a multi-age setting also have opportunities to interact with older children.

Controversial Issues

Subject Matter

Any topic which generates interest, enthusiasm and controversy has associated with it issues which must be clarified and examined. The most frequently heard criticism of open education is, "The kids don't learn anything." Some parents and teachers view open classrooms as nothing more than places where children wander around doing anything they want, in any way they wish, neglecting the traditional subjects of reading, writing and arithmetic. What is absolutely necessary in order for this issue to be adequately examined is for more parents and teachers to get into open classrooms and realize this need not be true. Once parents and teachers visit and get involved they generally see that open education has the potential for happy, learning children.

In the open classroom, the teacher substitutes standing in front of the room and talking about reading, with activities for involvement in reading. Instead of starting with a skill and hoping that the children get interested in something, children become interested in doing things and the enthusiasm leads to the development of the skill out of need. As a substitute for teaching children how to read and hoping they will be able to read a recipe for baking bread, the teacher uses the activity of baking bread and the need to read the recipe as a learning experience.

Perhaps one of the reasons it is assumed children aren't learning is that many of the things learned are not what parents or teachers traditionally expect learning to be. For example, it may be that, rather than spending all of his time learning to spell *El Salvador* or memorizing for a test all of the names of the Greek gods and goddesses, Andy is developing a set of interview questions which he will use when he interviews the local banker about the function of the bank in the community. One of the things open education has done is to force teachers and parents to examine the traditional content of learning and to recognize that schools can no longer be interested in teaching the trivia they taught in the past. Students are no longer interested in learning the "knowledge" many people think they ought to learn. Much of the school curriculum as practiced in the past is meaningless not only to the children, but also to the kind of lives they will live in a world much different from the one we now know.

Parents and teachers must understand that open education provides a setting in which children can develop and refine skills of data gathering, such as reading, interviewing, observing, and researching. In place of memorizing inappropriate facts they can have the skills necessary for finding the facts whenever they need them.

Structure

Many critics of education, and teachers as well, believe that without structure a child will not learn. By structure they mean providing discipline, a
routine in terms of *time* and *subjects,* and an emphasis on following instructions, paying attention and doing what one is told. We are all aware of the
results of this kind of schooling, and, depending on one's particular point
of view, the results have been either successful or lacking in some regard.
It would seem, however, that it would be possible to have both a structure
to provide the routine some educators think young children need and a
program which encourages active exploration and participation in the environment. Figures 9 and 10 help to illustrate some of the differences between
traditional education and open education in terms of structure and curriculum.

Interest of Children

An area that seems to present teachers with a great deal of difficulty is
teaching according to the interests of students, as we have already mentioned. They visualize that the way to get the children "going" is to say to
them, "Okay, kids—you're on your own, you can do anything you want to."
The problems associated with this strategy are several. First, students in
these situations may not know what they are interested in, so they act as
though they are interested in nothing. The second problem is the teacher
may interpret this apparent disinterest to mean the system won't work, so
he immediately returns to his old system of telling children what to do.

Quite often a strategy employed by teachers to get children involved
is to provide them with a series of choices. Unfortunately, the choices
provided may be beyond their experience level and outside of their interest
areas. Imagine someone saying to you, "Which Beethoven sonata would
you like to listen, no. 1 or no. 2?" Your reaction would probably be
synonymous to children faced with a similar decision—you wouldn't know
what to decide. When this occurs, the tendency on the part of the teacher
is to interpret this as a sign of immaturity for decision making and conclude
that the best way to get things accomplished is to make all the decisions.

Guilt Feelings

Another issue connected with open education, and one which may be more
imagined than real, is the feeling some teachers have that they aren't teaching anything in an open classroom. This issue exists on two levels. First, the
general public and the parents of children look at the teachers and their

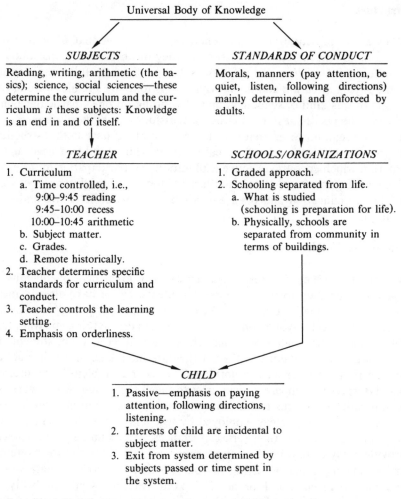

Figure 9 *Traditional Education Expressed through Traditional Classrooms*

performance in the classroom and say, "We don't see you teaching anything. We don't see you standing in front of the room or a group of children telling them what to do. We don't see you sitting down with thirty kids who have thirty books, so how can you be teaching anything?" The second level of this issue exists at the teacher level. Teachers, because they are not in the traditional role of standing in front of a group of children telling them what to do, the center of attention, manipulating as a whole group the actions of thirty children, directing the memorizing of dates and places, therefore

SCHOOLS

1. *Open concept*—encouragement of movement; opportunities to select areas of interest and become involved.

2. *Individualization* of instruction; continuous progress; nongradedness; multi-age grouping; family grouping.

3. *Freedom of movement* from arbitrary rules for children to "work out" standards of conduct.

4. *No rigid time schedule*—Interest becomes the determiner of how much or how little time is spent on an activity.

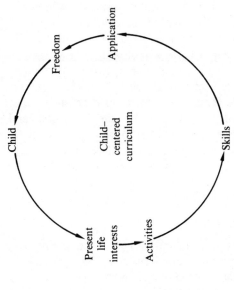

Child

Freedom

Application

Present life interests

Child-centered curriculum

Activities

Skills

TEACHER

1. *Learns with children*— teaching/learning a continuous process.

2. *Organization of experiences* so they are educative, i.e., reading is involved.

3. *Guide, director, catalyst*

4. *Teacher of children,* not subject matter.

CURRICULUM

1. *Child centered*—Activities and problem solving experiences are based on interests.

2. *Flexible* according to interests of children.

3. *Activity centered*—knowledge is not an end in itself, but a means to an end. Subject matter grows out of experiences.

Figure 10 *Progressive Education as Advocated by John Dewey and Expressed through Open Education*

think they are not teaching. Of course this thinking-that-you're-not-teaching syndrome leads to guilt feelings; rather than have these feelings, teachers respond by saying, "I can't do this any more," and abandon their attempt at openness.

It must be recognized that in this respect teachers are their own worst enemy and are responsible for the public believing they are not teaching. Such teachers may lack data necessary for reporting children's learning and progress to parents. This lack of data is due, in part, to very poor record keeping. At another level, teachers don't utilize many of the means available to them for communicating with parents. For instance, when parents express dissatisfaction with the school or say schools aren't doing their job, it is usually because they lack the evidence necessary to make enlightened decisions. A result of noncommunication with the public on the part of either the teacher or a school leads to suspicion, fear and criticism. Usually the most general criticism leveled against the school is the "how can you be teaching" criticism, for after all, it's the easiest charge to make. A most natural way of increasing information about schools is to involve parents in the schools as aides and tutors. This does not mean that the teacher surrenders her role as professional, but rather gains the time, help and support, through parental involvement, to become more professional. By involving the public in school programs, the public will become aware of the good things that are happening, and this awareness in turn helps to eliminate criticism.

Permissiveness

A charge frequently leveled against open education is that it is permissive, a charge that concludes that permissive children grow into permissive adults who are bad for society (so let's get rid of open education). I recently heard one parent in a public meeting state, "If you don't discipline kids when they are young, they are going to end up in the state penitentiary." This criticism is difficult to answer. Generally, the best way to deal with it is to invite the critics into the open education classroom and show them it is a setting where children are assuming responsibility and making decisions.

It is not uncommon for both teachers and parents to assert that chaos, noise and lack of discipline exist in the open method. Certainly the teacher who is used to having everything "super quiet" and throws dirty looks to those who even sneeze is going to find any classroom where there is an increased noise level disturbing. Admittedly, a teacher in an open education classroom must accommodate to an increased noise level. However, it is not the noise of chaos and destruction, but rather the noise and hum of activity which pervades any classroom where meaningful learning is taking place.

The "noise" in an open classroom is the noise associated with children laughing, excitedly sharing information with each other, talking to each other about how they should get involved in a task, asking directions from each other, sharing discoveries, and coming to teachers asking for advice and information.

Also, teachers who are used to having children lined up in nice, neat rows and who subsequently enter a setting where children are free to move about, go to the restroom on their own, and have freedom to get materials, are likely to perceive this freedom as chaos. Any teacher who conceives of discipline as only that which she administers and dictates as opposed to that which students impose upon themselves is likely to level the charge that children are undisciplined regardless of the setting.

Extra Materials

Most people I talked with concerning open education agree it necessitates providing, in one way or another, more materials for children. It is easy for critics to jump to the conclusion that these materials mean an increase in tax dollars and school budgets. Teachers may interpret the need for more materials to mean they must spend money out of their own pockets. Fortunately, neither of these alternatives is necessary, for there are ways of acquiring materials needed within the amount of money budgeted for any program. For example, instead of buying thirty textbooks on reading which are all the same, six books from five different publishing companies can be purchased. Utilization should be made of "found" materials that children bring from home. Teachers are only now beginning to explore possibilities that exist in using materials which have been discarded. Not too long ago, I witnessed a group of kindergarten children totally involved for several hours in the process of dismanteling an old radio. I suddenly became aware of the tremendous learnings that were occurring, especially in language development. This activity provided an opportunity for language interaction among students and between students and teachers. Students asked the teacher for certain kinds of tools with which to take the radio apart. They discussed what they were going to do and how best to do it. One young boy said, "I see a yellow wire here, maybe we'll find a blue one as we go along." His friend responded, "If you find a blue one, show me because I don't know what blue is." The classroom can become full of found things used to promote learning as a supplement for bought materials.

Teacher Suitability

A final issue surrounding open education is the assumption that all teachers are suited for teaching in the open classroom. A number of teachers have been made unhappy by being told they have to teach in an open classroom when they are not emotionally, physically or intellectually prepared to accomplish this. To insist that they do so will simply make matters worse. On the other hand, teachers who are excited by the possibilities open education offers and whose teaching styles "fit" the system are the ones who will give open education a decent try. One solution to this issue is to match the styles of teachers to requirements of the classroom. It would be helpful also to stop trying to convince all preservice teachers that they ought to be open classroom teachers. There is certainly going to be room for both kinds of teachers with both kinds of teaching styles for many years to come.

The Past and the Future

In reality, open education is not really new, for its ideas and principles are basically those teachers fostered and practiced when they taught a wide age group of children in all grades (usually one through eight) in the one-room school house that your grandparents or even parents attended. Its main ideas are those advocated by Montessori, Dewey and to a certain extent Piaget. As is so often the case, the pendulum of change has begun its inexorable swing. What we are experiencing now is a swing from a subject-centered, teacher-centered, efficient (in terms of time), highly organized system, to a child-centered, activity-centered program characterized by freedom. It is what might be called a humanistic approach. How far the pendulum will swing and how long it will take are matters which remain to be seen. Educators and parents should hope that the promises and potential embodied in open education are realized and should be encouraged to participate in the process.

Open education is full of excitement and challenge for teachers who have the desire to dedicate themselves. The opportunities for an individualized, self-paced program operated within a context of freedom, respect for children and relevancy are ones that ought to appeal to the teaching profession and communities who need their faith and confidence restored in the ability of education to provide meaningfully for the citizens of the future.

BIBLIOGRAPHY

Brown, Mary, and Precious, Norman. *Integrated Day in the Primary School.* New York: Agathon Press, Inc., 1968.

FOR FURTHER READING AND STUDY

Clegg, A. B., ed. *The Changing Primary School.* New York: Schocken Books, 1972.
Written by teachers who have been involved in the British Primary School and
open education, this book is for teachers who want to get involved but don't
know how. Deals with the problems encountered by actual teaching.

Hertzberg, Alvin, and Stone, Edward F. *Schools Are for Children.* New York:
Schocken Books, 1971.
Another practical approach to open education based on the authors' observations in British schools. Provides detailed descriptions for both physical arrangements and curriculum.

Howes, Virgil M. *Informal Teaching in the Open Classroom.* New York: Macmillan
Publishing Co., Inc., 1974.
Provides many helpful hints and ideas about organizing and implementing an
open classroom. Should prove helpful for those who want to know what to do
and how to do it. Contains a good section on record keeping.

Kohl, Herbert. *The Open Classroom.* New York: Random House, 1969.
Discusses method and rationale for setting up an "open learning" room. Kohl
emphasizes in an impressive manner the idea that we must allow students to
become who they are to become.

Rogers, Vincent R. *Teaching in the British Primary School.* London: The Macmillan
Company, 1970.
Thirteen chapters written by British educators for Americans. Emphasizes
individual learning and child-centered approaches.

Silberman, Charles E., ed. *The Open Classroom Reader.* New York: Vintage Books,
1973.
Provides a good overview of the open classroom in sixty–five selections about
practices in the United States, Canada and England. Can be used by anyone
who wants to begin to develop an open setting.

For Further Study and Involvement

1. Discuss briefly the differences between spontaneous and adult-directed classroom activities of children. Give one example of where adult direction seems to be profitable and another where adult direction could easily be detrimental.

2. Compare the ideas of Montessori and Piaget. What are the similarities and differences? Can you find examples of their ideas being applied to open education? What are they?

3. Many educators have different meanings for openness and open education. Interview teachers, principals and parents to determine their concepts of open education. Compare these meanings to those of your classmates. How many different meanings did you determine? Do you feel there should be one definition of open education?

4. Design a model open classroom and explain the reasons behind your arrangements.

5. After visiting an open classroom, list reasons why you think you would or would not like to teach there. What personal adjustments would you have to make? What problems might be encountered?

6

Head Start
Helping Children Win

History and Operating Principles

Evidence gathered from many sources indicate that when the parents' incomes are inadequate for social and educational needs, their children have an impaired ability to become contributing members of society. However, one of the most damaging consequences of poverty is the effect that lack of opportunity has on the self-image of those involved.

In order to overcome the negative effects poverty can have on the lives of adults and children, the federal government, in 1964, passed the Economic Opportunity Act. One of the main purposes of this act was the breaking of intergenerational cycles of poverty (which tends to be present from one generation to the next) by providing educational and social opportunities for children from low-income families. The Economic Opportunity Act created the Office of Economic Opportunity, and from this office Project Head Start was developed and administered. Head Start was implemented during the summer of 1965 and approximately 550,000 children in 2,500 child-development centers were enrolled in the program.

Head Start was established and currently operates according to certain basic premises. (1) Children who come from low-income families may be disadvantaged because they may not possess the cognitive, social and physical experiences normally associated with success in first grade. (2) Many problems created by poverty can be alleviated or compensated for if children are provided opportunities earlier than normally provided when they start school at ages six, seven or eight. (3) Intergenerational poverty cycles, whereby children of families living in poverty grow up also to live in poverty, can be "broken" by providing educational and social opportunities for children early in their lives.

The Economic Opportunity Act mandated that at the local community level, community action agencies should be created for purposes of coordinating programs and monies associated with Project Head Start. By *program* is meant the agency who receives the money to operate the Head Start program. It further specified that any nonprofit organization could apply for operational monies, develop a program and operate a Head Start Center. This meant that organizations such as churches, AAUWs, YMCAs, parent groups and public schools could design a Head Start program and apply to the community action agency for funds. It was also possible for an agency to apply directly to Project Head Start for funding rather than through the community action agency. Many organizations currently receive their money in this way (see Figure 11) and are therefore known as single-purpose agencies.

While many Head Start programs were initially established by public school systems, most operated for only six weeks during a summer program. The majority of Head Start Programs are currently operated by nonprofit organizations other than public schools; this fact accounts, in part, for why some programs are housed in churches, YMCAs, and community centers.

Presently at the federal level funding for Head Start comes through the Office of Human Development rather than through the Office of Economic Opportunity. Figure 11 depicts the organizational structure that governs the operation of Head Start programs.

Head Start has always endeavored to conduct a child-centered program, comprehensive in nature, that provides all of the services and developmental activities necessary for children enrolled in the program. The project is also committed to having children achieve a positive outlook on life through success in school and daily life activities.

> The program should maximize the strengths and unique experiences of each child. . . . Local communities must be allowed broad latitude in developing creative program designs so long as the basic goals and standards of a comprehensive program are adhered to.
>   The overall goal of Head Start is to bring about a greater degree of social competence in disadvantaged children. By social competence is meant the

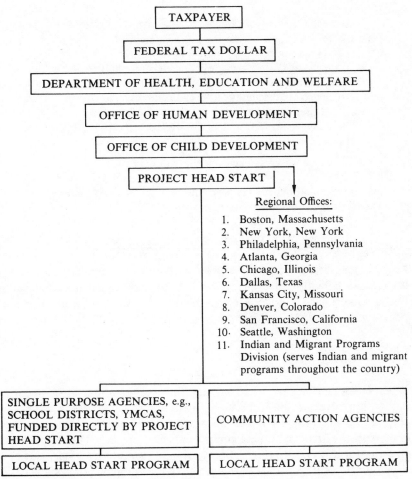

Figure 11 *Organizational Structure for Head Start*

child's everyday effectiveness in dealing with his environment and later responsibilities in school and life. Social competence takes into account the interrelatedness of cognitive and intellectual development, physical and mental health, nutritional needs, and other factors that enable a child to function optimally. Head Start is a comprehensive developmental approach to helping children achieve social competence. To this end, Head Start goals provide for:

A. The improvement of the child's health and physical abilities.

B. The encouragement of self-confidence, spontaneity, curiosity, and self-discipline which will assist in the development of the child's social and emotional health.

C. The enhancement of the child's mental processes and skills with particular attention to conceptual and verbal skills.

D. The establishment of patterns and expectations of success for the child, which will create a climate of confidence for his present and future learning efforts and overall development.

E. An increase in the ability of the child and his family to relate to each other and to others in a loving and supporting manner.

F. The enhancement of the sense of dignity and self-worth within the child and his family.

Head Start's approach is based on the philosophy that: (1) a child can benefit most from a comprehensive, interdisciplinary program to foster his development and remedy his problems, and (2) the child's entire family, as well as the community, must be involved.[1]

The implementation of these objectives occurs through child-development centers synonymously known as Head Start Centers. In discussing Project Head Start from the perspective of child-development centers, it is imperative that emphasis is placed on their comprehensive nature, meaning that a wide range of social, economic, educative and physical services are provided for both the child and his family.

Head Start Components

When Head Start began, it had six major program components: education, parental involvement, health service (including psychological services), social service, nutritional services, and career development for staff and parents. Now the first five of these components are considered major priorities. In order for us to have a fuller appreciation of Project Head Start and child development centers, we will examine all of the components in some detail.

Education

Objectives. The educational program of Head Start is guided by the following objectives:

1. Provide children with a learning environment and the varied experiences which will help them develop socially, intellectually, physically, and emotionally in a manner appropriate to their age and stage of development toward the overall goal of social competence.

---

[1]U.S. Department of Health, Education, and Welfare, Office of Child Development, *Head Start Program Performance Standards,* Head Start Policy Manual, OCD Notice N-30-364-1 (Washington, D.C.: U.S. Government Printing Office, January, 1973), pp. 6–7.

2. Integrate the educational aspects of the various Head Start components in the daily program of activities.
3. Involve parents in educational activities of the program to enhance their role as the principal influence on the child's education and development.
4. Assist parents to increase knowledge, understanding, skills, and experience in child growth and development.
5. Identify and reinforce experiences which occur in the home that parents can utilize as educational activities for their children.[2]

Most educational programs of child-development centers in the past have stressed activities generally typical of nursery school-kindergarten programs. These activities have emphasized the social skills which teachers traditionally believe are acquired by living and playing with other children. As such, emphasis in many Head Start programs has been placed on getting along with others, sharing, manners, and large group activities devoted to stories and play. In addition, activities associated with success in school such as taking and following directions, listening, becoming accustomed to routines, and interaction with materials of learning such as books, and adults are included. On visiting a Head Start child-development center, you will find routines similar to those in Figures 12 and 13, which are schedules for the Head Start centers of Meadville and Springboro, Pennsylvania. The Springboro Head Start is considered a one-half day, while the Meadville Head Start is a full-day program.

PROGRAMMATIC DIRECTION

One problem many Head Start centers have experienced with the educational component of their programs is they have had difficulty translating national Head Start goals into clear and meaningful goals for their local programs. This in turn has often resulted in an uncertainty on the part of individual programs about the kind of program they will conduct, making it difficult for teachers to select appropriate activities that would be significant for children.

The educational objectives for Head Start are sufficiently nebulous (or comprehensive, depending on your point of view) to permit a local program to conduct just about any kind of educational program it feels is appropriate. However, herein lies the problem. If a center director or teacher has had adequate preparation and has been able to conceptualize what a good program should include, then working within the guidelines of the Head Start educational objectives can be a strength. If, on the other hand, teach-

---

[2] *Ibid.* pp. 8–9.

9:00 A.M.   Children arrive, greetings and conversation, cursory health check, children choose work from interest areas and materials available in room, individual child activity (one adult to one child).

9:30 A.M.   Light snack served, classroom staff and volunteers interact with children during this time and initiate conversation. Children help set up and clean up.

9:45–10:00 A.M.   Group time stories, songs, fingerplays and conversation time. Amount of time devoted to this is determined by the needs of the children.

10:15 A.M.   Children choose own activities, teachers interact one to one or in very small groups to build cognitive skills (readiness type activities).

Outdoors activities occur anytime from now until children go home at 1:00 P.M.

About 12:00 Noon Lunch—family style. Children wash and set tables, serve themselves from serving dishes. When finished with lunch, children clean tables.

Manipulative materials such as games and puzzles used after lunch. These are self-selected by the student.

1:00 P.M.   Children go home.

NOTE: Reprinted by permission of the Conneaut Valley Head Start Center, Springboro, Pennsylvania.

Figure 12 *Daily Schedule—Conneaut Valley Head Start Center*

ers and directors do not have this background of preparation (as many Head Start personnel have not), then the individual program may be full of activities which are directionless. Unfortunately, a great deal of trivia wastes valuable time because of this type of planning. Too often a teacher (be it Head Start or public school) will hear about or see an activity and implement it without asking, Is it good for children? Does it relate to objectives of the program built around the needs of children?

Frequently when asked, "Why did you include this activity in your program?" a teacher will respond, "Because the children like it." However, simply because children like something does not make it sufficient, relevant, or meaningful to the goals of the program.

Predictably, when there is an absence of objectives that would provide clear programmatic direction, many Head Start centers operate programs which frequently consist of groups of unrelated activities. Many of these activities are structured around "free time," which can consist in some instances of eight children riding tricycles, terrorizing the other seven children.

Just as deadening has been the tendency of many centers to model their programs after those of public kindergartens. Unfortunately, this has led to some programs emphasizing free play, rest, and whole-group activities where everyone does everything together. While there is a need for freedom on the part of children, there is also a need for teachers to organize the environment so that the exercise of freedom can be meaningful.

Historically, Head Start has emphasized a social-emotional based program, which accounts for the lack of local conceptualization. Since many parents want their preschool children to learn how to get along with others, some programs have interpreted this to mean children should play all day long. Many Head Start programs could appropriately be named play schools. Socialization-oriented programs are more appropriate to middle-class children; socially and intellectually disadvantaged children need cognitively oriented skills that will enable them to achieve success in first grade.

8:30 A.M.	Arrival time. Hang up wraps, wash hands, participate in quiet activities including looking at books or magazines. Show and tell (where children bring in things of interest to them and tell about them to the class members).
8:40–9:00 A.M.	Breakfast—cleanup.
9:00–9:30 A.M.	Academic activity—language arts, number readiness, science activity.
9:30–10:15 A.M.	Outdoor play or walk.
10:30–11:15 A.M.	Organized activities for learning. Designed to meet individual needs of children.
11:15–11:30 A.M.	Games or activities dealing with spatial relationships.
11:45–12:00 noon	Rest. Preparation for lunch. This is an activity/learning experience for children.
12:00–12:45 P.M.	Lunch. Cleanup.
12:45–2:00 P.M.	Nap.
2:00–2:30 P.M.	Get up. Quiet preparation for dismissal.
2:30 P.M.	Dismissal.

NOTE: Reprinted by permission of the Meadville Head Start Center, Meadville, Pennsylvania.

Figure 13 *Daily Schedule—Meadville Head Start Center*

PERFORMANCE STANDARDS

Head Start, as a national program, seems to be making every effort to emphasize its role as a developmental program that will account and provide for the intellectual growth of children as well as the physical and social. In addition, since 1973, Head Start programs have conducted their activities utilizing performance standards. These performance standards are, in essence, requirements that must be met in order to continue receiving federal funding. For example, the educational objectives previously mentioned must be implemented in accordance with a performance standard. According to this standard, a program must be written to incorporate activities and services designed to meet the needs of all children in the Head Start center. Each objective in all the component areas has a corresponding performance standard. This effort of linking programmatic objectives to minimum standards of performance represents an admirable attempt by Head Start to strengthen its program of services.

COORDINATION WITH PUBLIC SCHOOLS

It is obvious then there also needs to be more coordination and liaison between Head Start and the public schools. Head Start may not have ever

Good early childhood education programs provide children with opportunities to do things for themselves. Here a child at a Head Start Center puts on her shoe "all by myself."

adequately dealt with processes, materials and activities (i.e., reading readiness activities) because they have long been considered the domain of kindergarten and first grade programs. The attitude has prevailed among Head Start personnel that whatever the public school professionals included in their programs, Head Start would not. Unfortunately, the crucial issues of personalizing instruction and doing what is best for children may have been overlooked. The guiding concept in Head Start should be, "If the child can benefit from certain activities, then we will provide them and rely on the public school to extend and go beyond what we have done." Now Head Start is finally starting to adopt this position.

It should not be assumed that the fault for this situation rests wholly with Head Start. Certainly the professionals of the public schools cannot remain blameless. Regardless of the type of program a child has experienced in Head Start, and in spite of what she is able to do when she comes to kindergarten or first grade, she often experiences what the teacher has previously and arbitrarily planned. In some instances, these plans may be repeated forever, in spite of what children are like or what is new in the world.

Parental Involvement

Objectives. Head Start has always been committed to the philosophy that if children are to be changed and improvements made in their lives, then corresponding changes have to be made in the lives of parents and teachers who are partners in the change process. One cannot hope to change the lives of children without involving parents. Therefore, part of the Head Start thrust is directed toward a parental-involvement program. Objectives for this program are:

1. Provide a planned program of experiences and activities which support and enhance the parental role as the principal influence in their child's education and development.
2. Provide a program that recognizes the parents as:
   A. Responsible guardians of their children's well being.
   B. Prime educators of their children.
   C. Contributors to the Head Start Program and to their communities.
3. Provide the following kinds of opportunities for parent participation:
   A. Direct involvement in decision making in program planning and operations.
   B. Participation in classroom and other program activities as paid employees, volunteers or observers.
   C. Activities for parents which they have helped to develop.
   D. Working with their own children in cooperation with Head Start staff.[3]

---

[3] *Ibid.,* pp. 19–20.

MODELING

It is not uncommon, therefore, to find parents with children in Head Start acting as paid aides and teachers in the program. The philosophy for this involvement is based on the belief that by helping parents learn, you are also helping their children learn. For example, parents who learn in the Head Start center that mealtime is a time for conversation are more likely to model this behavior by talking to their children at home. Also, by observing that Head Start teachers look at children when they talk to them, the parent will understand the importance of eye contact during conversation. In this respect a great deal of emphasis is placed on the Head Start teacher modeling appropriate behavior for parents in the belief that parents will tend to model for their children.

LEARNING HOW TO RAISE CHILDREN

Parents may not instinctively know how to raise children. Many parents want help with knowing the what, how and why of child rearing and education. Although some educators advocate that parents should not be involved in the education of their children because they are too emotionally involved, most educators are beginning to recognize that the most logical and effective way to deal with children is through the interactive process inherent in the parent-child relationship.

INCREASING PARENTAL INCOME, RESPONSIBILITY, AND PRIDE

Parental involvement is also a means of increasing income levels of families through employment in Head Start centers. Many parent volunteers have stayed to become bus drivers, cooks, and paid aides. Also, as a result of participating in seminars and training programs, some parents have gained the skills necessary to assume positions of increased responsibility such as assistant teacher, teacher, and program director.

In order to make the above process a reality, each Head Start center must develop and implement a career development ladder. This career development ladder is a plan whereby personnel, through training and involvement, can move from one position to another with increased responsibility and pay. Jobs in Head Start are not viewed as dead-end positions. Employees are encouraged to increase their skills through career development so that a higher position can be achieved. Of course, pay and responsibility are not the only benefits; self-image, an important factor in personal life, is also enhanced.

POLICY COUNCIL

Another level of parental involvement mandatory in Head Start is the Policy Council. Every Head Start program is operated within the context of policy established by this council. For example, if a single agency receives money to operate three Head Start centers, then each local center has a *parent committee*. Representatives from the parent committee would serve on the Policy Council establishing policy for the three programs. Half the Policy Council members are selected from parents with children in the program and half are selected from interested personnel from community agencies (day care, Family Services) and parents who previously have had children in Head Start. Policies established by the Council would include such things as determining the attendance area for the center (this might be based on the very practical question, "How far do we want to transport children?"), determining the basis on which children should be recruited into the center ("Which children need us the most?"), helping develop and oversee the program budget, and acting as a personnel and grievance committee.

The philosophy inherent in the involvement of parents in a Policy Council is two-fold. First, in many instances the people for whom programs are developed are the last to be consulted about the programs that affect them! Well-intentioned program developers sometimes have a preconceived idea of what they hope to achieve and no one is going to stand in their way, not even the people for whom the program is intended! Head Start, in an effort to minimize this phenomenon, utilizes the Policy Council system which insures input from parents.

The second rationale for the Policy Council is that parents can develop skills necessary for operating programs and meetings. Professionals who already know how to conduct meetings should not always be involved. Those on the council who have had few opportunities to make decisions will enhance their skills for making decisions. Chairmanship and group committee skills are developed through participation rather than through observation. A basic concept of Head Start is that people who don't possess certain skills should be placed in positions where these skills, through help and encouragement, can be developed. This not only provides skills that can be transferred to other settings; it also promotes self-confidence needed to become involved in other programs and activities.

Some college students have a tendency to be incredulous about parental involvement in decision making. Their attitude is generally expressed in the following way: "How can parents, who have had no college training or who may not even have graduated from high school, make decisions which in effect tell me, a college graduate, what to do?" Individuals with this point of view need to be aware of two things. First, just because a person has not had a formal education does not mean they cannot make good decisions. Second, the Policy Council does not operate in a vacuum. They have the resources of the center director as well as educational consultants and the center teachers to advise them. Generally, Head Start teachers attend these policy advisory committee meetings and give comments, recommendations and opinions, but do not vote. Not all Head Start policy comes directly from the Policy Council. The Office of Child Development has performance standards and guidelines which centers are required to observe. In this sense, the Policy Council is working within a framework designed by child development and educational experts. While teachers make certain recommendations to the Council about policy and procedures, the ultimate decisions concerning how the program is operated, within the framework of the performance standards, is the responsibility of the Policy Council. Consequently, it is not a case of having a committee that is doing anything they wish but a group of people learning responsible action through making decisions about things which affect them.

A Head Start teacher instructs a mother in the use of a manipulative material. The mother will then teach her child at home.

POSITIVE VIEW OF EDUCATION

While this explains the two main underlying reasons for parental involvement, there are also other associated benefits. Through involvement, parents who previously held a low image or concept of education come to appreciate the power and value of education in their lives, as well as in the lives of their children. This changed attitude toward education is reflected in parental attitudes and interaction with children. The cliche about educating a woman and thus also educating a family may seem trite in the current milieu of woman's awareness. Nevertheless, research has shown that the attitude of the child's mother toward education plays a major role in determining the child's attitude toward education. In today's society, the natural mother is generally the primary caregiver and therefore plays the dominate role in the development of attitudes and perceptions.

TRANSFER TO THE HOME

Parental involvement also provides opportunities to try in the home educational processes and activities observed in the center. If, as Head Start believes, home experiences can be used to reinforce center activities, then it would be logical to demonstrate these activities in the center or home depending on the availability of the parent. The parent who is shown that pots and pans can be used to teach size, shape and sequencing is not so apt to admonish the child for playing with the pots and pans. It may well be that the parent will spend time with the child (also an important process) and talk about size ("Show me the largest pot") and other classification concepts.

Health Services

Objectives for Medical and Dental Health. The health services component of Head Start means delivering a comprehensive program of medical, dental and mental services to the child, including related follow-up and follow-through procedures. The child's family is involved through a program of education and example. Objectives for the medical and dental components are:

1. Provide a comprehensive health services program which includes a broad range of medical, dental, mental health and nutrition services to preschool children, including handicapped children, to assist the child in his physical, emotional, cognitive and social development toward the overall goal of social competence.
2. Promote preventive health services and early intervention.
3. Provide the child's family with the necessary skills and insight and otherwise attempt to link the family to an ongoing health care system to ensure that the child continues to receive comprehensive health care even after he leaves the head start program.[4]

---

[4] *Ibid.*, pp. 24–25.

DIRECT SERVICE

When health services are ordinarily thought of in public school settings, we usually picture the child being examined and the parents informed of the results. Corrective and remedial care, if provided, is often left to the discretion of the parent. However, Head Start assumes a much more active role. The current health status of the child is monitored and reported to the parent and, in cooperation with the parent, corrective and preventive procedures are undertaken. For example, if the child needs glasses, corrective orthopedic surgery, or cavities filled, then these services are provided through Head Start programmatic monies that have been budgeted for such purposes. An alternative approach could be working with social service agencies to provide services or monies necessary for the health needs of children.

PARENTAL CARE IS PRIMARY

Regardless of the procedure, the parents' role of providing health care for the child is never bypassed. Although Head Start personnel would take the child directly to the doctor or dentist, every effort is made to see that the parent is provided the support and assistance necessary for securing appropriate services. The community worker for the Head Start program could conceivably play a supportive role by providing the parent needed transportation to a medical facility. If the parent had difficulty arranging an appointment with a specialist, then the community worker might help arrange an appointment. Regardless of the supportive role, the parent is involved. The philosophy inherent in this process supports the right of the parent as the primary provider of services for the child. Head Start does everything it can to encourage and enhance this role.

An associated rationale of the parent as primary care-giver is that through involvement in the process of providing health services for their children, parents gain knowledge, skills and confidence necessary to provide for the future needs of their children. This process of parental involvement is an extremely important one and is always an integral part of the health service delivery system of Head Start.

DAILY HEALTH EDUCATION

Health services in a child development center are not limited merely to providing services to children. Education related to healthy living is also stressed and taught by precept and example in the educational component of the program. In addition to examining children's teeth and filling cavities, each Head Start center conducts a program of dental health education whereby children are taught how to care for their teeth. This educational program includes stressing the importance of eating proper foods and care through brushing. Every child is provided his own tooth-brush and tooth-paste so that he can brush after every meal. In addition to being an important routine in each center, this activity involves children in the process of establishing good health habits, which, it is hoped, will become an integral and lasting routine in his life.

Mental Health Objectives. The mental health portion of the health services component refers to those services necessary for meeting the following objectives:

1. Assist all children participating in the program in emotional, cognitive and social development toward the overall goal of social competence in coordination with the education program and other related component activities.
2. Provide handicapped children and children with special needs with the necessary mental health services which will ensure that the child and his family achieve the full benefits of participation in the program.
3. Provide staff and parents with an understanding of child growth and development, and appreciation of individual differences, and the need for a supportive environment.
4. Provide for prevention, early identification and early intervention in problems that interfere with a child's development.
5. Develop a positive attitude toward mental health services and a recognition of the contribution of psychology, medicine, social services, education and others to the mental health program.
6. Mobilize community resources to serve children with problems that prevent them from coping with their environment.[5]

DEFINITION OF MENTAL HEALTH

By reading the objectives, it becomes apparent that the Head Start concept of mental health is not necessarily that which is held by the man on the street. The public usually conceives of mental health as a nice way of referring to mental institutions, schizophrenia and other mental disorders. However, Head Start's concept of mental health focuses on the early detection and prevention of problems that tend to prevent children from gaining full advantage of opportunities available to them. Since detection of problems and their subsequent treatment depends upon the ability and competence of Head Start staff members working with children, programs of staff training are initiated for the purpose.

DIRECT SERVICE

For example, a Head Start program might hire a psychologist to help it design and implement a program of diagnosis of children's problems

---

[5] *Ibid.,* p. 30–31.

through observation. The staff and parents would be trained in observational procedures and skills that would be used to detect children's problems. Using the data gathered through observation, the psychologist would then help the staff develop a set of "prescriptions" for dealing with particular behaviors. Thus a program to modify the behavior of an overly aggressive child who intimidates his classmates would be developed and implemented under expert guidance. In addition, appropriate follow-up activities for use with the child in the center and home would also be developed.

Head Start programs, through the help of a consultant, would also seek to involve, where necessary, children and parents in existing mental health delivery systems such as community health centers which already are operative in a community. It is not the intent or purpose of Head Start programs to duplicate existing services but to become aware of and utilize services currently available. If a particular child is suspected of having a hearing deficiency, then his parents are advised of this and put in contact with an agency that could provide a free hearing test.

Social Services

Problem-solving Objectives. The social services worker (or family services coordinator) also works with families in analyzing and finding solutions to their problems. Ultimately, the purpose of social services is to provide families access to those services which will enable them to lead full and meaningful lives. Solutions generally come through liaison with existing agencies such as departments of welfare, health agencies, and school systems. For example, it may be that a family is not receiving the full benefits of welfare, or that they could benefit from family counseling. These problems would be handled by the social services worker through linkage with an appropriate public agency. Objectives for the social services component are:

1. Establish and maintain an outreach and recruitment process which systematically insures enrollment of eligible children.
2. Provide enrollment of eligible children regardless of race, sex, creed, color, national origin, or handicapping condition.
3. Achieve parent participation in the center and home program and related activities.
4. Assist the family in its own efforts to improve the condition and quality of family life.
5. Make parents aware of community services and resources and facilitate their use.[6]

---

[6]*Ibid.,* pp. 16–17.

Eligibility. One of the problems facing many Head Start programs concerns who is eligible for participation according to the Head Start guidelines. It is the function of the social services component of Head Start to enroll those who are eligible. Once eligibility is determined, these children must be enrolled in the program. The basic criterion used for admission purposes to Head Start is family income level. Currently, a nonfarm family of four with an income of $4,320.00 is eligibile for Head Start services. Ninety percent of the children enrolled must come from families meeting poverty guidelines, while 10 percent may come from higher income families. In addition, 10 percent of all the children enrolled must be handicapped.

Nutrition

Objectives. Nutrition as a Head Start component includes providing children with nutritious meals as well as nutritional education for children and their families. Objectives for the nutrition component are:

1. Provide food which will help meet the child's daily nutritional needs in the child's home or in a clean and pleasant environment recognizing individual differences and cultural patterns and thereby promote sound physical, social, and emotional growth and development.
2. Provide an environment for nutritional services which will support and promote the use of the feeding situation as an opportunity for learning.
3. Help staff, child and family to understand the relationship of nutrition to health, factors which influence food practices, variety of ways to provide for nutritional needs and to apply this knowledge in the development of sound food habits even after leaving the Head Start program.
4. Demonstrate the interrelationships of nutrition to other activities of the Head Start program and its contribution to the overall child development goals.
5. Involve all staff, parents and other community agencies as appropriate in meeting the child's nutritional needs so that nutritional care provided by Head Start complements and supplements that of the home and community.[7]

A basic premise of Head Start is that if children are undernourished or malnourished they cannot live and learn as well. Therefore, children need to be properly fed so they can have the strength and energy to attend physically and intellectually to the learning process. This philosophy implies that if we teach children meaningful nutrition habits through daily practices, this will carry over for the rest of their lives and include their children as well. In addition, if we can provide mothers with basic nutritional education, then they, in turn, can continue the nutritional program

---

[7] *Ibid.,* p. 33.

of the child development center. Thus good nutritional practices are complemented and reinforced in the home. Nutrition education for parents can include seminars on buying food and how to read and compare grocery advertisements. I recently observed a Head Start sponsored program in consumer education for parents and staff. Emphasis in this seminar was placed on can sizes, number of servings per can, comparison of prices, nutritional value, and specific foods that can maximize dollar value.

Factors Determining Meals. For children, the nutrition program consists in part of a breakfast, snack and lunch. The decision to serve breakfast by a center depends on such things as the length of the Head Start day, how far children must travel to the center, and if particular mothers are able to provide their children with breakfasts. For example, one Head Start center which does not serve breakfast to the children provides breakfast for one child since his mother leaves home at 5:00 A.M. to begin her job as a bus driver with a large metropolitan transit authority.

Sample Menus and Methods. The menus listed in Figure 14 are not the traditional tomato soup and grilled cheese fare generally associated with cafeteria eating. They are purposefully designed to include food children like as well as foods indigenous to their ethnic background.

Nutrition plays a major role in Head Start programs such as this one. Children learn better when they are well nourished.

Just as children are not fed typical cafeteria food, neither are they fed cafeteria style. The type of feeding program generally utilized in Head Start is family style. In family-style eating, the children are fed as a family where food is served in bowls and children help themselves whenever possible. Of course there are variations from center to center but whatever the style, a

	Breakfast	Snack	Lunch
Monday	Orange Juice Oatmeal Milk	Graham Crackers with Apple Butter Citrus Cooler	Ham Loaf Sweet Potatoes Green Beans Cup Cakes Milk
Tuesday	Pineapple Juice Sausage & Milk Eggs/Biscuits	Cookies Milk	Macaroni and Cheese Peas Pudding Milk
Wednesday	Apple Juice Rice Krispies Milk	Peanut Butter and Jelly Sandwich Orange Juice	Roast Beef Spinach Buttered Potatoes Cookies Milk

Thursday	Grape Juice
	Corn Chex
	Milk
		Crackers and
		  Cheese
			Sauerkraut/Weiners
			Mashed Potatoes
			Ginger Bread /
			  Whipped Cream
			Milk

Friday	Grapefruit Juice Cinnamon Toast Milk	Corn Meal Mush	Meat Sandwiches Tossed Salad Corn Jello Milk

Figure 14 *Representative Head Start Menus*

major objective is a relaxed atmosphere. Adults eat with children and through this interaction conversation is encouraged, and manners and use of eating utensils are role modeled. The above process contrasts sharply with many public school cafeterias where the main purposes apparently are to discourage conversation and to rush children through the meal. Unfortunately, humanness seems to have left the arena of many public school cafeterias.

In Head Start child-development centers, opportunities are provided for combining nutritional concepts with learning experiences. The nature of foods such as taste, quantity, size, shape and color can be related to daily educational activities and programs. In this respect, the importance of cooking activities in any educational program cannot be overemphasized as a vehicle for the teaching of skills and knowledge. Instead of telling children about how pies are baked, they can make their own pies and experience these learnings firsthand. Of course, eating pie for dessert at the noon meal adds to the enjoyment and excitement of learning.

Career Development

While career development is no longer one of the major programmatic goals of Head Start, it nevertheless remains a part of the project in regard to parental involvement. Not all Head Start teachers have four-year baccalaureate degrees. Since there are no guidelines which mandate that teachers in Head Start must be graduates of a four-year college, there are many teachers and aides who have no previous college training. Much training in child development and educational practices occurs through career development. Generally, before a person starts to teach children, they are provided an intensive training program with on-the-job experiences as a volunteer, aide, bus driver, cook or other similar position. In this way they have contact with children, know about the program and are familiar with its goals and objectives and have an experiential basis for training.

In-service training is usually conducted by professionals hired at the local level or by representatives of the Head Start regional offices whose duties include assistance with the design of training programs, coordination of training personnel and training of staff.

Part of the career development program of Head Start is a college training program called Head Start Supplementary Training or HSST. This program is designed so that staff members have opportunities for involvement in college-level training and work. Many Head Start employees have taken advantage of this opportunity and, as a result, have earned baccalaureate degrees.

There is a growing realization that simply because individuals possess a college degree, this does not necessarily mean they have the competencies necessary to teach young children. Because of this, there is a trend toward programs whereby individuals, before they are certified in early childhood education, demonstrate competencies considered necessary for teaching young children. This national trend, known as competency-based teacher education (CBTE) has prompted the Office of Child Development to inaugurate the Child Development Associate (CDA) training program. This CDA program is designed to train child-care specialists who will have the basic competencies necessary to assume primary responsibility for the daily activities of a group of preschool children in center-based programs. It is hoped that this program will provide child development centers with trained personnel and also encourage colleges and universities to provide competency-based training for all students. It is anticipated that each CDA will hold a nationally respected credential certifying professional competency.

Components and Features of the CDA Program. The key feature of the CDA concept is that unlike the traditional approach to professional training based on courses, credits, and degrees, the CDA credential granted will be based on demonstrated ability to work effectively with young children in a center setting.

The CDA program is currently comprised of several components:

1. Compentencies necessary for working in a comprehensive, developmental program for preschoolers.
   a. Setting up a safe and healthy learning environment.
   b. Advancing physical and intellectual competence.
   c. Building positive self-concept and individual strength.
   d. Organizing and sustaining the positive functioning of children and adults in a group in a learning environment.
   e. Bringing about optimal coordination of home and center child rearing practices and expectations.
   f. Carrying out supplementary responsibilities related to the children's program.[8]

2. Pilot training projects to develop innovative training programs for the demonstration of competencies.

3. Competency assessment system to promote national uniformity in assessment processes and standards, as well as explore alternative procedures for assessing competencies.

4. Credentialing system developed by the CDA Consortium, a group of national organizations concerned with child development. The group works toward national recognition and acceptance of the CDA credential.

Head Start Improvement and Innovations

Local Options. All of the programmatic features have traditionally been delivered in a five-day, half- or whole-day program. However, there is a trend in Head Start toward what is known as the locally-developed option. Under this approach, Head Start programs at the local level are encouraged to plan, develop and implement alternative ways for delivering their services to children and parents. Centers have the option, for example, of having children attend centers on an "as needed" basis that precludes the necessity of their attending five days a week. In a program of this kind, a child would

---

[8]U.S. Department of Health, Education, and Welfare, Office of Child Development, *The CDA Program: The Child Development Associate, A Guide for Training,* HEW publication, no. OCD 73-1065, p. 3.

attend only one or two days a week depending upon his needs, capacities, and abilities.

All Head Start programs are encouraged to explore ways in which they can deliver their services directly to the child in the home. This approach is based on the premise that the parent is the most important person in the child's life and the home the optimum place for growth and development to occur. In brief, the locally designed option encourages Head Start programs to plan programs that fit their own needs, the needs of children and parents, while also taking into consideration the characteristics of the community they serve. In addition to encouraging local variations in the delivery of services, Head Start as a national program also periodically implements new delivery systems such as Home Start. There is a growing awareness that the parent can provide a meaningful developmental program for the child. Unfortunately, parents want to be good parents but sometimes lack sufficient knowledge and resources. In response to this, Home Start was designed to take Head Start expertise to the parent in the home. Trained home visitors work with parents and train them to work with their children. Since its implementation in 1972, Home Start has fostered sixteen experimental programs throughout the United States.

OBJECTIVES FOR HOME START

The primary purpose of Home Start is to implement various approaches to home-based education and to gather data about their effectiveness. Four major objectives of Home Start are:

1. to involve parents directly in the educational development of their children
2. to help strengthen in parents their capacity for facilitating the general development of their own children
3. to demonstrate methods of delivering comprehensive Head Start-type services to children and parents (or substitute parents) for whom a center-based program is not feasible
4. to determine the relative costs and benefits of center- and home-based comprehensive early childhood development programs, especially in areas where both types of programs are feasible.[9]

Health Care Program. Health Care, an innovative program initiated in 1970, explores methods for: increasing medical services provided to

---

[9]United States Department of Health, Education and Welfare, Office of Human Development, Office of Child Development, *The Home Start Demonstration Program: An Overview,* Publication no. (OHD) 74-1069 (Washington, D.C., 1973), p. 2.

disadvantaged children; increasing the number of such children receiving health services; and promoting better utilization of existing facilities and services.

Additional Health Problems. Since at least 10 percent of the enrollment in Head Start consists of handicapped children, two or three handicapped children may be in each classroom. Handicapped children have been defined by Head Start as "mentally retarded, hard of hearing, deaf, speech impaired, visually handicapped, seriously emotionally disturbed, crippled or other health-impaired children, who by reason thereof require special education and related services."[10] In order to provide adequately for these children, staff and parents receive training in methods and procedures related to these particular disabilities.

Head Start also provides training for their personnel in the identification, treatment, and prevention of child abuse and neglect, which may foster a staff-operated program concerning child abuse.

Head Start Issues

Funding

Head Start faces many issues, any one of which could determine if it will survive as a dynamic social intervention program. Probably the most crucial issue is funding. At federal budget time in particular, Head Start programs grow apprehensive until their fiscal fate is decided by Congress. The ultimate decision about the continued funding of Head Start will probably be decided by the attitude and feelings of the American public. First of all, if the public is willing to support child-development programs in general, Head Start will receive money. If, however, the public feels that such programs are unnecessary, are a threat to the dissolution of the American family, or portend totalitarian practices, then funds are unlikely. Second, the extent to which the public is willing to support a program for the disadvantaged remains to be seen. This is basically a question of universality. The public may well decide such a program should be for all children. If this is so, then Head Start will benefit. If on the other hand the public decides it cannot afford a program for all and therefore decides not to fund any program, Head Start might have to try to maintain its budget through a fee schedule based on family income and size. This proposal, based on past indications of feasibility, has encountered many political and social obstacles; it is questionable when, if at all, it will become a reality.

---

[10] *Head Start Newsletter,* vol. 7, no. 2 (DHEW Publication no. OHD 74-1068, November–December, 1973).

Socio-economic Mix

A second issue Head Start faces concerns the socio-economic mix of the families and children it serves. Some critics charge that under the present arrangements the program promotes de facto segregation of poor people. The 10 percent clause which is designed to encourage the enrollment of children from higher income families has apparently not been as successful as anticipated in dealing with this issue. It would seem that a more varied socio-economic mix would be desirable. How and if this mix can be achieved are issues which up to this time have eluded Head Start planners.

Influences on Family Life

A third issue deals with a problem confronting all early childhood programs and concerns the charge that they promote the breakup of the family. Many critics of early childhood education see any attempt to provide services (be they educational or care) for children outside their homes as a threat to the home. Head Start, with its emphasis on parental involvement and its Home Start program, demonstrates that it encourages and supports family life.

Articulation

A fourth issue facing Head Start involves articulation and it may ultimately be the issue which could decide the fate of Head Start. Basically this issue is a question of the ability of Head Start to explain its program to the American public in general and the public schools in particular. The more the American public understands what Head Start is accomplishing, the more inclined it will be to support and lobby for its continued success. The more understanding the public schools are of Head Start, the more likely it will be that teachers will cease duplicating services and content. More importantly, increased articulation could promote sharing of programs, services and training. If this were to occur, both Head Start and the public schools would benefit greatly.

Continuity

A fifth issue concerns the continuity of Head Start programs and services. As it currently stands, when a child leaves Head Start, he stops enjoying and benefiting from its services; Head Start is now challenged to seek ways and means of providing for a continuation of its services to children throughout their entire school career. This is why Follow Through programs were established and funded. Follow Through continues services for children in the primary grades. Such programs are not widespread.

The Future

Given these issues and problems, one can speculate on the future of Head Start. The clientele support based on the loyalty of parents will most probably be the determining factor, in the short term at least, that will insure continued funding for Project Head Start.

BIBLIOGRAPHY

Conneaut Valley Head Start Center. *Daily Schedule.* Springboro, Pa.

Meadville Head Start Center. *Daily Schedule.* P. O. Box 157, Meadville, Pa. 16335.

U.S. Department of Health, Education, and Welfare, Office of Child Development, *The CDA Program: The Child Development Associate, A Guide for Training,* no. OCD 73–1065.

Office of Human Development, *Head Start Newsletter,* vol. 7, no. 2, no. OHD 74–1068, November–December, 1973.

———, Office of Child Development, Head Start Policy Manual, *Head Start Program Performance Standards,* OCD Notice N–30–364–1 (Washington, D.C.: U.S. Government Printing Office, January, 1973).

———, Office of Human Development, Office of Child Development, *The Home Start Demonstration Program: An Overview,* no. OHD 74–1069 (Washington, D.C., 1973).

FOR FURTHER READING AND STUDY

Bell, T. H. *Your Child's Intellect.* Salt Lake City, Utah: Olympus Publishing Company, 1972.
Subtitled *A Guide to Home-Based Preschool Education,* this book provides many practical how-to-do-it approaches for helping children develop intellectually. Illustrated with many photographs that show concepts being applied in home situations.

Gattmann, Eric, and Henricks, William. *The Other Teacher: Aides to Learning.* Belmont, California: Wadsworth Publishing Company, Inc., 1973.
Head Start has focused attention on and created interest in the role of parents, aides, and volunteers in the classroom. This book offers practical information and techniques for all those who are or hope to be a teacher aide.

Maccoby, Eleanor E., and Zellner, Miriam. *Experiments in Primary Education.* New York: Harcourt Brace Jovanovich, Inc., 1970.
Discusses the efforts to enhance the education of disadvantaged grade school children through Project Follow Through. Compares and contrasts the national models for implementing the project.

U.S., Department of Health, Education, and Welfare, Office of Child Development, *Project Head Start—A Guide for Head Start Personnel,* 13 booklets. (Washington, D.C.: U.S. Government Printing Office).
A series of booklets called the *Rainbow Series* (because the cover of each booklet is printed in a different color) that provides excellent information about Head Start and its programs. Designed primarily for Head Start personnel, the thirteen booklets are devoted to practical ideas, suggestions, and rationale. The series can be ordered from the Superintendent of Documents, U.S. Government Printing Office, Washington, D.C. 20402.

For Further Study and Involvement

1. Discuss the range of your own community's economic and cultural differences. Give an example of a particular classroom problem that may occur as the result of economic and cultural variations.

2. What kind of federal education programs are there in a school district you visited? How is the money being spent? Do you agree or disagree with what you saw?

3. There has never been universal agreement that Head Start has been as effective a program as it was intended to be. Interview parents of Head Start children to find out what they feel has been the impact of Head Start on the lives of their family.

4. Visit several different Head Start centers. Compare and contrast their programs. How are they similar and different? How do you account for this?

5. Interview Head Start personnel to determine their opinions about the future of the program and the new variations within the organization.

6. Arrange to accompany Head Start personnel when they visit the homes of children. How do you think qualities of the homes (style, background, values, etc.) you visited affect the learning ability of children?

7

Day Care
What to Do with Children

Definition

Day care is probably the most confusing term associated with early childhood education because it is often used interchangeably with other terminology such as *child welfare, child care* and *child services.* Vagueness and confusion about what it stands for seem to be the standard state of affairs. (See Chapter 1 for a discussion of terminology.)

Not only does day care connote many different meanings, it also conjures up a wide range of varied emotions. Advocates of day care consider it the salvation of the nation's children and families; yet those who oppose it see it as a sinister evil, with power to destroy all that is good about childhood, parenthood, and the home. There seems to be no middle ground; either you're for it or you're against it. It is unfortunate that issues associated with children are often polarized to this extent.

One definition for day care often used is that of the Child Welfare League of America which conceives of day care in part as a service provided by the community, "because of its concern for children who might otherwise lack the care and protection essential for their healthy development."[1] Two key words in this definition are *care* and *protection,* which have

---

[1] *Child Welfare League of America: Standards for Day Care Services* (New York: Child Welfare League of America, Inc., 1973), p. 9.

traditionally involved assuring that children's physical needs are provided for, that they do not harm themselves, and that they are not harmed by others—including the parents. A negative connotation is often associated with this type of service since the primary emphasis is directed toward providing for basic physical needs of children. It is regarded by some as a "holding action" and is typically referred to as "custodial day care." While opportunities for free play may also be provided in such a program, it is not generally structured for any educational purpose nor are educational activities planned for as an integral part of the program. Children usually make use of the toys and materials provided. Learning, other than that occurring through maturation, is viewed as incidental.

Another view of day care is the one in which all the needs of children are accounted for:

> Child care or *supplementary child care* refers to the care and supervision which augments care provided by the parent(s) or guardian(s) of the children. The responsibility for supplementary care is delegated by the parents or guardians and is generally provided in their absence. Such care of children is considered *supplementary* since the parent or guardian maintains the primary responsibility for rearing their children. (This definition excludes the placement of children in foster homes for extended periods of time and the legal adoption of children.) The term *child* refers to any person under 14 years of age for whom care is needed. *Care* includes the variety of activities and services provided for the children by the delegated caregiver. The number and kinds of activities included in care may range from the provision of supervision, of food, and of other physical necessities for custodial care to comprehensive supportive services for meeting education, medical, dental, social and psychological needs of the children. The first is frequently called day care and the second, child–development services.[2]

While this definition uses the term *child-development services* to refer to a comprehensive program, the current tendency is toward using the term *day care* to mean a program of comprehensive services and unburden it of the custodial care image.

The comprehensive concept is more contemporary because of its emphasis on satisfying many needs. This emphasis also tends to remove the stigma of poverty, deprivation, and welfare traditionally associated with day care. Many center-type programs that handle groups of children use

---

[2]U.S. Office of Economic Opportunity, *Alternative Federal Day Care Strategies for the 1970's: Summary Report* (Washington, D.C.: Department of Health, Education, and Welfare, March, 1972), pp. 22–23.

A day care teacher gathers data from a parent about his children's growth patterns, behavior, interests, and habits. The parent also learns what he can expect from the center program and staff.

this idea. Head Start programs are also included as using this concept. It is not uncommon, therefore, for the public to refer to Head Start as day care and/or a child development program.

Types of Day Care Programs

Comprehensiveness of Care

In discussing day care programs, it is also necessary to distinguish conceptually between what a program is (as outlined above) and where the programmatic services are conducted. *Family day care,* sometimes called *home day care,* refers to the care given children in a home by a person other than the parent. In Pennsylvania, a family day care home is defined as "any premises in which day care is provided in a home setting to not more than six children at any one time."[3] Services provided in family day care homes, while not thought of specifically as babysitting services, generally amount to as much in practice and is considered a custodial service.

Group day care, sometimes called *center day care,* refers to the care of children in a center setting. In Pennsylvania, group day care is "any premises in which child day care is provided similtaneously for seven or

[3]Pennsylvania Department of Public Welfare, Office of Family Services, *Family Day Care Homes for Children under Social Service Auspices,* Regulations Title 4700, p. 1.

more children who are not relatives of the operator."[4] It is also possible to have a group day care program in a home setting and in such a case, about twelve children would be cared for by two adults.

Another type of service often provided by individuals is *at-home care.* This is care provided by a person other than the parent in the child's home, and can be considered babysitting. Sometimes these arrangements are made with adolescents or a combination housekeeper and babysitter.

The comprehensive services are usually found in center-type programs. However, simply because a center program exists does not mean it is conducting a comprehensive program. Many center programs operate glorified babysitting programs and some provide something less than good custodial care. One of the big criticisms of some center-type programs is that they fail to provide meaningfully for children.

It must be understood that just as the quality of public schools varies among districts, cities, and states, so also does the quality of day care services vary from between settings. This accounts in part for the difficulty with comprehending the term *day care.* Variations from state to state make it difficult to do anything but generalize. A common ground, specifying broad regulations and guidelines, is found in the *Federal Interagency Day Care Requirements,* a statement which is applicable to all day care programs receiving federal monies.

Time of Care

Day care programs can also be classified according to time. A program may operate a *twenty-four-hour day care program* in which the center or home is open for admittance of children twenty-four hours a day. For example, if the parents work from 3:30 P.M. to midnight, they can bring their child to the home or center and have him cared for while they are working. Likewise, if they work from midnight to 8:00 A.M., the child would have care during that time also.

There are also programs called *whole-day programs.* These are usually operated on a 6:30 A.M.–5:00 P.M. schedule to accommodate working parents. Recently I talked with a woman who was elated about being employed as a bus driver by the transit authority of a major city. However, she had to report at 5:00 A.M. for training. The problem of what to do with her three-year-old son was a major concern. Fortunately, there was a day care program available that was willing to meet her needs.

---

[4]Pennsylvania Department of Public Welfare, Office of Family Services, *Child Day Centers under Social Service Auspices,* Regulations Title 4600, p. 1.

Some programs offer before-school and after-school services in addition to their regular schedule. This means that, should the parents have jobs that require going to work before the time for the child to go to school or require going to work before the time the child normally comes home from school, the child can be brought to the center or day care home. Transportation is a problem. Some programs provide transportation; others require the parents to manage on their own.

There is also the *half-day program* such as those operated in many Head Start centers. These programs usually run from 8:30 A.M. or 9:00 A.M. to 1:00 P.M. or 2:00 P.M. Parents who work usually supplement this kind of service with a private babysitter or relative who acts as a babysitter.

Funding of Day Care

In addition to the above kinds of programs, day care can also be classified according to funding sources. Usually centers receive most of their funds from the federal government because they serve low-income families who are eligible for cash assistance under the Aid to Families with Dependent Children (AFDC) provision of Title IV-A of the Social Security Act. In this type of program 75 percent of the monies are federal and 25 percent are local. The local monies can come from such varied sources as foundations, United Funds, private donations, and school districts. When you hear of a day care program being referred to as a "Four-A" program, it is because this is a program which receives federal monies from Title IV-A. Families usually receive AFDC assistance because one parent is absent from the home through desertion, death or because the child or children of the family are illegitimate. Day care is currently provided to AFDC families for several reasons. First, day care is viewed as a means of enhancing the lives of those children who may not have available to them opportunities believed necessary for normal development. Second, these services can make it possible for both parents to work and thus supplement their income. Third, day care services can provide opportunities for parents to participate in job training, thus enabling them to be self–supporting and no longer dependent on welfare assistance. The government may also make job training available to welfare recipients through the Work Incentive Program (WIN), and usually encourages them to use day care services. They may receive an additional welfare supplement with which they can pay for child care. The use of day care services as an inducement for job training may raise in the reader's mind some intriguing moral and political questions. It should be obvious, therefore, that day care can be and usually is a political as well as a moral issue.

It should not be assumed that only families who are receiving welfare benefits can utilize day care services. While the head of a family may be employed, the income from this employment may be below the federal poverty guidelines. In this instance, the family would be eligible for federally supported day care services.

Proprietary Day Care

Day care can also be classified according to its profit-making or proprietary nature. There are day care centers run by corporations as businesses for the purpose of making profits. Centers such as the Singer Learning Center and American Child Centers are in the business of providing care for children with the intent of making a profit in the process. Some of the programs operated in this manner not only provide custodial services but also preschool and educational activities designed to take the place of regular school programs. Thus, it is possible in one center to have both preschool age children and elementary school age children at the same time. Many of these programs emphasize the educational component of their school program and appeal to middle-class families who are willing to pay for the promised services. Many of these programs are also of a franchise nature, meaning that the name and method of operation are sold to an individual who has the necessary money to purchase the franchise. This franchising process of child care constitutes one of the more controversial issues in day care. Critics are quick to make analogies between franchising child care, hamburgers and chicken. Apparently, it is legitimate to make a profit on the latter, but not on the former!

A day care program operated in a home for purposes of providing income must also be considered proprietary. Many homes are used for day care programs as a means of supplementing the incomes of those who operate the homes. The only restrictions usually placed upon these programs are those relating primarily to facilities and child caring abilities of the operator. For example, it is unlikely that a woman who had a history of child abuse would be licensed to operate such a program.

Increasingly, day care services are being provided by business and industries on their premises as a benefit for their employed personnel. This service enables parents to bring their children to work and utilize the day care services provided. The services provided may be considered fringe benefits or they may be an inducement to employment. On the other hand, they may be provided for an "at cost" fee. Hospitals in particular seem to be taking the lead in providing this type of benefit.

It is interesting to note that during the second World War, many industries provided child care services at the shop or plant so that women who were needed in the labor force would have a place for their children. Following the war, these services were discontinued, apparently because there was an emphasis on giving jobs to returning veterans and because of the view that the woman's proper place (except in times of national emergencies) was caring for her children. It may be that the current awareness of the equality of women will see a return to more child care services offered by employers either by establishing their own day care services or through consortia efforts where several employers band together and provide child care.

Cooperatives and Sitters

Also available is the *cooperative day care program* which is established by a group of interested individuals who come together for the purpose of providing day care services for their children. This venture is usually operated by parents who take turns staffing the program, or a board of directors who hire a staff. Rules which govern the programs are decided cooperatively by the membership.

Simply because a family is eligible or has need of day care services does not mean that it is available to them. Therefore parents must hire a babysitter or make arrangements with relatives. Most of the arrangements for day care services made by working mothers are now made in this way.

Reasons for the Current Interest in Day Care

Reasons for today's interest in day care are much the same as those forming the basis for the current interest in early childhood education. (See Chapter One.) Briefly, these reasons include:

1. Head Start began to focus attention on the need for adequate care for all children, not just for those from poverty-level homes.

2. Women's Liberation focused on the current lack of adequate facilities for child care. Women have traditionally been responsible for the care of children; now they do not want to be discriminated against because they have children who need care. The traditional role of women as solely housewives is rejected in favor of one that would give them equal opportunity in the home and job market. The need for women to work, to find fulfillment through involvement in a wide range of activities, and to lead meaningful lives in general can become realities only if there is good care of children.

3. Government officials offered day care to people on welfare who were enrolled in federal job training programs.

*According to day care advocates, these bright, alert children
have an inalienable right to day care that provides more than
custodial services.*

Arguments in Favor of Day Care

Many reasons for and against day care have already been mentioned. As
time goes by, it is inevitable that more issues will be advanced. Briefly, here
are the ones now most commonly used to defend this emotional topic.

1. Working women need day care. It is difficult for women to find
   adequate care for their children, and if they do find adequate
   custodial care, then the care provided may often be in direct
   conflict with their own theories and ideas of child rearing. Worse
   yet, some women may not know what their own ideas of child
   rearing are, or what the ideas are of the people to whom they are
   entrusting their children. For example, when talking with a working mother not too long ago, she expressed her dissatisfaction with
   the arrangements she had made for taking care of her only child.
   Her biggest complaint was that while the physical care given to
   the child was fine, the caretaker's theory of corporal punishment
   was almost in direct opposition to her own. Where the caretaker
   had a tendency to feel that if you spared the rod you spoiled the
   child, the mother's feelings tended to be more permissive. The
   mother felt that techniques of behavior modification and with-
   holding of privileges should be used as opposed to corporal punishment. However, because no other sitters were available, the
   only alternative to this dilemma was for her to quit her job.
   Because of such circumstances, working women will undoubtedly
   continue to press for adequate day care.

2. Women need day care in order to provide time for creative and recreational activities that will help fulfill their needs as persons. Twenty-four-hour services should be available so that women who want to go to school can have facilities open near to their homes or near to the institution where they will receive their education. Day care should be available to women who wish to receive job training in order to reenter the job market. In addition, women should have day care in order to participate in social events.

3. A question frequently asked by children's rights advocates is, "Do not children have a right to opportunities which will help them achieve all of their potential?" Day care is often viewed as a means of providing and/or supplementing these opportunities. If it is true that children are a nation's greatest wealth, then young children should be provided with the best a nation has to offer in order to protect and enhance this wealth.

Friendships developed in good day care programs provide a basis for future adult relationships.

Arguments Against Day Care

The issue of day care touches many fundamental values. The following are a few summarized arguments in opposition to day care.

1. Children should be the responsibility of the people who have them and not the taxpayer. The average person on the street will say, "If you're going to have kids then you take care of them; don't ask me to."

2. Day care services will lead to the destruction of the American family, a sacred institution on which the stability of the nation is based.

3. Children are emotionally or psychologically injured if taken away from their mothers and homes. Those who use this argument cite statistics and research conducted in institutional settings where children were obviously deprived and where care given them was certainly not the best. They also point out the inadequacies of many of the current day care programs where children are left to their own devices, which may mean sitting in front of a television set all day long.

4. Federally funded day care has the potential for controlling the minds and lives of children resulting in adults willing to obey a central government. Critics would have us examine the ways in which the Soviet Union educates its children through the utilization of centers. They ask, "Is Ivan the kind of child we want to rear?" Of course nobody wants to be guilty of Sovietizing the nation's children.

5. Day care is counter productive to zero population growth by relieving parents of the responsibility of child rearing, thus encouraging them to have more children. This reasoning is extended to include the idea that if you don't have to take care of your children, then you're not concerned about how many you have. It is further assumed that relief from the responsibility of child care for a part of the day will surely lead to increased procreation.

Issues Associated with Day Care

Many issues are outgrowths of the arguments for or against day care. The following are the basic controversies.

1. Should there be day care? Up to now, this fundamental issue seems to have been answered by "Yes, it should be provided for those who need it."

2. Who should be admitted to day care centers? Generally, the child who needs day care has been defined as that child who must have the care and protection his family either does not or cannot provide. There also seems to be some agreement that for working parents who can find no alternatives, day care services should be provided at their own expense. However, there are those who say

only the neglected child deserves these services. Where limited facilities exist, who has priority? Single-parent families? Low income families? Abused children? The emotionally impaired?

3. Who should control day care? In the light of the cost of day care services, the federal government will be called on to provide the basic funding for the programs, and will consequently mandate operational functions for individual programs within broad federal guidelines. The responsibility for local operation within these broad guidelines will be assigned to the parents it services in order to account for local needs. In this respect, day care will probably operate similarly to Head Start.

4. Is care outside the natural home bad? Some people feel that whoever bears a child can and should provide the care for that child. Care given by a surrogate parent is not necessarily bad and may be better than the care the natural parents can or are willing to provide. Those who advocate no day care fail to recognize that care provided by immature and inadequately trained adolescent girls at seventy-five cents an hour (or less) may do more harm than care provided by properly trained personnel in day care homes or centers. Children need an adequate environment and these conditions don't necessarily have to occur in the home. It may be that the conditions found in the center or in family day care settings may be much more adequate.

5. Are working mothers bad mothers? Persistent prejudice is aimed at the working mother. We still have a long way to go in terms of acknowledging the right of women to work irrespective of their status as mothers.

6. Should day care be used politically as an expedient to provide training in order to reduce welfare rolls?

Future of Day Care

Just as we have always had children, so too we will always have day care. Although the federal government's role will probably become stronger, providing more money for day care, it is doubtful whether or not the federal government will see fit to make comprehensive services available to all children. Not only would a national program of day care be tremendously expensive, it would also necessitate a reordering of budget priorities at a national level. For example, it is unlikely that money will be taken from the defense budget and funneled into services for the nation's children. Consequently, while the federal function and effort in day care will probably increase, the emphasis will be toward providing for children of low-income families, neglected children and children whose parents are in federal job training.

Because of the national attitude toward day care, other sectors of society must continue, out of necessity, to assume more responsibility for day care services. While institutions such as hospitals and industries will keep on expanding their day care programs as a benefit to their employees, this will provide day care for only a small number of the nation's children. The profit-making sector of day care will continue to grow and expand, but the extent to which this will occur depends upon the willingness of the public to pay. It seems likely that the profit-making organizations will still be limited to large metropolitan areas where demographic features such as a large population, a high percentage of college graduates, and high median family income will make their existence profitable.

While currently existing day care services for low-income, disadvantaged families will continue, probably not enough services will be provided to meet the needs of everyone adequately. At the other end of the economic spectrum, services for those who can afford to pay will always be available. Children of the middle class who don't qualify for day care services based upon income and whose parents can't afford fees charged by profit-making day care programs will remain the forgotten children of day care.

Futuristic thinking must also include conceptualizations about alternatives to day care. It is conceivable, for example, that, rather than pay parents to place their children in a day care program, they could be paid to stay at home with their children. This strategy could be combined with a program of training parents in child development and child-rearing practices.

The future of day care will undoubtedly depend upon how well it meets the needs of the nation's children. If, for example, day care becomes a service primarily aimed at meeting the needs of women, then children, for whom the service is really intended, will suffer.

BIBLIOGRAPHY

Child Welfare League of America: Standards for Day Care Services. New York: Child Welfare League of America, Inc., 1973.

Pennsylvania Department of Public Welfare, Office of Family Services, *Child Day Centers under Social Service Auspices,* Regulations Title 4600.

Pennsylvania Department of Public Welfare, Office of Family Services, *Family Day Care Homes for Children under Social Service Auspices,* Regulations Title 4700.

U.S. Department of Health, Education, and Welfare, Office of Economic Opportunity, *Alternative Federal Day Care Strategies for the 1970's: Summary Report.* (Washington, D.C.: March, 1972.)

FOR FURTHER READING AND STUDY

Brietbart, Vicki. *The Day Care Book.* New York: Alfred A. Knopf, Inc., 1974.
Generates a great deal of enthusiam for day care programs. A wealth of ideas dealing with financial support, community involvement, and how to begin programs. Written by actual participants.

Costin, Lela B. *Child Welfare: Policies and Practice.* New York: McGraw-Hill, Inc., 1972.
Presents philosophy and practices covering the broad spectrum of day care. A very comprehensive and in-depth coverage of basic child welfare services. An excellent reference for those who desire detailed information.

Painter, Genevieve. *Teach Your Baby.* New York: Simon and Schuster, Inc., 1971.
An excellent resource of activities for anyone who anticipates being a parent or working with children. Emphasizes what to do and how to do it for children up to thirty-six months. Nicely illustrated.

Seefeldt, Carol. *A Curriculum for Child Care Centers.* Columbus, Ohio: Charles Merrill Publishing Company, 1974.
Designed to "provide ideas, materials and methods for establishing a successful curriculum within a child care program." Of particular interest are chapters dealing with parents and community.

For Further Study and Involvement

1. Determine what the legal requirements are for establishing center and home day care programs in your state, city, and locality. What are the similarities and differences? What is your opinion of the guidelines?

2. Visit various day care programs, including center and home programs. How are they similar and different? Which of the programs do you think provides the best services for children's needs? Why?

3. Visit a day care center program for infants and toddlers. What makes this program unique? What special provisions need to be made for children for the success of these kinds of programs?

4. Gather information on franchised early childhood programs. What are the similarities and differences? In your opinion, what factors are necessary for the success of these kinds of programs?

5. Make a survey of parents in your area to determine how many are in need of day care services. Also, determine what services most parents desire of a day care program.

6. Design a day care program that you feel would meet the needs of children and their parents. How is your program similar to or different from those you visited?

7. Invite personnel from day care programs, welfare departments, and social service areas to speak to your class about day care.

8

Language Development
What Makes Us Human?

Symbols in Communication

Evidence of communication can be found everywhere in nature. Studies of the communication patterns of bees and dolphins make fascinating reading. Your dog wags her tail and you interpret it as her communicating to you that she is happy about her new toy dog bone. A baby cries and her mother immediately interprets this as a sign of distress and changes her diaper. A teacher in a classroom frowns at a child who is talking and the child ceases under fear of more tangible punishment. All of these are examples of communication, but none of them involve what we usually think of as language. While other animals, including humans, can communicate without language, we alone are unique in our ability to use symbols in communication. This ability is one of the attributes that makes us human and sets us apart from other living creatures. Language helps define the uniqueness of humanity.

While communication involves language, it is not necessarily limited to the use of language, for, as was indicated above, communication occurs in many nonlanguage ways. You communicate constantly on both the conscious and unconscious levels without using language. However, when vocal sounds and written symbols are employed, we move into the realm of language, which is defined by S. I. Hayakawa in the following way:

> Of all forms of symbolism, language is the most highly developed, most subtle, and most complicated. It has been pointed out that human beings, by agreement, can make anything stand for anything. Now, human beings have agreed, in the course of centuries of mutual dependency, to let the various noises that they can produce with their lungs, throats, tongues, teeth, and lips systematically stand for specified happenings in their nervous systems. We call that system of agreements *language*. For example, we who speak English have been so trained that when our nervous systems register the presence of a certain kind of animal, we may make the following noise: "There's a cat." Anyone hearing us would expect to find that by looking in the same direction, he would experience a similar event in his nervous system—one that would have led him to make an almost identical noise.[1]

This system of agreements which we have developed has some basic characteristics which we may, because of our very closeness to it, have a tendency to overlook. First it is a set of symbols that stands for certain ideas, thoughts, concepts, things, feelings, etc. We sometimes forget that these symbols are not the things or feelings themselves. The word *chair* is merely a written and spoken symbol for that object in which you are sitting while reading this chapter. The word *love* is a symbol for that emotion you have for your boyfriend or girlfriend. It is not a natural thing for children to understand this process that society has devised for assigning symbols to objects. When working with children who are deficient in language, it is often necessary to begin with learning the names for objects. Second, language is very arbitrary, since any symbol we wish can stand for anything we wish. It would be a totally confusing world if all of us were to practice this arbitrariness in our daily lives. Therefore, by convention and custom we agree upon certain symbols as standing for certain things. Third, language is constantly changing both in usage (the word *pot* has come to have many different meanings over the years), and in new words, such as *Watergate,* which are constantly being added to our vocabulary. Fourth, language involving symbols is a very human behavior. While baboons have a repertoire of sounds in their communication system, they never have, to my knowledge, created a new word to describe the anthropologist studying them. Fifth, because language is a uniquely human activity, it is also an integral part of the human society. It becomes a societal instrument for a wide variety of purposes and functions. In a discussion on early childhood

---

[1]S. I. Hayakawa, *Language in Thought and Action* 3d ed. (New York: Harcourt, Brace Jovanovich and Company, 1975), p. 30.

*Language plays an important role in determining what and
how learning occurs. Here children develop and extend
language skills through "reading."*

education, the most important use of language as a social instrument is for the induction of the child into society. The socialization of children would be difficult without language. Thus parents and schools have a great responsibility to provide optimum opportunities for language acquisition.

Language—The Acquisition Process

Language is something every child develops, provided, of course, she has the physical equipment and ability for making language. The physical attributes necessary for language development include the larynx (which contains the vocal cords), lips, tongue, palate, lungs, and teeth. Working as a unit, these bodily parts permit the formation of sounds which are recognizable to those who hear them. When they are missing or malformed, they sometimes can be restored or corrected through surgery or artificial devices.

At least some aspects of language must be learned. We often have a tendency to think language is innate (indeed some language authorities believe this idea) because of the naturalness and ease with which many children learn it. We take the language learning process for granted and assume that every child will learn her native tongue well. This assumption on the part of parents and teachers may do the child more harm than almost any other assumption we make about her development; for if the child does not learn language easily she is generally destined for failure in school. Many language development programs try to make parents and teachers aware of the vital role they play in the language development process, so that they can provide more input into the language learning process.

When a child learns her native tongue, it is a demonstration of her basic intelligence and ability to learn. It is now quite common to use the term *nonlearner* for children who cannot master traditional school activities, such as difficulty with the learning materials. Teachers use this term in spite of the fact that a child has already demonstrated, unequivocally, her ability for learning by mastering her native tongue! This is a theme Montessori emphasized repeatedly in her writings. Unfortunately, it is something that we have a tendency to neglect.

Not only does the child pass the basic intelligence test by learning language; she also engages in one of the most individualized learning activities possible. As Montessori indicated, the child literally learns language by herself, through self-motivation, in a manner and style all her own.

This process of learning language begins at birth and continues throughout an individual's lifetime. However, the period for most rapid language growth occurs prior to the age of eight; most children, by the time they enter first grade, can communicate with their peers. The ease and level of this communication, however, is individual for every child and includes a very broad range of ability for speaking, including size of vocabulary and quality of speech.

A child begins to make sounds from the moment of birth. We generally associate the life process as beginning with the sharp slap on the buttocks which causes the cry signaling life has begun. From this time, the child makes a combination of sounds we usually understand as coos, babbles and chuckles. Many of these sounds are strange to us and this is not surprising since the child makes sounds that she will probably never use again because they are not a part of the sound structure of the language she is destined to learn from her parents and peers. Through imitation and reproduction of sounds, the child generally produces her first "word," e.g., *mama,* somewhere between twelve and eighteen months; at eighteen months she begins to put words into simple, two-word sentences. The period for most rapid language growth begins at about 2½ years and continues until about 8 years.

Effects of Language

How Language Affects Life

The language a child learns and how she learns it will play a tremendously powerful role in her life; in many instances, it will set parameters for achievement at the cognitive and social levels. A child is affected by the language she learns, which is generally determined by the society or culture into which she is born, and more specifically by her home and community. She learns to speak Spanish, English or Urdu because that is the language of her home.

The language style of the child's mother (or primary caregiver) also plays a dominant and important role in the type of language a child learns and how she learns to communicate. Some factors which have an influence on the mother's language style are level of education, language style learned as a child, knowledge of child-rearing practices, and time and opportunity to use language with their children. In many instances we do visit the sins of one generation on the next generation and are not aware of it!

Labels Nationality. The language a child learns will label her as a native of a particular part of a state, nation, or world. English children identified me immediately as someone not native to their country. Many young children I talked with in England asked me if I were an American. When I asked them why they thought I was American, they invariably responded, "Because you have an accent!" And all along I thought they were the ones with the accent! Also, while living in a community in the deep south, I was invariably asked, "What part of the north are you from?" The implication was obvious; I had to be from someplace else because I spoke differently than the local natives.

No Choice of Language Learned. A child has almost no control over the kind of language she learns or how she learns that language. Children are given no choice over their original language. She is never asked "Would you like to learn this language, or this dialect?" Her language is determined for her by the environment in which she is reared. A child learns the language from the models available at the time of her language development. If the language model uses extended conversation and asks questions, then the child learns to speak with these qualities. If, on the other hand, the model from which the child learns emphasizes nonverbal communication, then the child learns this type of language.

Affects Achievement. What a child learns and how she learns it will invariably affect her school achievement and, to a certain extent, her self-image. If the child has learned nonstandard English in a nonverbal setting, she will undoubtedly have difficulty (probably fail) with the language of schooling and expectations of the teacher. School achievement as it is traditionally and currently measured in the early grades is based upon children's ability to learn to read. Children who do not speak well (generally standard English is used as the criterion) often have difficulty learning to write and read, which leads to failure, which in turn leads to poor self-image.

We must understand that the background of experiences that a child brings to school is not the only factor bearing on her achievement. What kind of learner she is will depend on the language patterns she has learned prior to entrance to school, and indeed often determine if she will be allowed to be a learner. The roots of school failure and subsequent life failure can be traced to failure to acquire the vocabulary and language patterns which encourage and are necessary for the active seeking of knowledge.

A problem often encountered with the language of children is that it is tied to school success. Failure of children to do well in school can often be traced to the language they bring to school, not because their language or dialect is intrinsically "bad," but because schools have tended to view certain kinds of dialects as inappropriate for learning. Teachers do not adjust themselves and their activities to the language of the child, but rather expect the child to do the majority of the adjusting. Of course, given the setting and the nature of the task, this is impossible for the child to accomplish, and she fails. Not only does she fail, but the gap between what she knows and what her classmates know increases over the school years rather than decreases. This gap is commonly known as the cumulative deficit phenomenon.

Marks Personality. A child is further affected by the language she learns because her language, her particular way of speaking, choice (or lack) of words, inflections and all the other factors and nuances associated with language are uniquely hers. A person is often identified by her particular language and how she uses it. It is unique to her and marks her as an individual. How often have you tried to mask your voice and failed? It has long been recognized that it is possible to identify an individual by her fingerprints, and there is a growing body of evidence to support the hypothesis that each person's voice print is also entirely original. We should give more attention to the processes responsible for this uniqueness.

Reasons for the Current Interest in Language Development

Rediscovery of the Poor: Language Deficit or Language Different?

The renewed interest in early childhood education in general and disadvantaged children in particular has promoted a current interest in the language of children. During the 1960s and continuing to the present, there have been many federally supported programs for disadvantaged children such as Head Start and day care that seek to counteract environmental factors detrimental to child growth and development. With the "rediscovery" of the poor and associated research studies into the effect poverty has on the lives of children, there has been a renewed interest in the role language plays in the educative and learning processes. This interest has resulted in the development of two rather sharply contrasted concepts about the language utilized by such children. These two concepts are popularly termed the *language deficit* and *language different* points of view.

According to the language deficit theory, any child's language is deficient if it does not "measure up" or if it is not similar to middle-class English. This middle-class English has been labeled Standard English and is the language of most schools. If a child comes to school and cannot speak the language of the school she is deficient. One of the problems with the deficit theory is that it would be possible to classify just about any child or adult as deficient in language in some way or another, using Standard English as the criterion. However, this is not always the case, for the child who is usually considered deficient is the poor or disadvantaged child, often a member of a minority group such as migrant workers, rural families, and inner-city residents. Unfortunately, too, if one holds the deficit point of view, it is easy to doom a child to failure immediately, because if a child doesn't have the language of the school, she fails. If teachers have expectations of children coming to school with a background of Standard English and a child does not meet these expectations, it is very easy to ignore her language problem and not provide her with a program whereby she can learn. In addition, it is very easy to blame the child, her parents and her home and because the fault lies elsewhere, not do anything at all about it. Another problem with the deficit point of view is that it creates a situation whereby the child must be "brought up to" the level of language usage of the school. This situation can lead to feelings of student inferiority and teacher superiority, creating an atmosphere that is not conducive to the best mental health or self-image of children. The language deficit theory has an elitist air about it and promotes a concept of a particular way of communicating as "right and proper" as opposed to an acceptance of the communication systems children bring to school.

The language different theory views all language as a means of communication, and it is this power to communicate that renders all languages or dialects as equal in effectiveness. The ability of the child to use language renders her capable of communicating. From this point of view, then, a child is not inferior because she does not talk using Standard English. Rather, she is merely using her dialect to communicate and, depending on who she is talking with and where she is, communication occurs with varying degrees of understanding. Thus the task of learning to communicate rests with both teacher and child, whereas in the deficit theory almost all of the burden of adjustment is placed on the child. In the language different theory, the teacher models Standard English and extends the child's dialect. The teacher also accepts the language the child uses to communicate, avoids "correcting" her and refrains from insisting she speak in Standard English. The language different theory has also promoted the development of strategies and programs for teaching children to read utilizing the dialects they bring to school.

Once one accepts these ideas it becomes possible to think of some children as needing a second language for school success. *Bilingualism* is a term that is used when referring to someone with two languages. In a narrower sense, bilingual programs are designed to teach children a second language when their primary language or dialect is not that of the school. Thus a child who speaks Spanish or Black English may sometimes be taught English as a second language. Generally, in a bilingual program, the child is taught to read in his native tongue and dialect while he is taught the second language. A problem that can exist in bilingual instruction is that insensitive and unknowing teachers may insist that the major portion of the child's instructional program occur in the second language rather than in the native tongue.

Language Deficiency of the Disadvantaged

Another reason for interest in the language of children is the interest in the disadvantaged child. As programs such as Head Start and day care focus on the needs of children, it has become increasingly clear that many children from disadvantaged homes bring to school with them a different language system. In addition, many children lack the experiential background often required for school success. Evidence indicates that this lack, while in and of itself a barrier to learning, is also a cause of language deficiency. Experiences establish the context for listening, discussing, conversing, and related activities upon which language development is dependent. Efforts at correcting and alleviating these language deficiencies have led to the designing of language development programs which we will discuss later.

Linguistics Study

Linguistics, a science devoted to the study of language, has also caused renewed interest in the teaching of language. While the study of language is new, there has been an increased interest in language per se during the past decade. As knowledge about language and its learning processes increases, more interest and attention is generated.

What Constitutes Language?

There are basically four broad areas of language responses that a child must master and have in his repertoire of language responses in order for effective communication to occur. These elements of language are phonemes, morphemes, morphological rules, and syntactic rules, and constitute what we refer to as the structure of the language, including the rules, sounds, and units governing language.

Phonemes

Sounds such as vowels and consonants refer to phonemes. Many phonemes occur naturally in children's early sound reproductions. Through learning and practice these sounds come to resemble the ones we as adults are familiar with. There are about forty phonemes in the English language.

Morphemes

Morphemes, made of phonemes, are the smallest units of meaning it is possible to have in the language. A morpheme may or may not be a word. Examples of morphemes would be *no* and *man,* which cannot be divided and still have their meaning remain the same. In addition, elements of words such as the endings *ed* and *by* are also morphemes. Those morphemes that can stand alone such as *man* are called *free morphemes.* One that cannot stand alone is called a *bound morpheme.* An example of a bound morpheme would be *ed.* Whereas the word *jump* would be a free morpheme, *jumped* would consist of the free morpheme *jump* and the bound morpheme *ed.*

Morphological Rules

In any given language, there are certain rules to govern and control how morphemes are put together. These rules are morphological and include such things as tenses (*ask—asked*), and possessives (*John—John's*), just to mention a few.

Syntactic Rules

How words are put together into meaningful sentences is governed by syntactic rules. In the English language, a basic syntactic structure is the noun-verb pattern. A child learns that the noun *John* precedes the verb *ran* so that the sentence "John ran to his house" results instead of "ran John to his house." Such rules are studied in the name of grammar.

Approaches to Grammar

TRADITIONAL GRAMMAR

Beginning in the 1960s and continuing into the present, there has been a great deal of controversy and change in the area of grammar. Not only is the concept of what constitutes grammar under attack, but also how it should be taught. Traditional grammar is concerned with the application of precise rules of language. The purpose of this attention to rules is usually justified on the basis that it promotes "correct" usage on the part of the practitioner. Thus a student would study and learn to use the language by learning rules, e.g., "a noun is the name of a person, place or thing," and through application of these rules analyze and classify sentences according to how words fit the definitions. The epitomy of this approach is applying these definitions in the diagramming of sentences. The basis for traditional grammar is Latin models, and its rationale presumes to instruct people how they should talk; in this sense it is prescriptive. The teacher who continually "corrects" children's language operates according to the correct model of grammar.

STRUCTURAL GRAMMAR

An almost opposite approach to traditional grammar is structural grammar which tends to distinguish between how the language is put together (syntax) from what the language means (semantics). Instead of prescribing how people should talk, it is concerned with how people actually do talk. This has led to a great deal of criticism of structural grammarians on the assumption that they are not concerned with "proper" usage and are therefore vulgarizing and lowering the standards of good usage. In a structural approach to the language, a child would learn about nouns by studying how they are used in sentences. Instead of memorizing that a noun is the name for a person, place or thing (the "thing" part was where much confusion always occurred for me), the child would experience through sentence analysis that nouns are different from other parts of speech. For instance, a noun can be transformed to be a plural and a possessive, but an adjective cannot.

TRANSFORMATIONAL GRAMMAR

A newer approach to grammar was developed by a linguist, Noam Chomsky. Known as transformational grammar, it tends to bridge the gap between structural and traditional grammar by dealing with both meaning and structure. According to the transformational grammar approach, language is composed of certain kernel sentences which form a basis from which all other sentences can be transformed or generated. A basic kernel sentence would be, "John has a ball." A transformation of this sentence would be "Does John have a big ball?" The child begins by working with a simple declarative sentence, such as "John has a ball", and learns "rules" for transforming this sentence into an almost limitless number of other sentences: "Does John have a big ball?" "John does not have a ball."

A child must not only learn and master the elements of what is involved in language responses, but he must also master the meaning of the language. I have indicated the meanings of words are arbitrary in the sense that any sound or word can stand for any object or feeling, as long as there is agreement to this effect. Thus it is through the learning of meanings that the child learns to say, "Here comes a cat," as opposed to "Here comes an elephant."

Linguistics, involving the study of the structure of the language, has become very popular. The linguist is concerned with studying language as it exists in operation, not as it ought to be. Therefore, rather than prescribing a right or wrong way to speak, the linguist would have us aware of the usage of language at different social levels. Children should be made aware of this difference and taught to develop the ability to change their level of usage to meet differing social occasions. Also, the emphasis on linguistics has encouraged an acceptance of language used by differing social and ethnic groups. It would appear that the influence of linguists and an emphasis on transformational grammar will be a dominant force in language study in the years to come.

How Is Language Acquired?

While this question would seem easy to answer, it is by no means possible to do so. Not only is the question difficult to answer because of the complex and in many respects mysterious nature of language development, but there are also conflicting theories and data about how the process occurs. Again, as is the case in so much of child development and educational methodology, it is up to the particular individual to weigh the evidence and make choices involving what his beliefs will be and on which he will ultimately base his teaching.

Innate Ability

Chomsky. One proponent of the theory that language acquisition is innate is Noam Chomsky, who hypothesizes that children possess within their system a structure or mechanism called a Language Acquisition Device (LAD), which enables children to acquire language. The LAD of the young child receives all the sounds of a language to which she is exposed and uses these sounds to process many grammatical sentences of the language, even ones to which she was never exposed. The child hears and takes in a particular language and processes it to form grammatical rules, the grammar enabling her to communicate with other people and also to understand reciprocal communication.

Lenneberg. One of the leading proponents of the concept that language acquisition is innate is Eric Lenneberg, who has studied this process in considerable detail in many different kinds of children, including the deaf. According to Lenneberg:

> All the evidence suggests that the capacities for speech production and related aspects of language acquisition develop according to built-in biological schedules. They appear when the time is ripe and not until then, when a state of what I have called "resonance" exists. The child somehow becomes "excited," in phase with the environment, so that the sounds he hears and has been hearing all along suddenly acquire a peculiar prominence. The change is like the establishment of new sensitivities. He becomes aware in a new way, selecting certain parts of the total auditory input for attention, ignoring others.[2]

The "biological schedules," states of "resonance" and "new sensitivities" Lenneberg talks about would appear to be similar to the condition Montessori intuitively perceived through observation and called sensitive periods. In addition, Lenneberg would tend to support Montessori's position that sensitive periods, once having passed, never occur again. He feels that "Language development thus runs a definite course on a definite schedule; a critical period extends from about age two to age twelve, the beginning and the end of resonance."[3] It should not be assumed that Lenneberg

---

[2]Eric H. Lenneberg, "The Biological Foundations of Language," in Mark Lester, *Readings in Applied Transformational Grammar* (New York: Holt, Rinehart and Winston, Inc., 1970), p. 8.

[3]Lenneberg, p. 12.

dismisses entirely the role of the environment in language development, but he does consider it a minor role.

> Children will never learn language unless they hear it, and we fulfill our function simply by talking, the more the better. Beyond that and offering moral support there is little for us to do, because biology takes over. Biology takes over in basically the same fashion as it does when the child metabolizes protein after eating. He uses the protein but not in ready-made form.[4]

The fact that children generate sentences they have never heard before is often cited as proof of innate ability. What would language be like if we were only capable of reproducing the sentences and words we heard! In addition, the ability of children in all cultures and social settings to acquire language at a relatively immature age would tend to support the thesis that language acquisition and use is more than a product of imitation and/or direct instruction. Indeed, children learn language without formal instruction.

Lenneberg also offers other reasons to support his contention that language is a "biological propensity."

1. Language development begins at about the same time in children's physical development and follows a fixed sequence;
2. Language is learned by all children, even those who have severe handicaps;
3. Non-human forms do not have the capacity for language development;
4. All languages are based on the same principals of syntax, semantics and phonology.[5]

Environmental Factors

However, before we jump to any conclusions about innate processes being entirely responsible for language acquisition, and lest we throw the baby (language) out with the water (factors affecting and governing language development), let us think about the role of the environment. Reasons cited for the biological base of language should not be interpreted to mean that children innately acquire *the* particular language they will speak, for this

---

[4] *Ibid.*

[5] Eric H. Lenneberg, "A Biological Perspective of Language," *New Directions in the Study of Language,* ed. Eric H. Lenneberg (Cambridge, Massachusetts: M.I.T. Press, 1964), pp. 66–68.

is not the case. While the ability for language acquisition has a biological base, as Lenneberg indicates, the content of the language, i.e., vocabulary, must occur with the context of a particular environment, which includes other people as models for language. Therefore, development depends on language interaction between children and adults, and between children and children. Optimal language development ultimately depends on the kind and quality of interaction children have through experience with the best language models possible. While the biological process of language development may be the same for all children, the content of that language will be different according to environmental factors.

Children at this table freely contribute their ideas while reinforcing and extending language skills.

Without a doubt, environment determines the quality and kind of language a child develops. A child left to his own devices will not learn the language as well as the child who was reared in a linguistically rich environment.

The Product of Interaction

The question of innate language acquisition versus language acquisition based upon environmental factors is akin to the controversy of nature versus nurture in intellectual development. One simply cannot reject one viewpoint at the expense of the other. We must consider language acquisition as the product of both innate processes, of which we know little, and environmental factors. Very likely the product of the interaction of both innate mechanisms and environmental influences equals more than the sum of the two operating separately.

Language Development Programs

Because of the current interest in language, and due to the tremendous role it plays in the life of an individual, there are increasing numbers of language development programs being designed and marketed for use in early childhood settings. Some of these language development programs are discussed following. The discussion is not meant to be either exhaustive or a substitution for a critical examination of the individual programs by anyone who proposes to use them.

The Peabody Language Development Kits (PLDK)

Method. These kits are an oral language development program designed to promote language as well as intellectual functioning and school success.[6] The program consists of four separate programs, Levels P, 1, 2, and 3. Level P is for children 3–5, Level 1 for children 4½–6½, Level 2 for children 6–8, and level 3 is for children 7½–9½. The name for the program reflects its initial development by personnel associated with George Peabody College for Teachers in Nashville, Tennessee.

All of the levels stress a broad oral development approach and materials are provided that encourage children to use their senses of touch, sight and sound so that they are actively involved in seeing, hearing and touching. The program also encourages expression at the vocal and motor levels through saying and doing. In addition, cognitive processes of divergent, convergent and associative thinking are also part of the learning model of the program. For example, in lesson sixty-eight of Level P, children are involved in reception of data during a touching-describing session by touching objects, listening to their descriptions, seeing the differences of textures in objects, and feeling how objects differ according to touch. The cognitive process (conceptualization) of associative thinking would be encouraged by having children think of objects other than those used as examples that are rough. The expressive process of vocalization would be achieved by having children describe how the object feels.

Each of the four levels provides 180 daily lessons making it possible to have a lesson for each day of the school year. In Level P, each daily lesson is divided into two units, each unit having two parts for a total of four learning episodes. For example, Daily Lesson No. 1, Part A consists of Listening-Conversation Time and Listening-Activity Time. Part B consists of Looking Time and Activity Time. Each of the 180 daily lessons takes

---

[6]Dunn, Lloyd M., Horton, Kathryn B., Smith, James O. *Peabody Language Development Kits Manual for Level #P.* Circle Pines, Minnesota: American Guidance Service, 1968.

about forty minutes, each part receiving an equal emphasis of twenty minutes. The directions for teaching recommend that Part A of the lesson occur early in the morning and Part B occur early in the afternoon. Depending on the group being taught, one part of the lesson can be taught after the other if a short break is provided for the children. A total of twenty children can be accommodated in a learning session, which is conducted in a circle or semicircle around the teacher. Particular emphasis is placed on:

1. Involving all of the children.
2. Overall group language development (as opposed to individual speech correction).
3. The role of the teacher as a language model.
4. The encouragement of spontaneity and creative thinking.

Teachers are encouraged to make each lesson enjoyable, reward children for their participation, and continually make the activities child centered.

Materials. Materials for Level P, packaged in two metal carrying cases, consist of a teacher's manual, stimulus cards, puppets, boy and girl manikins, plastic fruits and vegetables, geometric shapes, records, xylophone, magic wand, and plastic chips.

Reinforcement for participation by the children consists of praise and tangible rewards with the color chips and stimulus cards; behavior modification is based on the processes of rewarding desired behavior and ignoring undesirable behavior. Following correct responses and participation in an activity children are praised verbally ("Very good, John!"), and given a plastic chip or a stimulus card (an 8 X 11 picture card) to hold. The use of the plastic chips may be extended to include a token system or economy whereby children "trade in" their tokens (plastic chips) for objects (a toy truck), activities (time to write at the board), or other suitable reinforcement.

Pros and Cons of PLDK. Special features of the PLDK are specific, structured daily lessons; emphasis on the involvement of children in learning activities (as opposed to passive involvement); inclusion of a behavior modification component; and the packaging of materials necessary for the program.

The PLDK program has several strengths that may be lacking in other prepackaged oral language programs. First, the program is based on learning and linguistic theories that result in models for the following behaviors:

1. Reception—Seeing, hearing, and touching
2. Conceptualization—Associative, convergent, and divergent thinking
3. Expression—Describing and doing

The behavior modification process is also based on positive reinforcement theory. However, teachers should examine program materials to ascertain if their own philosophies are in agreement with these theories, and if the program objectives are congruent with local program and school objectives for children. Second, the program has been widely field tested and many research studies have been conducted to determine the adequacy of the materials in achieving programmatic objectives. Results of this research are reported in the teacher manuals that accompany each level and are also available in the professional literature. Third, no special training appears to be necessary for using the materials since the teacher's manuals are very specific and detailed.

On the other side of the ledger, it seems as though there are certain features which would tend to detract from the program. First is its structured nature. While this can be a strength to the program, it can also be a weakness. This will depend to a large extent on the natures of particular teachers. While the manuals do encourage teachers to modify lessons and depart from suggested activities, teachers may fall into the dull routine of merely parroting instructions and presenting activities in a stilted manner. This of course can happen even with the best of materials. On the other hand, some teachers do express a difficulty with modifying activities in spite of the encouragement to do so. Some teachers also object to the constant preparation involved in conducting the program. This fault, however, is concerned with the teacher's use rather than with the materials themselves.

The PLDK was one of the first language development programs designed to provide teachers and children the help they need in this crucial area. As such, it is probably one of the most widely known and used language development programs.

Breakthrough to Literacy

Method. This program is unique in several respects. First of all, it is a language program developed by the Schools Council Programme in Linguistics and English Teaching in Britain. The program, therefore, represents practices used by good primary teachers in schools in Britain and is a less structured approach than is usually found in American schools in the basal textbook approach to reading. The application of a language program developed in Britain and imported to the United States reflects the current interest by American educators in British practices of education particularly as it relates to open education.

The program also has merit in that it deals with language at both the spoken and written levels by providing instruction for initial reading and writing. It starts with children's own language as the base upon which to encourage these skills; therefore, the program does not try to separate language from reading artificially, but rather treats it as a part of a necessary requisite for the writing and reading process. In addition, the program does not try to make children learn new and unfamiliar words in order to begin the reading process, but utilizes their current language ability and vocabulary. This approach to language is reflected in some basic assumptions underlying the program, which are:

> Children should become well acquainted with language through listening to it and experimenting with it before they are expected to read it or write it. . . .
>
> Printed materials from the beginning, should be linked to the child's spoken language. The children's neighborhood dialect may be the only resource that they have for learning to read and write, and to present them with written language unrelated to their own is to cut them off from what they know.[7]

Other unique features of the program include the integration of writing and reading and the utilization of concrete, manipulative objects. Montessori believed that writing comes before reading and that children are able to develop skills necessary for reading through writing. *Breakthrough to Literacy* also involves written language to the extent that children make their own first reading books. They are also involved in written language through the materials which accompany the program. "My Sentence Maker" and the "Classroom Sentence Maker" (both accompanied by plastic stands in which word cards and letter cards are inserted) invite "hands on" involvement and encourage children in the production of sentences. Through the use of the "Sentence Maker" and "Word Makers," children can not only see and hear language, but they can physically—as well as intellectually—manipulate letters, words, and sentences. This process is similar to the process utilized in Montessori settings for writing and reading.

> The design of the Sentence Maker is based on the fact that children can produce written sentences without prior knowledge of handwriting and spelling. The Sentence Maker is a word store that contains words widely

---

[7]Reprinted from *breakthrough to literacy Teachers Resource Book* by David Mackay, Brian Thompson & Pamela Schaub, American edition © 1973 BOWMAR and used by permission of Bowmar Publishing Corp., Glendale, California 91201, p. 4.

used by children. With the vocabulary, a very large number of sentences can be produced. In addition, children can add personal words that enable them to draw on private experiences and personal interests.

The plastic Stand is used to hold the word cards while children are composing their phrases and sentences. From thoughts and feelings that arise from discussions of their own experiences, the children decide what they want to compose.

By means of the Sentence Maker, children convert short stretches of thinking and speaking into writing. In this way, they begin to build up expectations of what words and sentences look like.[8]

Materials. Materials which accompany the program in addition to the "Classroom Sentence Maker" and "My Sentence Maker" include *Story Figures,* twenty-eight books (all of which are sixteen pages long and are based on actual stories told by children), *Lollipop Books* (books on rhyme and poetry), a "Project Folder," and "My Word Maker."

Initial Teaching Alphabet

Another British approach to the teaching of language and reading is the Initial Teaching Alphabet of Sir James Pittman. This approach utilizes forty-four symbols, each with its own sound, in place of the twenty-six symbols of the traditional alphabet. Children who learn to read using the Initial Teaching Alphabet gradually make a transition to the regular alphabet when they and the teacher feel it is appropriate to do so. While this program was very popular in the United States during the 1960s, its popularity has diminished considerably and it is not currently used by a great number of school districts either in the United States or Great Britain.

The Distar Language Instructional System

Rationale. Distar, developed by Bereiter and Engelmann, is a structured approach to teaching and learning language that has as its primary goal teaching the procedures and language of instruction used in schooling.[9] Their approach is based on two major ideas. First, they believe that cultural deprivation is synonymous with language deprivation. As Bereiter and Engelmann indicate:

> . . . disadvantaged children of preschool age are typically at least a year behind in language development—in vocabulary size, sentence length, and use of grammatical structure. Indeed, in practically every aspect of lan-

---

[8]*Ibid.,* pp. 13–14.

[9]Siegfried Engelmann, Jean Osborn and Therese Engelmann, *Distar Language I,* Teacher's Guide (Chicago, Illinois: Science Research Associates Inc., 1969).

guage development that has been evaluated quantitatively, young disadvantaged children have been found to function at the level of average children who are a year or more younger.[10]

If this belief is correct, then one way of attacking cultural deprivation is through a program that will provide children with the language development they need.

Second, they think that children deprived in language ability will fail when they come to school and do not understand the language of instruction. Bereiter and Engelmann further explain:

> Cultural deprivaton, then, has a double edge. The lower-class child is not without culture, but he is deprived of that part of culture that can only be acquired through teaching—the knowledge, the meanings, the explanations, the structured beliefs that make up the conceptual furniture of culture. Beyond that, the child spends his early childhood in an environment where teaching does not take place and where the language with which teaching is carried out is not used; therefore, he may not even learn *how to be taught,* and when he is exposed to teaching, he may behave much as if he were mentally retarded or devoid of language altogether.[11]

Therefore, they believe that preschool teachers should be sensitized to the language problems of children; and in addition, that teachers should provide their students with the appropriate language experiences necessary for school success by focusing on the language used in instruction.

Method. The Distar Language program is designed to fulfill these needs through the application of a direct instructional approach to teaching and learning. With a small group of children, the teacher teaches language skills (e.g., identity statements) in a fast-paced, oral, no-nonsense approach. Utilizing materials provided with the program, the following verbal interaction dealing with preprogram identity statements would be typical:

> Teacher, (pointing to a picture of a shoe), "Everybody, what is this?"
> Children, "A shoe."
> Teacher, "Yes, this is a shoe. Say the whole thing."
> Children, "This is a shoe."
> Teacher, "Everybody, what is this? Say the whole thing."
> Children, "This is a shoe."[12]

---

[10]Carl Bereiter and Siegfried Engelmann, *Teaching Disadvantaged Children in the Preschool* (Englewood Cliffs, New Jersey: Prentice-Hall, Inc., 1966), p. 4.

[11]Bereiter and Engelmann, *Teaching Disadvantaged Children in the Preschool,* p. 33.

[12]Siegfried Engelmann, Jean Osborn, and Therese Engelmann, *Distar Language I, An Instructional System* (Chicago, Illinois: Science Research Associates, Inc., 1969), p. 10.

Materials. Materials for the Distar Language I program consist of six presentation books, a Storybook, a Color Book, and Take-Homes (worksheet-like papers given to children at the end of each lesson as a reward for good work).

The materials in the presentation books are organized in a sequential manner so that language concepts presented first (e.g., identity statements) can form the base for concepts presented later in the program. Thus the sequencing of materials is done for teachers so they can follow the program and have some assurance that concepts presented first are used as a foundation for later language concepts. This emphasis on sequencing tends to minimize the haphazard approach to teaching. All that the teacher needs to do is follow the program and teach the lessons as they are presented.

Teacher Role. Another interesting and sometimes controversial feature of the Distar program is the different role it specifies for teachers. Teachers are encouraged to present program materials in the manner specified in the presentation books. In this sense, following directions and teaching how and what the program materials prescribe constitute the key ingredients of teacher behavior. Sometimes teachers resent this role, causing them to be "turned off" by the program. It has been my experience that the teacher who enthusiastically presents the lessons is more effective than the teacher whose presentation is mechanical and listless.

Other teacher tasks which specify a different teacher role emphasize classroom management techniques (rewarding students for correct responses and on task behavior), instructional pacing techniques (e.g., not spending too much time on one topic or with the response of one child), involving all children in programmatic materials, and group management techniques (e.g., using hand signals as a means of cueing students to respond).

Strengths and Weaknesses. One of the strengths of the Distar program is the systematic and sequential way in which it presents materials for the instructional process. This eliminates the uncertainty many teachers face in not knowing what concepts should be taught next or the order in which they should be taught. Also, language concepts taught in the program are recycled and therefore reinforced throughout the school year, which is a much better format than teaching a concept and never mentioning it again.

A second strength of the Distar program would appear to be its explicit, concise and detailed instructions for teachers. There is no guessing about what to do or how to do it. What is required of teachers is reading the lessons ahead of time so they are familiar with the content and then implementing the lessons as specified.

Another strength of the Distar program concerns the content and is a feature which cannot be minimized. The materials do present a program designed to have children deficient in the language of instruction gain the proficiency and understanding necessary for school success. This feature, in and of itself, is a worthwhile and commendable approach. In addition, it is also a refreshing one from the typical attitude schools and teachers have of failing children because they cannot, on their own, learn the language of schooling.

There appears to be no middle ground as far as proponents and opponents of Distar are concerned. Some teachers object most to its structured nature, explicit directions and direct instructional approach that discourages deviation from programmatic strategies. These elements seem to run counter to teachers' ideas of good teaching. The commonly accepted idea of what constitutes good teaching generally consists of allowing children to experience a language-rich environment (usually the teacher's) and through this process hope that children deficient in language will become proficient. Thus teachers would rather provide a setting that may promote language rather than one that teaches it directly. Distar also does not fit the typical image of what children do in a play-oriented preschool designed to foster social-emotional growth.

A problem sometimes encountered with the program, which is not necessarily a weakness of the program, is that teachers have a tendency not to use the program consistently, eventually discontinuing the entire program. In order for Distar to be effective it is necessary for it to be used with consistency.

From my observations of the Distar Instructional System in operation it appears that the program works best when implemented by teachers who understand the importance of language in the learning process, are enthusiastic about teaching, and realize they can learn more about teaching. On the other hand, if a teacher feels prior to an introduction to Distar that they know what constitutes good teaching, and are generally apathetic to the teaching process, then they are not likely to care for or find success with the Distar program.

An important thing for all educators to remember is that no materials in and of themselves ever made a poor teacher a good one. It is quite possible that some teachers with potential for being good teachers were ruined because they didn't think they had to do anything but use a packaged curriculum program. Poor teaching can occur in spite of the best materials. A frequently heard expression is that a certain program is "teacher proof." This is supposed to imply that if teachers use a particular set of materials, they can't foul it up. This attitude is not only demeaning to teachers but, if followed to its logical conclusion, it also encourages teachers blindly to accept prepackaged curricula and cease from thinking.

Selection of Prepackaged Curricula

Use of preschool curriculum packages is an area with which educators of young children should be more concerned, and rightly so, because their use is becoming more popular and frequent. The development of these packages in not only the language area but in all subject matter areas has increased substantially in the last several years and it is likely that this trend will continue.

ADVANTAGES

These curricula have a number of advantages. First, they are prepackaged. The work of gathering materials has already been done and they are assembled in a convenient format. While the materials may not be of the quality that could be had were an individual teacher to assemble them, they do save time, energy and work. Second, the materials have generally (but not always) been field tested so publishers have some idea of what will and will not work with particular children in particular social and economic settings. This field testing should eliminate the "bugs" of a program and problems of trial and error associated with teacher-designed materials. Third, the materials are usually recommended for use with a particular age or intellectual level. Consequently, a teacher has some idea on what level to use the materials. Fourth, the manual which accompanies a program is usually detailed, specific, and prescriptive in its design and format. The teacher is told what to do, when to do it, and how to do it. This offers a great deal of comfort and support to a weak teacher or to a teacher who needs the support of detailed lesson plans. The manual can also provide teachers with ideas and suggestions which might not have been readily obvious had they not had access to the program. Fifth, the lessons presented in the manuals are sequenced to provide an orderly introduction of skills progressing up a hierarchy of difficulty and complexity.

WHY USE A PREPACKAGED PROGRAM?

While the effectiveness of prepackaged curricula in some areas of early childhood education cannot be denied, there is the danger in the profession that too little emphasis has been placed on the utilization of these packages. Sometimes it is a case of merely using a program because it is present and available. It is a temptation to believe that simply because the programs are on the market they should be bought. Little critical attention is given to the purchase of them. Because curricular packages are advertised as easy to use, easy to implement, with little or no training required, they are often bought for that purpose.

Critical considerations for teachers are who will decide if the programs are worth buying, and on what basis that decision is going to be made. The decisions should be based on such questions as: "Is it good for children? Is it what we want to teach children? Is it material that will help children learn best?" Certainly one cannot make this decision through the brief orientation supplied by the publisher of the materials. Only individuals who have a background of experience with children and who work with them day in and day out can make decisions of this kind. These are the decisions for teachers to make; even paraprofessionals who are often assigned to work with the programs should attempt to aid in these decisions. Being a good teacher does not depend on how well one implements a prepackaged curriculum, but on how well decisions can be made concerning the educational needs of children.

WHAT IS THE TEACHER'S ROLE?

What is also frequently overlooked in the utilization of prepackaged curricula in early childhood education is that, while the program can benefit children, a great deal of the benefit ought to accrue to the people who are using the program. That is, can the program materials teachers or paraprofessionals are working with change their behavior? If the answer to this question is no, then the program may not be worth buying. Many publishers of curriculum packages are becoming more aware that their programs are only as good as the in-service training that accompanies them; these in-service sessions must be designed to foster change in the behavior of the personnel involved in the program. An area which is also frequently overlooked in the utilization of prepackaged curricula in early childhood education is how the program can be extended once a prescribed lesson with children is over. In other words, the personnel who are using and implementing the curriculum should be looking for ways to add to the program based upon the needs and interests of children they teach and the concepts of the packaged curriculum. This extending cannot be done in a setting where the only job of the implementor is following directions, implementing the program, and then forgetting about it. Probably one of the greatest dangers involved in utilizing these packages is to think that by implementing a program, the program itself will work miracles. Nothing could be farther from the truth. In many instances it is what happens *after* the program is implemented that is most important. What the teacher does when the training and teaching sessions are over frequently makes the difference between whether or not the program is a success or a failure.

Another recommendation frequently attributed to prepackaged curricula is that they are "teacher proof," which means that no matter how bad you are, these materials will get you through. Of course this attitude is dangerous to accept.

WHAT IS THE THEORY?

Yet another area that is often ignored is the theoretical base upon which a program operates. For teachers to effectively implement any curricular program, one of the requisites is that they possess a broad knowledge of the philosophy of the program. Only by knowing the theoretical base of a program can the teacher extend the concepts taught.

CRITERIA FOR IMPLEMENTATION

A last observation about prepackaged curricula is that people who implement the program may not know what the program does to children, or may not have asked the question, "Is the program good for children?" The question can be answered best by those whose responsibility it is to work with children on a day-to-day basis. The danger in the utilization of the prepackaged curricula does not come from the development of licensing procedures to exclude paraprofessionals from using prepackaged curricula (as is being advocated by teachers in some quarters). Rather the danger comes from not knowing what you are doing in the classroom, a danger that teachers in all times and places have had to contend with. One way of overcoming this danger of ignorance in the use of early childhood curriculum packages is to determine if:

1. The people who implement the program are knowledgeable about the theoretical base of the program.
2. It is a program which will help children learn better.
3. It has potential for helping teachers change their behavior.
4. The consultant service that accompanies the program (for which you may have to pay extra) is designed to insure a successful implementation.
5. The program has potential for integration in the total school program.
6. The people who implement the program are willing to seek ways to extend and supplement the program.
7. Provisions are made for an evaluation of the program after it has been implemented for a period of time.
8. The cost can be justified in terms of the potential of increasing learning with the particular package.

TOWARDS MEANINGFUL LEARNING

A comparison can be drawn between selecting materials and taking certain drugs. Programs have a great deal of potential for helping both children and teachers, but they also have the potential for becoming habit forming and if used to excess, they can deaden the learning environment.

Also, no language development program is a complete program in and of itself. Regardless of the merits which a publisher or author attributes to their product, it is only as good as the teachers and the efforts they make in making the materials and concepts relevant to the lives of children in the real world. If a concept is presented and used only within the context of the packaged program and in the time allotted for it, then it is doubtful if that concept will be as rich and meaningful as it could have been had it been extended to the world outside the lesson and classroom.

The Teaching of Reading as a Language Issue

In language teaching and learning one of the issues that is frequently encountered concerns reading. In most elementary schools, the total focus in the primary grades is the teaching of reading. The majority of students' and teachers' time and energy is spent in this process and related activities. Methods of organizing the classroom for instructional purposes such as grouping and scheduling are usually based on reading. Social patterns are often artificially established according to one's membership in the bluejays or redbirds.

Learning to read is not an unreasonable expectation on the part of parent or child. Children look forward to it with anticipation, and rightly so. Parents assume that when their children enter school they will be taught to read, or at least an attempt will be made to teach them. Ask any parent what they think schools are for and they will certainly reply, "To teach children how to read." Learning to read is not only a social dictate, but it is also an academic necessity, for how well a child succeeds in this venture often determines how successful he is in his school career.

A recent advertisement in a national magazine stated that twenty-one million Americans over sixteen years of age can't read a want ad. It is estimated that one-third of the population of the United States or about seventy million people have reading disabilities which keep them from being effective members of society. Why is it, however, given the expectation of the schools to teach reading and their efforts to do this, people often fail to learn how to read? It is my opinion that some of the answers to this question can be found in the poor approaches schools and teachers make to the challenge of teaching reading.

Poor Approaches to Teaching Reading

All Children Are Not Ready. One poor approach frequently made is to assume that all children, upon entering school, must immediately learn to read. Teachers persist in this venture in spite of their intuitive and objective recognition that a particular child does not have the experiential or social background necessary to benefit from beginning reading instruction. First grade and kindergarten teachers can generally assess, in a very short time, if a child will experience success or failure in completing predetermined activities associated with beginning reading. In spite of the results of this initial assessment, teachers often insist on beginning the formal reading process. Teachers must refrain from requiring children to do activities which promote failure and instead provide activities that will result in success. If a child cannot discriminate one letter from another, a program should be provided which emphasizes, among other things, shape discrimination.

Lack of Individual Attention. A second poor approach to the teaching of reading is the practice of providing "special classes" for children who have been in school for a year and yet have not learned to read. These classes are known by a multitude of names including "transitional kindergartens," "pre-first grades," and "transitional first grades." These classes generally become dumping grounds for children flunked by "regular" teachers who hope they won't have to teach them again. By providing separate classes for these children educators think their problems and those of the children will be solved. With this attitude, educators are sidestepping the real issue of providing an individualized program for all children.

Lack of Respect. Schools traditionally have not given enough consideration to the self-image of children. What emotional damage do educators cause children by placing them in groups and classes based on their disabilities? Isn't a good self-image also associated with learning to read? I would suspect it plays a greater role than we realize. Although there are signs of change in this area, we must base more of our teaching on respect for children as we have been encouraged to do by great educators such as Froebel, Montessori, and Dewey.

Disunified Teaching. A fourth poor approach which is interwoven with the ones above is the practice of singling out children for "special" reading instruction. In actual practice this usually means a child is sent to a "specialist" where she is diagnosed (can't discriminate between letters), reclassified (nonreader), and is told to report to a remedial reading class. This often involves leaving her own reading class during reading to go somewhere else to learn to read. This opportunity to a "right to read" can occur daily, biweekly, or weekly, depending on the schedule and temperament of the special reading teacher who usually prefers not to work with too many children at one time.

This fragmentation of the reading process results in several conditions:

1. Although the teacher already knows the child cannot read, a great deal of time is wasted in classifying the child as a nonreader.

2. An artificial dichotomy is created when the child leaves her own classroom and goes to a special reading class. The child does not see a relation between what she is doing (the reading process) and what her teacher is doing (the instructional process).

3. Because there often tends to be a lack of correlation between what the special reading teacher does and what the regular classroom teacher does, the activities of the child in these two settings are also unrelated.

4. The classroom teacher feels that because the child goes to a special reading class she is relieved of any responsibility for the child's learning how to read.

5. If the child continually fails to learn how to read, the "blame" is placed with the special reading teacher rather than on the classroom teacher.

6. Fragmentation is expensive. The more reading specialists added to the staff, the less money there is to be utilized in an instructional approach that can benefit all children. The classroom teacher should be provided help within the context of her classroom. If a teacher has a class of thirty to thirty-five first graders, she can be helped most by being given classroom aides and instructional materials so that children will have the type of instruction they need. A teacher does not need to have a small group of three or four children taken out of her class by a specialist.

There appears to be a national tendency toward producing a great number of reading specialists. There are training programs that lead to certification as diagnosticians, remediationists, supervisors, and coordinators. Such special training is counterproductive in that it takes the teacher out of the classroom where there is opportunity for prolonged contact with the child. The trend toward reading specialists overlooks the role of the classroom teacher in providing basic reading instruction. It seems that everyone wants to be a specialist, resulting in a lack of "general practitioners."

Lack of Interest in Children. The trend toward specialization of reading teachers is not always accompanied by a desire to help children. In place of the needs of children, education has created a religion of reading and endowed it with a mystique (not everyone can teach reading), a priesthood (reading supervisors), a language (*dyslexia, reading age*), paraphernalia (controlled readers), a physical setting (clinics), and initiation rites (graduate classes for a duration of thirty or more credits) from the holiest of holies (directors of reading clinics and professors of reading). Not only does the mystique and prestige make for a constant supply of candidates, but there are other more mundane benefits as well. Increased salaries (usually subsidized through federal programs) and reduced contact with children ("I can only handle a few at a time") provide the motivation necessary to maintain a waiting list of initiates. I recently heard an elementary teacher remark how happy she was about receiving her reading specialist certificate because now she wouldn't have to teach a regular classroom of children!

Emphasis on Teacher Needs. It is time that teachers of reading stopped doing what is comfortable for them, and started fulfilling the needs of children. Today we encourage a hierarchy of specialists who spend less and less of their time with children actually teaching reading. Education may be in danger of becoming secondary to the perpetuation of the reading profession.

Lack of Confidence. The emphasis on the training of reading specialists and the mystique of reading leads to the seventh factor, which is the brainwashing of college students into believing they are not competent teachers of reading. In conversations I have had with recent college graduates, they express a lack of confidence in their ability to teach beginning reading. Beginning teachers quite often believe they can gain competence to teach reading only by returning to school and taking graduate courses in reading in spite of the fact that they have just spent four years in college!

It should not be assumed I'm against formal courses in the training of specialists or the encouragement of teachers returning to the college classroom. Neither is this a "Why Johnny Can't Read" attack of the schools. I am suggesting, however, that whatever schools do in the name of reading instruction, it should benefit children, who are the ultimate consumers in any educational process.

Good Approaches to Teaching Reading

In response to the seven poor approaches that I feel inhibit the teaching of reading, I suggest the following responses:

1. Demystify the reading process. Many good teachers have done a good job of teaching reading by processes and procedures that are

easy to understand and implement. These procedures have and can lead to an almost spontaneous ability to read on the part of children. It would be beneficial and fruitful for all teachers and children if the profession would examine, identify, and promote the conditions under which some children have learned to read without undue emphasis on reading instruction or strict adherence to a basal approach. A question that should be asked in this regard is, "If a child can learn to speak his native tongue without formal instruction, cannot reading also be learned in this way?"

2. Discontinue making nonreaders of children in the name of teaching reading. Teachers often structure as part of the child's curriculum tasks and activities that she is not capable of accomplishing. Remedial readers don't just occur. A child does not suddenly develop a reading problem in the second, fifth, or eighth grade; the reading problem develops when she comes to school and is confronted with tasks that preclude her success. Educators are so busy diagnosing children as remedial readers that they never stop to realize they "create" such children.

3. Teachers should stop acting as though spending more time on reading will make children better readers. I think perhaps what children need is relief from reading instruction. If a child is involved in activities that interest her and that are pleasurable for her to accomplish, then these activities can be used as a means of learning to read. Performances, storytelling, writing, conversations with peers and adults, fieldtrips, and related experiences that promote language all provide a natural approach to reading, which can be supplemented by formalized reading instruction. After all, isn't reading an *extension* of oral language and writing?

4. Schools should devote their talent, energy, and money to the language process in the early years as opposed to the growing preoccupation with junior high school remedial reading programs. Remedial programs are attempts at correcting mistakes. With proper language instruction in the early years, there should be few, if any, nonreaders in junior high school.

5. There needs to be more accountability associated with the process of how well children learn to read. Usually the failure for learning to read is shifted to the child ("lacks ability," "dyslexia," etc.) or to his parents ("poor home background"). Curiously, teachers have been omitted from this accountability process. What I am suggesting is that while teachers accept the praise, they should also be willing to admit that they might be at fault. The attitude

of doing as little as possible in anticipation of passing the child on to the next teacher should be replaced by procedures which hold the teacher accountable.

6. Administrators should reallocate resources to help the classroom teacher help all children in the reading process. Monies currently being spent for salaries of reading specialists could better be utilized by providing regular classroom teachers with aides, increasing the amount and kinds of materials needed to individualize instruction, and conducting meaningful, ongoing programs of inservice education. The salary of a reading specialist who earns $10,000 a year could be used to hire six or more teacher aides. This reallocation would encourage the teaching of reading within the child's own classrooms with his peers. There are many reasons why children can benefit by remaining in their own classroom for reading instruction, one being that children can help and learn from each other.

While the above ideas do not represent all the strategies educators can use or implement which will put reading in its proper perspective, they do, I believe, constitute a means for a long overdue new beginning. In light of our past accomplishments with reading, it would at least be worth an effort.

Issues in Language Learning and Teaching

Teaching Oral Language

While there seems to be no problem with the concept of teaching reading and writing (after all, why do children come to school?), there does seem to be some question about providing oral language development for children. The question ultimately becomes, "If a child does not have a sufficient background of language, can he learn to read well?" The answer has to be, probably not. Perhaps teachers are so concerned and preoccupied with the reading process that the language process is ignored. It is frequently assumed by many teachers that all children have been provided a language background by the home that is sufficient for school learning. However Bereiter and Englemann have pointed out that the language a child brings from home may be totally inadequate for learning in school. When this is the case, what frequently occurs is that instead of being provided with the language skills needed, the child is introduced to the reading process and failure occurs.

The whole issue of whether or not to teach language is closely associated with the artificial separation of language and reading by teachers. This dichotomy is encouraged by many schools of education who have separate methods courses devoted to the teaching of language arts and the teaching of reading. Also, the subject matter of the curriculum of the elementary schools has traditionally separated reading from language (English) so there is a tendency to conceive of them as separate subjects on the elementary level also. In practice, then, teachers teach these areas as unique, without integrating them into one unified whole. There seems to be, however, a growing awareness in education that these processes need to be taught together. Hopefully this trend will continue.

Reading Readiness

Another persistent issue deals with the readiness-for-school issue. I think the issue is really one of schools getting ready for children rather than children getting ready for school. Specifically, however, the issue is also one of language development in children and how best to promote that process. Should schools deny admittance to children who do not have the language ability the schools think they need for school success? Some people maintain that to admit children to school without a background of language skills is not only inviting failure but encouraging it. The other side in this issue just as strongly maintains that schools should provide the child with the background of language skills needed for academic success. It appears as

These children are surrounded by a wide variety of printed materials, which help promote language development and provide an incentive for writing and reading.

though this issue will not be readily resolved and that the nation will continue to have schools and teachers embracing both points of view. The problem with this state of affairs, however, is that as long as children are not provided with the skills they need for success, those individuals and eventually society are the losers.

How To Teach Language

Method. How to teach language to children is and will probably continue to be a vital issue. Should language be taught through a structured approach such as the Distar Instructional System, or through a less structured approach such as the Peabody Language Development Kits? Of course, these are not the only options available to teachers, for language can also be taught through the teacher's own method. Whatever the method employed, the language needs of children should receive top priority.

Bilingualism. Bilingualism will continue to be an issue which educators will have to face with more forcefulness than they have been willing to face it with in the past. As our nation emerges and grows toward a more open society, cultural pluralism will be more accepted and encouraged. This will necessitate more attention to the teaching and fostering of languages and dialects that children bring to school.

Packaged Materials. The wide range of packaged language programs already on the market almost exceeds our ability to know about them, and, if anything, this number is likely to increase. Some of these programs have different and opposing goals. The process of selection for adoption and use of such materials will become more difficult and complex in the future.

BIBLIOGRAPHY

Bereiter, Carl, and Engelmann, Siegfried. *Teaching Disadvantaged Children in the Preschool.* Englewood Cliffs, New Jersey: Prentice-Hall, Inc., 1966.

Dunn, Lloyd M.; Horton, Kathryn B.; Smith, James O. *Peabody Language Development Units Manual for Level #P.* Circle Pines, Minnesota: American Guidance Service, 1968.

Engelmann, Siegfried; Osborn, Jean; and Engelmann, Therese. *Distar Language I, An Instructional System.* Chicago, Illinois: Science Research Associates, 1969.

———. *Distar Language I, Teacher's Guide.* Chicago, Illinois: Science Research Associates, Inc., 1969.

Hayakawa, S. I. *Language in Thought and Action.* 3rd ed. New York: Harcourt, Brace Jovanovich and Company, 1975.

Lenneberg, Eric H. "A Biological Perspective of Language." In *New Directions in the Study of Language* edited by Eric H. Lenneberg. Cambridge, Massachusetts: M.I.T. Press, 1964.

————, "The Biological Foundations of Language." In *Readings in Applied Transformational Grammar,* edited by Mark Lester. New York: Holt, Rinehart and Winston, Inc., 1970.

Mackay, David; Thompson, Brian; and Schaub, Pamela. *breakthrough to literacy,* Teachers Resource Book. Glendale, California: Bowmar Publishers, 1973.

FOR FURTHER READING AND STUDY

Engelmann, Siegfried. *Preventing Failure in the Primary Grades.* Chicago, Illinois: Science Research Associates, Inc., 1968.
An excellent discussion of reasons for failure in schools and techniques and strategies that can be used to prevent this failure. A good section on classroom management is also included. Specific activities in the areas of reading, arithmetic and language are provided.

Tiedt, Iris M., and Tiedt, Sidney W. *Contemporary English in the Elementary School.* 2d ed. Englewood Cliffs, New Jersey: Prentice-Hall, Inc., 1975.
A very good book for the preservice teacher taking a language arts course. Deals with all aspects of language development and teaching including creativity, oral communication and wordplay. Includes a discussion of preparing children for the future and practical ideas for individualized instruction.

O'Brien, Carmen A. *Teaching the Language–Different Child to Read.* Columbus, Ohio: Charles E. Merrill Publishing Company, 1973.
Very worthwhile reading for all preservice and inservice teachers. Does a good job of providing a rationale for bilingual education. A balanced blend of theory and practical suggestions.

Pflaum, Susanna Whitney. *The Development of Language and Reading in the Young Child.* Columbus, Ohio: Charles E. Merrill Publishing Company, 1974.
Excellent reference for future teachers. Includes theories of language development with related research. Also includes discussion of reading readiness and instructional procedures for beginning reading.

Stewig, John Warren *Exploring Language with Children.* Columbus, Ohio: Charles E. Merrill Publishing Co., 1974.
Explores how infants learn their language, purposes of language programs, language programs built on children's interests and specific areas such as handwriting, spelling and literature. There are chapter supplements written by undergraduate students which add a nice dimension.

For Further Study and Involvement

1. Observe a first, second, and third grade classroom. Note how the teachers vary their use of language in order to further the language development of the children in their grade levels. Discuss these variations.

2. How does human communication differ from animal communication?

3. What are some social and educational sources which influence the child's communication? In what way does childhood communication affect how individuals communicate as adults?

4. List five ways parents influence children's language development.

5. How does a child's language ability affect her ability to cope with frustrations and anxieties?

6. Observe three children, one 2½, one 4, and one 5½. Note the differences in their use of language. Is there a greater difference in pronunciation and fluency between the 4 year old and the 5½ year old or between the 4 year old and the 2½ year old?

7. What can parents do to help children's language development? Can you think of any methods that would be helpful in the home?

8. Observe an early childhood classroom and chart instances and examples of nonverbal communication between teacher and students, and students and students. Cite specific examples of ways in which a teacher's nonverbal communication has a negative or positive influence on children and the classroom.

9. As a class, critique the criteria for the evaluation of prepackaged curricula found in this chapter. What other criteria do you think should be added?

10. Visit classrooms where a prepackaged curriculum is being used. Interview the teachers to determine the strengths and weaknesses of the program.

Behavior Management
What You Reinforce Is What You Get

Renewed Interest in Behavior Management

Traditionally there has been an emphasis in education on managing classrooms and classroom control. However, today there is more of an emphasis than there has been in the past. This renewed emphasis on classroom management can be attributed to several reasons. First, there is currently a renewed demand on the part of the public for schools to exercise a greater amount of discipline than they have in the recent past. Parents view new methods such as open education, as signs that the schools have gone "soft" on discipline. In order to counteract this "soft" discipline, parents are demanding that the schools return to a more fundamental system where control and authority prevail. A second reason for the renewed emphasis on classroom management and control comes from teachers themselves. Teachers are finding themselves confronted with new innovations in education but are increasingly reluctant to try procedures that encourage student freedom, movement, and independence. This reluctance is due, in large measure, to some teachers' inability to manage a classroom. Some teachers are afraid that their students will "get out of control," and perhaps more importantly, that they will lose authority. Therefore, a dichotomy exists between what parents want and what teachers are encouraged to try (but are afraid to accomplish). As a college professor who works daily with inservice teachers, I find some teachers aren't sure of themselves in terms of how to handle individual children, and therefore concentrate on whole-group procedures. Typical comments from teachers are, "I would try to make my classroom more open, I would try to individualize instruction, but how am I going to handle the children?" Recently, I had an opportunity to work with a group of teachers in microteaching sessions in which they videotaped themselves teaching small groups of children. Following the microteaching sessions, a debriefing period was held in which I asked the teachers to express their main concerns prior to the microteaching experience. All the teachers, without exception, said that one of their main concerns was the problem of what they were to do with the other children while they were videotaping. The teachers felt apprehension that some students would cause trouble while they were working with the other children. In short, the teachers' concerns were for problems of managing behavior.

At first we might think most teachers' concerns would be those associated with what to teach children or curricular matters, this is not necessarily so. Problems expressed by inservice teachers often are associated with how to teach children, and specifically with how to manage them. These problems are of a physical nature, i.e., how to keep children busy, how to keep children from being discipline problems, how to keep children in their seats, and how to keep children from bothering one another. Essentially, then, most classroom problems are concerned with the behavior of children and how to control or manage that behavior.

Basic Expectations of Schooling

Most parents want their children to come to school, and most children are anxious to come to "school," be it a Head Start, day care, or kindergarten program. When children come to school they expect that they will learn something. Generally, when asked why they want to go to school, children will say "to learn." Parents generally respond with the same answer. Teachers also have expectations that they will teach and students will learn. Learning as an expectation of all three parties is a foregone conclusion. It is often thought of as change in behavior, and is reflected in the expectation that schooling or the educative process will change children in the following areas:

1. Quantity and/or quality of knowledge acquired.
2. Increased cognitive skills such as reading, writing, and arithmetic.
3. Beliefs and values held, forming the basis of behavior.

4. Interpersonal relationships.

5. Social skills such as manners and meeting people.

6. Physical maturation.

Thus schooling as we have come to know and understand it is not really a question of if children will learn. We need to consider what the child will learn, and how it will be learned. We neglect these issues because although we think we know the answers to these questions, we really can't specify the specifics when pressed to do so. We deal with these issues with a casualness which borders on carelessness.

Behavior

Definition

Behavior is a term teachers and students often take for granted. We talk about particular behaviors, how students behave, or the way students should behave without much consideration for what it is we are really discussing. Behavior can be defined as that which the individual does. What the individual does can be external and internal. It is possible for an individual to view his own external behavior by looking in a mirror or at a videotape. Through observation, we may see the behavior of another individual. Behavior is also internal in that one can "talk to himself," and "think to himself." This behavior, of course, cannot be observed by someone else. We can determine this internal behavior by written or verbal questioning of a person. The process of having individuals answer questions via writing is a normal and frequently used device for "testing" what individuals know. For purposes of classroom management, however, when we talk about behavior we generally mean that behavior which we can observe. We are concerned with behavior such as the child not completing his work, walking aimlessly around the room, hitting the kid next to him, going for a drink of water every minute, crumpling up his paper and throwing it away before he is done, biting, kicking, yelling, etc., as opposed to what the child is thinking. While we can observe the child sitting in his seat and although we can presume that he may be daydreaming, we are not so much concerned with the topic of his daydreaming. What we are concerned with is the sitting-in-the-seat, staring-into-space behavior. I don't mean to imply that we are concerned only with what the child shouldn't be doing or what we don't want him to do. We are also very much concerned with how to get individual children involved in tasks that are beneficial to them.

Principles of Behavior Modification

All Behavior Has A Cause

There are important concepts that must be taken into consideration and understood before the underlying ideas and principles of classroom management make sense. The first of these concepts that we must become familiar with is that all behavior, according to the behaviorist, is caused. This does not mean some particular behavior or randomly selected behavior, but that *all* behavior is caused. Everyone acts the way they do for reasons although these reasons may not always be evident or apparent to us. In fact, in many instances these reasons may be hidden from even the person involved. How often have you heard the expressions, "He didn't know what he was doing," "I don't know why he acts like he does," "I can't understand why I did that," and "I didn't know what I was doing"?

Implications of Modification Research

Thorndike. Basically, people act the way they do because the behavior that they exhibit to other people brings them pleasure. In other words, individuals have been reinforced to exhibit a particular behavior. This concept is based mainly on the Law of Effect of Edward L. Thorndike (1874–1949), a noted American psychologist. Thorndike's Law of Effect in essence says that in individuals there is a tendency to do pleasurable things and avoid those things which bring annoyance. This law has gradually grown into what has come to be known as the Imperial Law of Effect, which says that the consequences of particular responses determine whether or not the response will be continued and therefore learned. In essence, what happens to an individual after he acts in a particular way will determine whether or not he continues to act the way he did. A child who cries and who is immediately given a cookie by his mother will probably learn to cry in order to receive cookies. Receiving cookies reinforces crying behavior. We should understand that this behavior is not always planned. A child does not necessarily say to himself, "I'm going to cry because I know my mother will give me a cookie." The child may very well have accidentally cried, and his mother, wanting to cease the crying behavior, gave the child a cookie. The child then came to associate the two events.

Pavlov. Another person who immediately comes to mind when one thinks of rewards and reinforcement is the Russian psychologist, Ivan P. Pavlov (1849–1936). Pavlov was concerned with the conditioned response. He worked with dogs in conditioning a reflex (salivation) with a new stimulus (the ringing of a bell). What Pavlov did was to condition the salivary response of a dog by providing the dog with meat simultaneously to the ringing of a bell. After several occurrences in which the dog was presented with both meat and a ringing bell, Pavlov could merely ring a bell and the dog would salivate. What this means is that bell ringing was a conditioned reinforcer and took the place of a primary reinforcer, food.

Many of the things that reinforce us as adults are also conditioned in that they stand for something other than a primary reinforcer. In this context, we can define primary reinforcers as events to which we respond without much previous experience, including such things as food, water, air, and sex. However, many of these have been replaced by what can be called *conditioned reinforcers* in that we have been conditioned to respond to something else rather than responding to a primary reinforcer. A college teacher no longer teaches and researches for so many bushels of soybeans. Rather, he practices his profession for money, which has replaced food as a reinforcer. Just as Pavlov's dog salivated when he heard the bell, so man is motivated to work for money rather than a primary reinforcer such as food. Some critics of behavior modification will often cite Pavlov's experiment and what conditioned responses can lead to as evidence that behavior modification and reinforcement practices are dehumanizing. It is certainly true that behavior modification can dehumanize; undoubtedly this criticism can be very well illustrated with classroom practice. The difference is slight between a dog salivating when a bell is rung and children coming to attention in a classroom when the tardy bell is rung. Reinforcement is not evil in and of itself; but both the user and the ends to which it is employed have the capacity for evil.

Skinner. Another person who comes to mind in a discussion of behavior modification is B. F. Skinner (1904–). Skinner is often called the father of behavior modification and is given credit for many of the technological and pedagogical implications of behavior modification, including programmed instruction.

Classroom Guidelines

Conscious Use For Good. What we are concerned with in classroom management is the application of findings and procedures established in laboratories with animals to classroom situations. Specifically, we are concerned with behavior modification or the changing of the behavior of students who are under the guidance and direction of schools. As used in this chapter, behavior modification means the conscious application of the methods of behavioral science, with the intent of altering student behavior.

Teachers have always been concerned with changing the behavior of children, but it is implicit in the term *behavior modification* that we mean the use of modification techniques to *consciously* change the behavior of children. I would like to stress the difference between the conscious changing of behavior and the ignorant changing of children's behavior. The behaviorists, who are concerned with how behavior is learned, changed, altered, and controlled, have always maintained that all behavior is learned—and in this sense that all behavior is caused by reinforcers from which individuals have gained pleasure of some kind. The problem, however, is that many teachers in the classroom have been changing the behavior of children ever since children have been under their direction, but they have not been aware of it. Future teachers of children such as yourself should be more aware of the power and effect that you will have on the behavior of children. To use power ignorantly and unconsciously in a way to achieve ends that are basically dehumanizing to children is not in keeping with good teaching practices. When you become aware of the power you have over the lives of children, try to use that power in such a way that children will benefit from it. For example, a child may come to school and may not understand that sitting in a seat quietly is a premium that some schools and teachers have established as a goal. Therefore, the teacher will nag and scold the child to the point where he not only sits quietly but he also sits quietly and bites his nails. Now I'm sure that in cases such as this, the teacher did not intentionally set out to reinforce the child in such a way that he ends up biting his nails. Regardless of the teacher's original intent, this is the terminal behavior of the child and the teacher is totally unaware of how it happened! It may well be that the teacher also ends up blaming the home and parents for the behavior of the child. If it is true that teachers have changed student behavior for better or worse whether they knew it or not, then we can extend this idea one step further and say we have all had our behavior changed whether we knew it or not and even whether we liked it or not!

Reinforced Misbehavior. One of the facts of classroom life which we must recognize and face is that teacher behavior, attitude, predisposition, and inclination actually cause a great deal of student misbehavior. Many children actually misbehave because they are being or have been reinforced into what we call misbehavior. The main difficulty with this issue is how to get teachers to realize that they often reinforce undesirable student behavior. For example, children enjoy receiving the teacher's attention. Therefore, when a child receives any kind of teacher attention, it reinforces the behavior which the child overtly exhibited to get that attention. A child who is noisy and talking to the child beside him receives teacher attention by being spoken to (scolded, etc.). This particular child may never have received any kind of teacher attention before and he likes it! The chances of his exhibiting the same behavior (talking to the child beside him) to elicit the same response from the teacher is greatly increased because he has been reinforced. I have seen children in early childhood settings who never "misbehaved" before do so in order to receive attention from a new teacher!

This girl has selected an art activity. Providing time for children to do the things they like acts as a positive reinforcement for desired behavior.

I have also observed one instance where the teacher in charge of a day care program was preparing to take the children to another room for music activities. As the children were lining up, the teacher said to the group, "The last person in line can turn off the lights." Now with young children, turning the lights off is a very strong social reinforcer. The effect of the remark was such that five of the more aggressive boys began pushing and shoving to see who would, indeed, be last in line. In this case, the teacher's remark had the effect of reinforcing pushing and shoving behavior on the part of the children.

Another example may also help us gain more insight into the same issue. One of the myths of many early childhood programs is that young children are supposed to have a short attention span. I know I have heard, and you probably have too, teachers say, "Oh, Susie can't do that because her attention span isn't long enough," or "We could never do that activity in kindergarten because the children can't pay attention long enough." What teachers may not realize is that their own behavior and attitudes, as well as the classroom setting, may actually reinforce short-attention-span behavior! If teachers provide activities interesting to children, and if teachers use strategies to strengthen children's length of concentration, then they will become more attentive. In some early childhood programs, I observed children who were allowed to run randomly and indiscriminately from one activity to another so that they literally resembled bees seeking nectar from flowers. These children were never, in a sense, reinforced to attend to a task for increasing periods of time.

Positive and Negative Reinforcement

Before we can apply the principles of behavior modification to classroom settings there are certain concepts we need to be familiar with. First of all, when we talk about positive reinforcement we are talking about providing or giving children rewards or reinforcers that will promote those behaviors which teachers and parents have decided are desirable behaviors. The process of providing children with a reinforcer or with reinforcement in the nature of a reward, following the performance of a behavior which is desirable, is called positive reinforcement. Technically, positive reinforcement is a maintenance or increase in the frequency of behavior following a particular stimulus. That which the child receives, be it candy, money, or a hug, is called the reinforcer, the reinforcement, or the reward. A positive reinforcer is generally defined as any stimulus which maintains or increases a particular behavior. The way a positive reinforcer is generally viewed in classroom settings is that children find receiving rewards for desirable behavior a pleasant activity. Figure 15 may help you conceptualize positive reinforcement as a teaching-learning procedure. Negative reinforcement on the other hand is usually defined as the maintaining or increasing of a behavior by the removal of withdrawal of an aversive stimulus. An example of negative reinforcement is the instance in which the child increases his paying-attention behavior so that the nagging of the teacher will cease. This is a negative reinforcement situation since the removal of a stimulus (nagging) increases a behavior (paying attention). In this case the child found the nagging behavior of the teacher aversive. It may have been that another child liked the nagging behavior. If nagging behavior increased disruptive behavior, then nagging would be a positive reinforcer, leading to further misbehavior so that more attention may be received.

In the strict sense of the definitions, positive and negative reinforcement have nothing to do with whether or not a reward or reinforcer is intrinsically or generally "good" or "bad." The layman, however, usually labels positive reinforcement as that which is "good" (praise, money, etc.) and negative reinforcement as that which is "bad" (punishment, etc.). When considered within the classroom context, negative reinforcement is thought to be synonymous with punishment or the application of stimuli which children find undesirable. Therefore the layman usually thinks of positive reinforcement as giving the child something good such as candy for doing something good, i.e., "Since you've done such a good job on your reading, here's a piece of candy." On the other hand a child may be

Nonverbal

Nod.
Smile.
Hug.
Pat on the head, shoulder.
Proximity (being close to
    someone).
Eye contact.
Attention.
Wink.

Verbal

Good.
Right.
Correct.
Wonderful.
Very good.
I like that.
Good boy/girl.
Hey! That's great.
I knew you could do it.

THE CHILD
IN A SETTING
UTILIZING
POSITIVE
REINFORCEMENT

Tokens/Privileges

1. Extra time to do things.
2. Recess.
3. Games and puzzles.
4. Parties.
5. Classroom chores.
6. Food.
7. Premack (those activities
   which children engage in on
   their own).

Classroom Setting

1. Organized to help make
   desired behaviors possible.
2. Provides opportunities for
   novelty.
3. Gives children opportunities
   for control over their
   environment.
4. Reflects desires, interests,
   and ideas of children.

Figure 15 *Positive Reinforcement in Early Childhood Settings*

reprimanded or even spanked for doing something that he is not supposed to do. The child who gets up out of his seat and hits the child beside him may be punished by the teacher through spanking for his behavior. This is generally conceived of as negative reinforcement.

Understanding Behavior

The above are not the only concepts we need to understand about behavior modification in order for it to have meaning in the classroom. Another extremely important concept focuses on behavior rather than on the causes of such behavior. Teachers should not be concerned with why the child acts the way he does. This idea usually takes some getting used to on the part of many teachers since it is almost opposite of the way they have been taught to think. Generally, teachers feel it is beneficial to spend most of their time finding out why a child acts the way he does, and consequently they spend a great deal of time and effort in the process. Johnny, for example, cannot attend to his work in class; he is fidgety all the time and is inclined to daydream. When he is not engaging in one of these behaviors, he gets up out of his seat and wanders aimlessly around the room. The teacher, in an effort to solve Johnny's problem, spends six weeks investigating the causes. Through the investigative process the teacher finds out Johnny's mother has been divorced three times, is about to leave the man she is living with, and has a tendency to ignore Johnny at home. On the basis of this information, the teacher concludes that Johnny acts the way he acts because of his mother's influence. However, the teacher is no closer to solving Johnny's problem than he was six weeks previously since nothing has been done about Johnny's behavior! A teacher's time and energy should be spent in developing strategies to help children with their problems. This should not be interpreted to mean that we should not be sympathetic toward children with problems. Also there are instances in which underlying causes may help us in dealing with the behavior we wish to modify. At issue, however, is the practice of gathering information and not doing anything about the behavior under consideration. We as teachers and parents need to recognize that the behavior a child exhibits is a cause rather than a problem; it is behavior that we need to attend to. By solving the problem of the child, we can demonstrate warmth and support.

Another issue frequently encountered in an analysis of children's behavior is the attitude of the teacher toward the behavior of the child. Frequently teachers act as though they think children do the things they do because children are innately bad. You may hear them remark "That's the way he is," and "It's just his nature to do that." Teachers also feel sometimes that children do the things they do deliberately as a means of disturbing the teacher. Both of these attitudes show a lack of understanding of child development. To view children as doing "bad" things because they are innately bad is dehumanizing to all children. They are not born with a tendency to do bad things, nor do they spend their time plotting against teachers. The responsibility for changing and directing behavior rests with teachers, for they are the ones who should possess the maturity and understanding to help children.

Since teachers probably cause 99 percent of the behavior problems that occur in the classroom, we should understand the following ways in which such problems are fostered:

1. A teacher may allow a child to refrain from participating in a desired activity. For example, the child who didn't pick up his building blocks and put them on the appropriate shelf may not

have known what was expected of him. Since he did not know, he did either what came naturally to him in the situation, or he did what he was used to doing. In either instance, if the teacher allowed the child not to pick up his blocks, then this behavior was being reinforced.

2. A child may enjoy the attention that he receives by the teacher coming over and nagging at him to put the block away because it is the only attention he has received all day.

3. A teacher may be lax in reinforcing appropriate behavior. A child may not place any particular value on picking up blocks and putting them where they belong. If the child is reinforced positively for picking up blocks, then this activity will increase in frequency.

4. A teacher may be so busy attending to the wrong things students do that he may have neither the time nor the energy to attend to the good things students do. If you have ever observed young children role-playing the part of a school teacher during a "play school" session, you were probably aware of the way the children exhibited many of the behaviors attributed to teachers. The scene usually goes something like this: "All right, class, it's time to get down to work. Johnny, get in your seat; Susie, stop talking; Mary, pay attention; Harry, stop shuffling your feet," and so it goes ad infinitum. Ignoring inappropriate behavior is probably one of the most overlooked and least utilized strategies that can be employed in the management of an effective learning setting. As a matter of fact, in helping teachers develop procedures for positive reinforcement in the classroom, it has been my experience one of the major difficulties they experience with this strategy is guilt feelings. Teachers often feel that by ignoring undesirable behaviors they are not doing a good job of teaching. In addition, teachers often say they fear that should a visitor or principal walk into the classroom during their attempt to ignore undesirable behavior, criticisms of their teaching methods could result. It is extremely important, therefore, for teachers to have the cooperation of parents and school administrators in any effort which tends to deviate from what is normally considered "school teacher" behavior.

Building New Behavior

Behavior Classifications. In classroom settings, we can generally classify student behavior in two ways. It is either on-task or off-task behavior. On-task student behavior is appropriate either in terms of teacher approval or on the basis of a previously agreed upon contract between teacher and child. On the other hand, the child demonstrates off-task behavior when he is doing something which is not appropriate to the learning setting, such as not picking up toys or aimlessly wandering around the classroom. While one of the most effective strategies in changing student behavior may be ignoring off-task behavior, simply ignoring off-task behavior in and of itself will not necessarily change the behavior. Ignoring has to be combined with a system of positive reinforcement of another desirable behavior. Therefore the strategy becomes one of ignoring inappropriate behavior while at the same time reinforcing an appropriate behavior.

Ability to Change. Another concept that is sometimes overlooked is that a child is generally not capable of acting or thinking his own way out of undesirable behavior. I have heard teachers say to children, "You know how to act," when indeed he may not know how to act. Another common teacher device is to say of the child, "He could do better than that if he wanted to." The problem with this, however, is the child may not know what he wants to do, or he may not know what's appropriate for him to do. In other words, he needs help, and he needs teacher help through an organized procedure for how to act.

I have frequently heard teachers say of children, "You could do it if you wanted to," and "If you would really try you could do it," and also "You promised me you would do it and you've broken your promise." Teachers attribute more willpower (or ability of self-discipline) to children than they themselves possess! How often have you made a promise to yourself that you were going to do something (be nice to your roommate, for example) and yet you ended up doing just the opposite? How many people have promised themselves they were going to stop smoking cigarettes, yet didn't? Just as adults cannot think their way out of old behavior, even so is it more difficult for children. Thinking does not build new behavior; acting does. Building new behavior then is a process of getting children to act in new ways.

The new behavior that we want children to demonstrate must be within their power and ability to achieve. Quite often the behavior we ask of a child is nowhere near his physical or mental level. How is a child supposed to pay attention to and be interested in materials he cannot read? How can a child with no experiential background at sitting still and paying attention do so for the periods of time we require of him, especially when we want him to do something that is totally uninteresting to him? Suppose I were to give you a Greek passage to translate and informed you that you couldn't leave your room until it was completely translated. This is comparable to what we ask of children.

Strategy to Determine Practical Changes. Not only must the behavior we ask a child to demonstrate be within his ability to achieve, it must also be *practical* for him to achieve. Recently a teacher related to me a first grader's behavior that she found disturbing. Specifically, the behavior was talking out loud all the time and constantly coming to her to have his work checked. After determining that the child liked to listen to stories on the tape recorder, she told the child, "If you don't talk out loud and stay in your seat for fifteen minutes, I'll give you extra time to listen to stories with the tape recorder." This strategy didn't work and the child continued his talking out and coming up to the teacher. The teacher complained to me that positive reinforcement didn't work. Sitting in his seat *and* not talking out was simply too much to ask of the child. What the teacher probably should have done as an alternative strategy was to have the child begin by sitting in his seat for a short period of time and receive reinforcement for that behavior.

When determining which of the child's behaviors you are going to modify, pick the one behavior that is the most annoying or detrimental to the child and/or class, or pick the one behavior which is the most severe. If a child is exhibiting a series of annoying behaviors, or if the child is not attending to on-task behavior because he is talking out loud, biting other children, and walking around the room, pick *one* of these behaviors to modify; don't try to modify all three behaviors at once.

We need to also keep in mind that a particular behavior which is annoying to one teacher may not be annoying to another teacher. One teacher may feel that a child who talks out is a disturbance while another teacher may view the child's talking out as something to be prized. I recently talked with a young teacher who is very verbal, eloquent, and delightful to listen to. However, she vividly recalls her second grade teacher putting her in a corner for talking too much! One wonders if, indeed, children can talk too much, particularly when language is one of the qualities which makes us human.

Reinforce Approximations. Another concept that should be kept in mind can be summed up pretty well by the folksaying, "You have to learn to creep before you walk." First, the task we want the child to demonstrate must be broken down into manageable and easily attainable steps. Rather than ask a child who cannot make the letter *A* to make it at one sitting, ask him instead to draw straight lines. Second, reinforce approximations of the correct response or appropriate behavior. If a child prior to making the letter *A* makes a slanted line, reward that effort and achievement. If a child doesn't usually use the reading corner, reinforce him when he goes close to it.

As she achieves success in a coloring activity, she will become anxious to be involved in other writing activities.

When to Reinforce. In building new behavior, it is generally a good idea to reinforce the child immediately following the desired behavior. How nice it is to know that we have done something well and that others appreciate us. Children are no different. To wait till the end of the learning session, the period, or the day to reinforce behavior is totally inappropriate and, in addition, is nonreinforcing. The child's reinforcement should be not only immediate, but also consistent. Although there are reinforcement schedules that are built on random reinforcement, the reinforcement that works best with young children is that which is given continuously, at least until the desired behavior is well established.

Program for Behavior Modification

Specifying Terminal Objectives

The first step in the development of a program of behavior modification that is often overlooked by teachers is the specification, on the teacher's part, of the behavior that they want to reinforce in children. Teachers need to focus their attention on those desirable behaviors, which are referred to as "terminal" or "on-task" behaviors. One reason that such specification is difficult for many teachers is that they have been so used to identifying or paying attention to off-task behavior. In addition, the teacher is often in a quandary about what behaviors are ultimately desirable for the children; if given no direction, the teacher may be out of step with the home, the community, and the rest of the school. Ideally, those behaviors the teachers ultimately want their students to demonstrate should be consistent with and based on the goals and objectives established for the school and classroom program. If terminal objectives for a particular program or curriculum have not previously been established, it is extremely important that the teacher, in cooperation with other staff members and administrators, undertake this task.

Let us consider a school where terminal objectives have been agreed upon. The school faculty has set as goals for its program the development in children of a good self-concept, independent learning, decision-making skills and the basic skills of reading, writing, and computing. These broad goals are then subdivided into the areas of academic competency, social competence, and personal competence, including self-image. These three areas of academic, social and personal competence are then translated into specific classroom activities and procedures. The faculty has decided that a specific terminal behavior in the academic area includes the child learning to write his name. One way of attaining this terminal behavior would be to design specific learning tasks which deal with writing the letters of the alphabet or combining the appropriate ones to form the child's name. However, if the child cannot or did not know how to identify specific letters and needed help with shape discrimination, then this activity would be provided for him. As the child engaged in activities to promote shape discrimination and writing letters, he would be positively reinforced for this. Social behaviors exhibited by the child that are reinforced in this school are following instructions, paying attention to the teacher, and working for a period of time on writing letters. Personal behaviors identified as terminal behaviors for the child include health habits such as using a handkerchief and putting away materials when he was finished with them, all of which relate to a positive self-image. Arriving at terminal behaviors through this kind of planning provides teachers with a framework within which to provide instruction and is more appropriate than the uncertainty that exists in many classrooms and results from not having objectives to follow.

Gathering Baseline Data

A second activity that the teacher must engage in is the gathering of what is frequently termed *baseline data*. Gathering data can be accomplished concurrently with specifying objectives, our first step. Pertinent data consists of the precise identification of the off-task behavior performed by the child, the frequency with which it occurs, and the conditions under which it occurs. Generally, these data should be gathered over a period of time ranging from several days to a week. The reasons for gathering baseline data are several. First, it helps teachers isolate and identify the behavior that they want to ignore and/or modify. Frequently when pushed to explain what behaviors they find annoying in children, teachers respond in vague terms or list a whole series of behaviors. There may not be any behavior in particular that is annoying, but rather it may seem that the whole child is annoying. Gathering baseline data can help teachers clarify their feelings toward children and be more precise in specifying behavior. Second, the data can show the frequency with which a behavior occurs. Teachers are often surprised with this part of the data base because sometimes a particular behavior does not occur with the frequency a teacher thinks it does. A typical teacher response may be, "He is always out of his seat." Gathering data will help to determine if this is true. Third, baseline data can help pinpoint the conditions under which an off-task behavior occurs. While the teacher may think the child is out of his seat all of the time, he may be out of his seat only when he has nothing to do. Fourth, such data can help show progress in the program of behavior modification. A teacher can tell by comparison with the baseline data what improvement has occurred in the child's behavior as a result of the behavior modification.

Reinforcing Behavior

Appropriate Reinforcers. Once teachers have identified those behaviors that they want to reinforce in children, then it is necessary to reinforce the behaviors when they occur. Although this statement may seem obvious, all teachers are not aware of it. The "what" of reinforcement, or more specifically, what is to be given children for a reward, is a question that has to be answered within the context of what is appropriate for children, what teachers find appropriate, and what the school and community find appropriate. We have indicated that the use of food or other primary reinforcers is an excellent means of providing reinforcement. However, many people object to using food as a reinforcer since it conjures up images of animals in cages, rats in mazes, and other procedures which tend to be identified as dehumanizing. Regardless of whether or not the teacher uses a primary reinforcer of food, or a social reinforcer (praise), or manipulative objects (games), it is important to keep in mind that the reinforcer one uses is only as good as the desire of the individual to have it. In other words, if the reinforcer has the power to reinforce the behavior that precedes it, then it will work. A method that has been used in determining the nature of the reinforcer is the Premack Principle, which takes its name from David Premack. This psychologist determined that behaviors with a high probability of occurrence can be used to reinforce behaviors with a low probability of occurence. The activities that children participate in when they have free time can determine what they like to do best, and teachers can use those activities to reinforce terminal behaviors. In many early childhood classrooms, using the chalkboard or using easels to watercolor is a highly desirable activity. Therefore, time to use the chalkboard or the art easels could be used in reinforcing desired behavior. Figures 16, 17, and 18 give examples of reinforcers commonly used in early childhood settings. The following sections discuss some main ideas involved in reinforcement strategies.

CONTINGENCY MANAGEMENT

In reinforcing behavior, teachers frequently find it helpful to engage in what is generally known as *contingency contracting* or *contingency management.* When this strategy is used, the child is told, for example, "If you put the materials that you are working with away when you're done with them, you can use the chalkboard for five minutes." Basically, it is a matter of "if x, then y." Sometimes contingency management is accompanied by a written contract between the teacher and the student. This of course depends on the age and maturity of certain children.

Interesting work encourages this child to become involved in on-task behavior.

Frequently, teachers object to managing contingencies on the basis that it is bribery; however, teachers have always managed contingencies. If the class gets quiet, then children are allowed to pursue some activity. Appar-

PRIMARY REINFORCERS	CONDITIONED REINFORCERS
Reinforce behavior without the respondent having much previous experience with the item.	Reinforce as a result of the experiences children have had with the reinforcer.

PRIMARY REINFORCERS

A. FOOD

M & M's	Sugar-coated
Cookies	cereal
Juice	Raisins
Peanuts	Popcorn
Celery	Gum
Carrots	Cheese
	Fruit

CONDITIONED REINFORCERS

A. VERBAL

I like the way you . . .

Great	Fine	A-Okay	Tremendous
Right on	Wow	Excellent	
Beautiful	Way to go	Fantastic	
Terrific	Super	Fine job	

B. NONVERBAL

1. *Facial*

Smile
Wink
Raised eyebrows
Eye contact

2. *Gestures*

Clapping of hands
Wave
Forming an A-Okay sign
(thumb + index finger)
Victory sign
Nod of head
Shrug shoulders

3. *Proximity*

Standing near someone
Shaking hands
Getting down on a
child's level
Hug, touching
Holding child's
arm up

C. SOCIAL(Used here to mean they occur in or as a result of social consequences)

Parties
Group approval
Class privileges

Figure 16 *Reinforcers Used in Early Childhood Settings*

Games
Puzzles
Time to do Things
Cooking Activities
Coloring
Using the chalkboard
Classroom chores
Turning the lights off
Watering the flowers
Caring for pets
Playing the piano
Using books and records
Getting the teacher's mail

Figure 17 *Ways to Positively Reinforce Children in Early Childhood Settings*

Get the teacher's mail
Water the plants
Wash the chalkboards
Run errands
Extra recess
Pass out papers, supplies
Use audio visual equipment
Go outside
Bring books from home to read
Play games with friends
Lead games
Watch TV
Do flash cards
Cutting and pasting

Figure 18 *Examples of Activities and Privileges Children Say They Like to Do*

ently what makes this type of contingency management acceptable to a teacher is that it occurred almost intuitively. However, some teachers feel once contingencies are planned for, then it constitutes bribery. The distinction seems to be an artificial one.

TOKEN SYSTEM

When reinforcement techniques are used in the classroom, we must realize that reinforcement works best when it follows closely that behavior which we want to reinforce. Also, the closer the reinforcement follows the desired behavior, the better it works. Particularly when building new skills or shaping new behaviors it is important for the child to be reinforced immediately for the behaviors that he exhibits. In order to provide for this immediate reinforcement and to avoid having children wait for reinforcement, some teachers operate a classroom reinforcement system utilizing tokens. In this token-based system, the child is given an item of some kind, e.g., plastic discs, buttons, trading stamps, or beans, which he uses to "buy" or "trade" for the activity he wants. If the children desire to participate in an activity using the art easel, the teacher may have determined that when a child receives ten tokens, he can use the art easel. Therefore, during the work sessions, as a child works and performs the appropriate tasks and exhibits teacher-specified behavior, he is given a token. When he accumulates ten tokens, they can be traded in for time to use the art easel. While it is important in any reinforcement setting that a child should be reinforced often, it is more important in a token economy. The reason for this is that the child must have enough tokens to spend or trade for an activity. In a token economy, another strategy that is often employed is "time out." If a child is exhibiting disruptive behavior to the extent that it is impossible for the teacher to ignore, then the child is isolated in a booth or corner of the room. During this isolation period, the child is not able to earn tokens. The length of time that he spends in his "time out" period depends upon the behavior that he exhibited. The effect of this "time out" period is to associate the undesirable behavior with the time out during which he cannot earn tokens. The consequence of course is that the child will not have the necessary tokens to trade for desirable activities if he spends much of his time in "time out."

COMBINATION OF TECHNIQUES

In using behavior modification principles in an early childhood setting it is most desirable to use a combination of positive reinforcement and ignoring which can lead to extinction of the undesired behavior. Using the combination of these two behaviors, the teacher reinforces the desired behavior that she wants while she ignores the undesirable behavior a child has exhibited.

The Classroom as a Reinforcer of Behavior

When thinking about behavior modification strategies, we have a tendency to view modification as a relationship that exists only between teacher and child. However, there are many applications of the theory that can be applied to the early childhood education setting itself. Teachers must examine the physical settings in which they teach and determine if the classroom is structured and arranged so that this structure is conducive to the behaviors they want to reinforce. If a teacher desires to encourage independent work, physical places and time for children to accomplish individual work must be provided. Also, although one of our targets is to reduce disruptive behavior on the part of the children, such behavior is often encouraged by making children literally walk over other children in order to get the learning equipment and materials they need to accomplish a task. Through an examination of the classroom setting, a teacher may determine the classroom actually contributes to off-task behaviors. I'm sure all of you as students and learners have been in settings you found uncomfortable and in which you wished you did not have to spend any more time than was necessary.

The atmosphere of the classroom or the learning environment must be such that what is asked of a child in terms of a new behavior is possible within the context of the environment. For example, a child likes to hit other boys in the classroom. The teacher decides that he wants to reinforce nonhitting behavior on the part of the child and concludes that when the child does not hit his friends, he will be rewarded. The child, however, in order to engage in a particular task requiring the use of colored paper, must walk right by his friends. In this instance, the hitting behavior is probably being reinforced by the way the classroom is arranged!

Although teachers want to encourage independence on the part of children, they often make the children ask for materials, which the teacher must then locate for the children. This practice not only discourages independence, but also probably makes teachers old before their time. If a teacher wants to promote independence, then the classroom should be arranged so that independence is encouraged and reinforced.

Seven Processes for Modifying Behavior

The following are steps that should be followed in modifying the behavior of children:

1. Identify the terminal behavior
2. Gather baseline data.
3. Determine the reward or reinforcer.
4. Arrange the contingency or write the contract.
5. Reinforce the behavior.
6. Compare the results to the baseline data.
7. Modify the behavior modification program as necessary.

Issues Associated with Behavior Modification

Is Modification Dehumanizing?

The main criticism leveled against behavior modification deals with the dehumanization of people. There are several points associated with this issue.

Should We Use Lab Techniques? First, many of the insights, findings, and procedures associated with behavior modification were conducted in laboratories under experimental conditions. Some people have a tendency to think that the application of laboratory findings to human beings in social settings is inappropriate. It is further argued that you cannot and indeed should not manipulate children with the same techniques and procedures that are used to manipulate rats.

Is Reinforcement Bribery? The second feature of modification critics find dehumanizing is its resemblance to bribery. Critics maintain it is neither good, appropriate, nor moral to bribe children. The problem with this criticism seems to be that teachers have always "bribed" children ("When everyone is sitting quietly with their hands folded on top of the desk, we will line up for lunch"). Teachers have always managed contingencies but often have been ignorant of what they were doing. Then is contingency management appropriate only as long as you're ignorant of what you are doing? This of course is a question that teachers in early childhood education settings have to answer for themselves. The fact remains that teachers and parents have managed contingencies and will continue to do so. Whether or not it is called bribery seems to be merely a matter of semantics. It is unfortunate that the word *bribery* is associated with contingency management. We usually use the word *bribery* when referring to an illegal or immoral act. In fact, a bribe is usually illegal when used in business and political contexts. A bribe, usually money, is used to "buy" someone's influence, favor or knowledge, for personal or political gain. In the classroom, however, society, schools, teachers, and hopefully parents have agreed on and found acceptable the ends which will be modified.

Does Modification Threaten Freedom?

The issue of individual freedom and how much that freedom can be or should be restricted by the use of behavioral techniques is one that is not easily addressed. Many critics of behavior modification see it as a threat to individual freedom. When stated in question form, the issue is, "If individuals are manipulated and their behavior managed, are they then really free?" Of course, someone may argue that since we are products of managed behavior, we have never been as free as we would like to believe we are.

However, it is true that knowledge about behavior modification makes us freer than we once were. Then, too, is it really possible for us to be "free spirits" and "free" in the sense that we have no external restrictions at all? Perhaps one approach to the dilemma of behavior modification and individual freedom is to make the people who are in charge of early childhood settings as aware as possible of behavior modification strategies. Through this awareness perhaps they will not use the power they possess to overcontrol the lives and minds of children. Also, the more awareness that can be provided the public about the techniques, procedures, and underlying philosophies for controlling behavior, then the more guarded society and individuals can become concerning the procedures used and the ends to which these procedures are used. In this way knowledge indeed can bring freedom. It is when man is ignorant of many of the strategies and institutions which tend to limit his freedom that he is really not free.

Ignorance is an issue that we need to examine and deal with at any level where "behavior modification" occurs. How much damage is effected through ignorance? Probably more than we realize. The child who is nagged until he sits still, and in the process starts to bite his fingernails, is a victim of ignorance. The child who is denied the freedom to urinate when he needs to and develops a urinary infection is a victim of ignorance.

Can Modification Foster A Police State?

Another issue associated with behavior modification is the spectre of a police state. Visions of a society where the lives and minds of people are controlled through behavior modification techniques is one that causes many people to have misgivings about behavior modification strategies. Some critics maintain that if through the utilization of behavior modification techniques, individuals can be conditioned for the behavior other individuals desire, then the individuals doing the manipulating or reinforcing can structure any type of society they desire. Of course this is a problem that exists in early childhood education settings as well. Teachers utilizing behavior modification techniques for the wrong purposes can adversely affect the lives of children. For this reason, there is a need for a discussion of the issues, and an agreement by all parties, including parents, on the goals which govern the procedures that are used in classrooms.

Modification Towards What Goals?

There are also ethical issues and concerns with the ends of behavior modification techniques. What kinds of goals should be set? The individuals who advocate the use of positive reinforcement believe that the objectives established for behavior and the techniques used to achieve these goals are not the same. Basically, the behaviorist does not want to confuse the means (how to modify) with the goals (what to reinforce).

What goals to work towards is a crucial question for teachers in any early childhood education setting. As I have indicated before, however, it is not a question that has been adequately addressed or answered; many teachers don't know what they are reinforcing and therefore are reinforcing, in many instances, inappropriate behavior. As teachers address themselves to the question, "What do I want children to learn?" only then can they answer more clearly the ethical and moral issues involved in behavior modification.

Regardless of the issues that are involved in behavior modification, it would appear that modification principles, particularly those concerned with positive reinforcement, have a great deal to offer both teachers and children in learning settings. If teachers want to implement and be successful with learning procedures such as independent learning and open education, they will have to become more efficient and more effective in managing classrooms than they have been in the past. Behavior modification offers the opportunity to achieve this goal.

FOR FURTHER READING AND STUDY

Becker, Wesley C. *Parents Are Teachers.* Champaign, Illinois: Research Press Company, 1971.
    Written for parents to help them become better teachers of their children. An easy-to-read and systematic approach to positive reinforcement techniques.

Clarizo, Harvey F. *Toward Positive Classroom Discipline.* New York: John Wiley and Sons, Inc., 1972.
    A blend of research and practical experience resulting in solid ideas and techniques for managing the classroom. Actual case studies of particular behavioral problems with the techniques used to alter the behavior are also included. Informative reading.

Skinner, B. F. *Beyond Freedom and Dignity.* New York: Alfred A. Knopf, Inc., 1971.
    A very provocative and far-ranging discussion of the issues and implications of a technology of behavior. Will provide the reader with many new insights into himself and society in general.

Sulzer, Beth, and Meyer, G. Roy. *Behavior Modification Procedures for School Personnel.* Hinsdale, Illinois: The Dryden Press Inc., 1972.
    Discusses the principles of operant learning in classroom settings. Each chapter begins with objectives to guide the reader and concludes with practical exercises designed to extend and clarify textual concepts.

For Further Study and Involvement

1. What are the advantages and disadvantages of using tangible rewards to stimulate and reinforce desired behaviors?

2. Some critics of controlled education argue that the primary reason teachers need to devote so much time to managing student behavior is because the pupils are being forced to engage in contrived learning. Discuss this claim.

3. What is the difference between normal behavior and acceptable behavior? Give an example of a case where normal behavior may not be acceptable and of another where acceptable behavior may not be normal.

4. Visit a classroom where behavior modification is being used. Interview parents, teachers and students to find out how they feel about the program.

5. Observe an early childhood classroom. What reinforcement system (either implicit or explicit) is the teacher using to operate the classroom? Do you think the teacher is aware of the systems of reinforcement in use?

6. Interview children and determine from them what they find reinforcing. How do they compare to the reinforcers mentioned in this chapter?

7. I have indicated in this chapter that behavior modification, i.e., the use of contingencies, is practiced by parents and teachers without their being aware of what they were doing or the processes they were using. Observe a mother-child relationship for examples of contingency management by parents. What were the contingen-

cies? The rewards offered? What was the resultant behavior of the child? After further observation answer these questions for the teacher-child relationship. In both situations what were some ethical implications involved in the adult actions?

8. Observe an early childhood classroom and determine which behaviors earn the teacher's attention. Does the teacher pay more attention to on-task or off-task behavior? Why do you think the teacher acts the way he does?

Humanizing
Early Childhood
How Can Children
Become More Human?

Achieving a Humanistic Setting

Reaction Against Institutions

A great deal of the critical and radical literature (radical meaning those who advocate significant changes in the schools) of the past decade has been directed at the dehumanizing qualities of schools and classrooms. With increasing frequency schools are depicted as places that injure the mental health of children.

Charles Silberman in his widely read and discussed work, *Crisis in the Classroom,* which documents at length some current problems with schools and schooling, states, "What schools do to both students and teachers can be understood best if one realizes that in a number of respects, schools resemble 'total institutions' like hospitals, armed services, and even prisons."[1] In institutional settings that are walled, fenced, and in other ways isolated from the community, the lives of children are not their own, for "Getting through school also involves learning how to suppress one's feelings and emotions and to subordinate one's own interests and desires to those of the teachers."[2]

---

[1]Charles E. Silberman, *Crisis in the Classroom* (New York: Vintage Books, 1971), p. 146.
[2]*Ibid.,* p. 151.

In effect, schools are viewed as places that are not good places to be put in because they are antithetical and inimical to the species Homo sapiens and detract from the dignity of people, which has traditionally been thought to be a little less than the angels. A dehumanized classroom or learning setting is a place where the individual feels less about herself than she ought to because of the conditions and atmosphere of that setting. On the other hand, a humane setting encourages the full development of children as children of God and treats them as good and worthy individuals.

Interrelationship of Intelligence, Emotions, and Behavior

We have a strong tendency to talk of the cognitive (intellectual) domain, the affective (feeling, emotions) domain, and the psychomotor (behavioral) domain as though they were separate and distinct entities. A child or a teacher cannot turn the cognitive or affective on or off like a light switch. Neither should it be viewed as possible to teach the cognitive for a while and then teach the affective for a while. A line of demarcation does not separate the three domains and I think that our failure as teachers to understand this idea adequately has gotten us into trouble. Figure 19 shows the relationship that exists among the three domains; it should help us understand that all three areas should be accounted for in the instructional process. From this figure, it is apparent that the three domains cannot be easily compartmentalized. Neither is it possible to assign topics or activities to one of the areas with absolute assurance that it belongs to that area and only that area, nor should we attempt to draw such sharp divisions. To view these domains as other than integrated is not only inaccurate, it is also misleading and can cause us to view children as consisting of these three areas as though they were three separate compartments. Furthermore, it encourages a fragmentation of teaching which can be deadening to children and also has had a tendency to place an emphasis on the cognitive domain to the exclusion of the other two domains, particularly the affective. In addition, there has been a tendency to think that education could not have both achievement and a humanistic orientation. However, there is a decided movement toward humanistic education and more educators are realizing that it is no longer a question of if a school or classroom is going to have the basics (achievement) or a humanistic setting (values) but that it is possible and desirable to have both.

Terms Used to Discuss Humane Settings

In talking about the affective, it is very easy to discuss a great many different concepts employing a number of terms that are frequently used interchange-

	Intrapersonal	Interpersonal
Cognitive	Learning about body parts, and how the body functions. Learning right from left. Identifying the letters of her name. Identifying colors of foods.	Identifying likenesses and differences between people.
Affective	Identifying what foods the child likes to eat. Making decisions about what she wants for a snack.	Deciding by themselves what they want for snack time. Group discussions where everyone gets to tell about their favorite foods.
Behavioral (Psychomotor)	Being able to walk well. Playing games requiring knowledge of right and left. Writing her name; eating favorite foods. Cutting carrots for a snack.	Planning a trip to a food store to shop for foods. Shopping for food. Making cookies with everyone getting a chance to help.

Figure 19 *The Interrelationship of the Cognitive, Affective and Psychomotor Domains in a Humanized Early Childhood Setting*

ably and synonymously. Although some experts might quarrel about the precise meanings of terms, there seems to be no general agreement about what term or word is best to use to describe educator and lay interest in the area of values, feelings, emotions, and intra- and interpersonal relationships. Some words and terms in addition to *affective* that are currently being used are *values, value education, value clarification, moral education, humane, humanistic, personalization, congruency* (meaning the meshing of the cognitive and affective), and *mental health education.* I'm sure there are other terms and perhaps you can add some of your own. I used the term *humanizing* in the title of this chapter because for me, it emphasizes and places people at the center of the educative process. Humanizing seeks to maximize time and talent of both teachers and children in seeking and implementing those conditions and processes that will recognize and promote an image of people which is uplifting rather than degrading and that will make people more human and therefore, hopefully, more humane.

Attributes of Humane Settings

One of the interesting educational questions that arises, however, is precisely what is embodied in a humane educational setting and what are its attributes? This of course is a question which every teacher and school district must answer for themselves. However, in attempting to address itself to a new vision of education in which education is viewed as a lifelong process, the Citizens Commission on Basic Education in Pennsylvania articulated the following:

> The Commission believes that this goal [lifelong education] is achievable only in an educational environment which is committed to the worth of persons rather than systems. The Commission's signal word for this philosophical stance is "personalization." This concept recognizes that learning is a process of enhancing inherent potential rather than one of gilding the student with facts. Good teaching is this process of enhancing potential, and not merely dispensing information. To be most effective, schools must meet the needs of students. Emphasis should be given to learning: to helping students develop decision-making skills, not to imposing decisions upon them. In large part, personalizing education requires profound changes in the organization and methods of education. The needs of students should never be sacrificed for administrative ease.
>
> The organizational corollary to the philosophical concept of personalization is flexibility. Although the Commonwealth should play a more active role in evaluation, the primary thrust of state regulation in this area should be guiding and facilitative. Within the limits of state regulations, and available financial resources, schools should operate more like libraries than factories. Administrative and instructional patterns must accommodate the differing growth rates and learning styles of students. Neither local nor state policies should tie schools to the 12-year concept of public education. Counselors should be skilled in advising teachers and administrators in designing such programs. The legal definition of the length of the school day and the school year should encourage year-round programs, evening classes and out-of-school experiences. Student progress toward graduation should be measured in terms of actual skills and knowledge acquired—not by the completion of arbitrary numbers of courses or years. This orientation should prevent the mass-packaging and mass-merchandizing of curriculum.[3]

This attempt at spelling out what a program that is "committed to the worth of persons" should embody is the same kind of process that all teachers and parents who are responsible for maintaining or sending their children to early childhood programs should experience.

Requirements of Humane Settings

A humanized classroom is not so much a place as it is a condition or atmosphere in which a whole series of forces interact to provide an enabling

---

[3]Milton J. Shapp. U.S. Department of Health, Education and Welfare, Office of Education, Commonwealth of Pennsylvania, *The Report of the Citizens Commission on Basic Education*, Title IV, Section 402, and Title V–A, Section 503 E.S.E.A., pp. 3–4.

Learning is enjoyable for these two children in a humanized classroom.

setting for meaningful learning and living. Figure 20 depicts these forces. It should not be assumed that the items listed in the figure are either prescriptive or all-inclusive. Specific items will vary according to the social setting, different groups of children, and teacher attitude. However, it is the existence of such factors that is important.

Mature Teachers. A humanized classroom requires, in part, a teacher who does not feel threatened by the children. While this statement may at first appear to be denigrating to teachers, it is not meant to be. However, some teachers are afraid to deal with values, and view as presumptuous some children's effort to disagree with what the teacher says or does. It is extremely easy in an early childhood setting for teachers, because of their physical size and position as teacher, to impose their views and values on children through the process of intimidation. Teachers and parents must be

The School

1. Is open to the community.
2. Encourages community involvement.
3. Promotes student freedom.
4. Encourages student growth toward independence.

The Teacher

1. Respects and trusts children.
2. Is honest and accepting.
3. Believes in, promotes, and provides for individual differences.
4. Promotes a feeling of human warmth.
5. Avoids imposing values on children.
6. Encourages children to express their own ideas.

THE CHILD IN A HUMANISTIC, PERSONALIZED SETTING

The Learning Setting

1. Is individualized and self–paced.
2. Is flexible in time (no rigid time schedule) and space (learning can occur anywhere).
3. Is an emotionally secure atmosphere.

The Curriculum

1. Is based on the interests of children.
2. Learning is considered a lifelong process.
3. There is an integration of subject matter.
4. Is based on the whole student (not just as he exists in school).
5. Utilizes real–life problems in place of hypothetical ones.
6. Integrates the cognitive, affective and psychomotor.
7. Is based on the planning efforts of both teachers and children.
8. Provides for the development of the affective.

Figure 20 *Aspects of a Humanized Early Childhood Program*

very perceptive and sensitive. Many classrooms I have visited emphasize (sometimes with physical punishment) the need for children to demonstrate respect for the teacher's value system. There is also an obvious need, as we have discussed, for teachers to respect children. In an atmosphere which does not treat the child with courtesy, dignity, and respect, it is difficult if not impossible for the child even to feel good about herself, not to mention how she feels toward her peers and teacher. What we need are teachers who are mature in the fullest sense of the word.

Emphasis on Interaction. A surprising thing about some schools is that although they are places where people congregate, they all too often seemingly operate on the assumption that children and adults should not have any interaction with or among each other. As a matter of fact, except for periods such as recess, the opportunities for interaction may be very limited indeed. Humanizing the classroom involves more interpersonal relations than have existed in the past. Again, while open education does not necessarily guarantee that child-to-child interactions will increase, it does increase the tendency that these interactions will occur.

Schools have also had a tendency in the past to be isolated from the community in that their physical structure (fortress-like with fences around them) have discouraged people from entering. School policies (an open house once a year for visitation) have also communicated to the public that it is not always welcome.

The isolation which schools foster makes learning and teaching a very lonely business. Classrooms and the graded nature of schools, both from an age and from a curriculum point of view, make it difficult, if not all but impossible, for much interpersonal interaction to occur. Sadly enough, when teachers enter their classroom in the morning and shut the door, they are alone in two senses. First they are isolated from contact with other adults. Except for brief periods of the day, either in the cafeteria or in the teachers' lounge, opportunities to interact with other adults are extremely limited. In a profession based upon the importance of interpersonal relationships, the quantity and quality of these relationships very often leave a great deal to be desired. When we think of the tremendous opportunities that can and do exist for having other adults in classrooms (parents, aides, artisans, etc.), we cannot help but wonder why these opportunities don't occur more frequently.

The second way in which teaching is a lonely profession is that not only are teachers cut off from adult contact, they are also cut off from the caring process. By this I mean that nobody really cares what a teacher does as long as they don't make waves or problems. Principals don't care and parents don't care. Nobody cares either what teachers teach as long as it doesn't offend the prevailing moral codes or community standards. If teachers should ask, "What do you want me to teach?" the reply is usually, "Don't be silly, teach what is in the text," or "You ought to know what to teach if you went to college." Teaching indeed can be a lonely feeling and a lonely process.

Schooling is lonely for children too, for they also are cut off from significant relationships with their peers, other adults, and older and younger children. Our schools, with their sorting and sizing practices, isolate children into the same age group and sometimes a further step is taken to isolate by ability groups. Play periods are frequently taken by age and grade level so that interage contact is reduced. Lunch times are frequently a case of "hurry up and eat" with no talking to anyone. Is it any wonder schools are criticized as fostering and promoting dehumanization?

Pleasant Surrroundings. The physical nature of schools and classrooms frequently makes them unpleasant places to be. Instead of bright, airy, aesthetically pleasing places they are often drab, dreary and even in some instances unsafe. The physical structure of schools reminds one of boxes with the interior resembling egg crates with a color scheme typically institutional. There is also something about the way schools smell that sets them apart from the real world and adds to their dehumanizing nature.

Learning Happens Anywhere. There has also been the tendency to think that it is only in schools and with teachers that learning can occur. If it can't be learned in school, then it isn't worth knowing, has often been a justification for schooling. With this attitude, adults are literally kept out of schools even though they have many talents and skills to share with children. Fortunately, this attitude is rapidly changing so that children's experiences and interactions with more adults will promote a more humane atmosphere and introduce a wide range of values.

Openness. One practice which holds a great deal of promise for making school more humane and personalized is openness. One of the reasons open education tends to be more humane is that it focuses in on the individual as the center of the learning process. Any learning setting or curriculum which tends toward child-centeredness will stand a better chance of being more humane than one which is not. It is difficult to maintain humanness in an atmosphere which is subject centered rather than child centered because of the preoccupation with subject matter instead of children. Openness can also allow for different learning styles in both students and teachers. In my opinion, open education offers a viable alternative to the isolated, graded system used in many classrooms.

Developing Values

How Do Children Acquire Values?

Preaching. There are several views of how children gain a value system. One of the more popular views is that the value system is "taught" by the adult, be it teacher or parent. Generally, this teaching occurs through telling or exhortation on the part of the adult, teacher or parent. For example, a child may be told that it is not nice to be mean to other people and that when someone does something to you, you should "turn the other cheek." Also, children are told they should never tell a lie. This exhortation is reinforced by examples of people who have lived such a life, i.e., George Washington never told a lie. Several problems with this approach, however, are that the child usually does not have much of an opportunity to act her way into and through a value system. There is no opportunity to try out different value systems. Also, there may often be a dichotomy between what the adult advocates and what the adult actually does. This has a disconcerting effect on the child and creates a situation in which she doesn't really know how to act. Eventually she may come to the conclusion that many adults act differently from the way they say you are supposed to act and a double standard prevails, a value system for children and one for adults. In other words, don't do as I do, do as I say.

Modeling. Another view of how children develop a value system is through a modeling system by adults. Some adults think the child will develop a value system if the adult is a proper model or paragon of virtue. In this approach it is hoped that the child will imitate the adult. Several problems with this approach become rather apparent also, as many parents are quick to attest. First, a person operating on the modeling point of view assumes that the child cares enough or knows enough to model the behavior and that she wants to model the behavior. As more than one would-be modeler of behavior has discovered, much to her chagrin, it might not make any difference at all how the model behaves. Simply because we model a behavior is no guarantee that it will be copied by a child. Secondly, the modeler often assumes the behavior she models will be the behavior the child will model. It may be that another aspect or facet of the adult's behavior may be that which is modeled. For example, let's say an adult consciously models neatness for the child by being clean and well dressed. The child may not model this behavior; instead, she may model an undesirable behavior of the adult, such as playing with her hair.

Unguided Method. A third view of how children develop values is what I call the Little Bo Peep approach. Just as Little Bo Peep left her sheep alone and hoped or assumed they would come home, so also do some adults hope that if given enough time and freedom, children will develop a value system. This approach is also based on the premise that the adult is being "honest" with children by not providing a setting for value development. This believe-what-you-want-to-believe, don't-ask-me approach is directly opposite to the do-as-I-tell-you approach. The main problem here is that the child may not know what values to believe or know what he does believe.

Then, too, since no one exists in a vacuum, the value system the child does develop may lack the testing and clarification that can occur in a setting of support, guidance, and direction.

Indoctrination. Moral development is commonly fostered and encouraged through indoctrination. The schools in particular usually do a pretty good job of indoctrination by enforcing and imposing a system of values within the context of the institution. Schools believe they could not exist without certain values such as obedience and respect for authority. A second way schools promote and enforce values is through the curricular materials they adopt for use. Materials used often reflect the values of the teachers and the community. As a teacher of young children, I often read stories to my students about great Americans who demonstrated qualities of honesty, thrift, hard work, and persistence.

In a discussion of the schools and the role they play in teaching values, it is easy to lose sight of the fact that a purpose of schools is to teach or implant values in children. One of the reasons schools have been created and are funded by society is to perpetuate society and those values which society embraces and holds dear. Schools are not created to destroy society but to preserve it. They are not designed or intended to teach revolutionary practices because society wants the status quo, which is promoted by instilling the existing values.

Theorists on Moral Development

Piaget. During the past decade, a system of moral development based on a cognitive-developmental conception of morality has received a great deal of attention. Two individuals who are the leading proponents of a developmental concept of the moral growth of children are Jean Piaget and Lawrence Kohlberg. Piaget identifies the two stages of moral thinking that are typical for children in the elementary grades as "relations of constraint" and "relations of cooperation."

> The analysis of the child's moral judgments has led us perforce to the discussion of the great problem of the relations of social life to the rational consciousness. The conclusion we came to was that the morality prescribed for the individual by society is not homogeneous because society itself is not just one thing. Society is the sum of social relations, and among these relations we can distinguish two extreme types: relations of constraint, whose characteristic is to impose upon the individual from outside a system of rules with obligatory content, and relations of cooperation whose characteristic is to create within people's minds the consciousness of ideal norms at the back of all rules. Arising from the ties of authority

and unilateral respect, the relations of constraint therefore characterize most of the features of society as it exists, and in particular the relations of the child to its adult surrounding. Defined by equality and mutual respect, the relations of cooperation, on the contrary, constitute an equilib- eral limit rather than a static system.[4]

The stage of moral thinking characterized by the relations of constraint is when the child's concept of good and bad, right and wrong (and therefore what is moral) is determined by the constraints placed upon her by adults. An act is "wrong" because one's parents or the teacher says it is wrong. The child's understanding of morality is based upon the authority of adults and those values which "constrain" her.

Gradually, as the child matures and has opportunities for interaction with peers and adults, her moral thinking changes to the "relations of cooperation." This stage of personal morality is characterized by agreement among children and between children and adults about what is right, wrong, good, or bad. This level of moral development is not achieved by authority, but rather by social experiences within which opportunities are available to try out different ideas and discuss moral situations with other children and adults.

The moral stage of "relations of constraint" is characteristic for chil- dren up through grades one and two, while the stage of "relations of cooperation" would be characteristic for children in the middle and upper elementary grades. However, the real criterion for determining which devel- opmental stage a child is operating in is to determine how she is thinking, not how old she is.

Kohlberg. Lawrence Kohlberg, a follower of Piaget, also believes that the moral thinking of children occurs in developmental levels. The levels and substages of moral growth as conceptualized by Kohlberg are shown below.[5]

Level I, Preconventional Level

Morality is basically a matter of "good" or "bad" based upon a system of punishments and rewards as administered by adults in authority posi- tions. In this sense, the child is basically "hedonistic."

---

[4]Jean Piaget, *The Moral Judgment of the Child,* trans. Marjorie Gabin (New York: The Free Press, 1965), p. 395.

[5]Lawrence Kohlberg, "The Claim to Moral Adequacy of a Highest Stage of Moral Judgment," *The Journal of Philosophy* 70, no. 18 (October 25, 1973): 630–646.

Stage 1. "The punishment-and-obedience orientation." The child operates within and responds to physical consequences of behavior. Good and bad are based upon the rewards it brings her and she bases her judgments on whether or not an action will bring her pleasure.

Stage 2. "The instrumental-relativist orientation." The child's actions are motivated by the satisfaction of her needs. Consequently, interpersonal relations have their basis in arrangements of mutual convenience based on need satisfaction. "You scratch my back; I'll scratch yours."

Level II, Conventional Level

Morality is doing what is socially accepted, desired, and approved. The child conforms to, supports, and justifies the order of society.

Stage 3. "The interpersonal concordance or 'good boy—nice girl' orientation." Emphasis is on doing what a "good boy" or "nice girl" would do. The child conforms to images of what good behavior is.

Stage 4. "The 'law-and-order' orientation." Emphasis is on respect for authority, and doing what is one's duty under the law.

Level III, Postconventional Level

Morality consists of principles beyond a particular group or authority structure. The individual develops a moral system which reflects universal considerations and rights.

Stage 5. "The social-contract legalistic orientation." Right action consists of those individual rights which have been agreed upon by all society. In addition to democratic and constitutional considerations, what is "right" is relative to personal values.

Stage 6. "The universal-ethical-principle orientation." What is right is determined by universal principles of justice, reciprocity and equality. The actions of the individual are based on a combination of conscience and these ethical principles.

Just as Piaget's cognitive stages are fixed and invariant for all children, so too are Kohlberg's moral levels. All individuals through the process of moral development begin at Level I and progress through each level. No level can be skipped, nor does an individual necessarily progress through all levels. Just as intellectual development may become fixated at a particular level of development, so too can an individual become fixated at any one of the moral levels.

Implications for Classrooms

Given the theories of Piaget, Kohlberg and other programs for promoting affective education, what implications do they have for classroom practice?

First, the teacher must like and respect children. Second, the classroom climate must be accepting of individual values. Respect for children means, in part, respect for and acceptance of the value system the child brings to school and which she develops. It is usually rather easy to accept an individual with a value system similar to our own. It frequently takes more self-discipline and maturity to accept an individual with a value system different from our own. Third, teachers and schools must be willing to deal with issues, morals, and value systems other than those which they promote as a means of self-perpetuation, such as obedience and docility. During the time our nation was involved in the Watergate affair, some teachers were concerned about whether or not they should discuss in the classroom the issues involved! Their attitude should have been, dare the schools not deal with the moral issues of the times? Fourth, Kohlberg maintains that a sense of justice must prevail in the schools. This atmosphere would be the opposite of that which currently exists in many schools where students contend injustice exists based upon arbitrary institutional values. Fifth, opportunities must be provided for children to interact with peers, different age groups of children and adults in order to promote development to the higher levels of moral functioning. Sixth, students must have situations and opportunities to make decisions and discuss the results of decision making. Developing a value system cannot occur through telling or through a solitary opportunity at decision making.

Humanizing early childhood settings involves providing opportunities for children to become involved with other adults. Here a carpenter helps a child build an airplane.

Programs for Promoting Affective Development

The current interest in affective education is accompanied by the development of programs to help teachers enhance the affective atmosphere of their
classroom and provide for affective development in children. It also may be
that the present emphasis on the affective is due in part to some of the
programs designed to promote it.

Emphasis on Process

In promoting value development there is an emphasis in many of the
programs on providing an atmosphere which is conducive to valuing. This
atmosphere consists in part of a warm, supportive adult who is willing to
help children clarify their values in an honest and nonthreatening way. One
such program is detailed by Raths, Harmin, and Simon in their book *Values
and Teaching*. In their program, they do not place an emphasis on what
values children have or develop, but the emphasis is on the process by which
they acquire values. *Values and Teaching* lists the following seven processes:

1. *Choosing freely.* If something is in fact to guide one's life whether or
   not authority is watching, it must be a result of free choice. If there is
   coercion, the result is not likely to stay with one for long, especially
   when out of the range of the source of that coercion. Values must be
   freely selected if they are to be really valued by the individual.

2. *Choosing from among alternatives.* This definition of values is concerned with things that are chosen by the individual and, obviously,
   there can be no choice if there are not alternatives from which to
   choose. It makes no sense, for example, to say that one values eating.
   One really has no choice in the matter. What one may value is certain
   types of food or certain forms of eating, but not eating itself. We must
   all obtain nourishment to exist; there is no room for decision. Only
   when a choice is possible, when there is more than one alternative from
   which to choose, do we say a value can result.

3. *Choosing after thoughtful consideration of the consequences of each
   alternative.* Impulsive or thoughtless choices do not lead to values as
   we define them. For something intelligently and meaningfully to guide
   one's life, it must emerge from a weighing and an understanding. Only
   when the consequences of each of the alternatives are clearly understood can one make intelligent choices. There is an important cognitive
   factor here. A value can emerge only with thoughtful consideration of
   the range of the alternatives and consequences in a choice.

4. *Prizing and cherishing.* When we value something, it has a positive
   tone. We prize it, cherish it, esteem it, respect it, hold it dear. We are
   happy with our values. A choice, even when we have made it freely and
   thoughtfully, may be a choice we are not happy to make. We may

choose to fight in a war, but be sorry circumstances make that choice reasonable. In our definition, values flow from choices that we are glad to make. We prize and cherish the guides to life that we call values.

5. *Affirming.* When we have chosen something freely, after consideration of the alternatives, and when we are proud of our choice, glad to be associated with it, we are likely to affirm that choice when asked about it. We are willing to publicly affirm our values. We may even be willing to champion them. If we are ashamed of a choice, if we would not make our position known when appropriately asked, we would not be dealing with values but something else.

6. *Acting upon choices.* Where we have a value, it shows up in aspects of our living. We may do some reading about things we value. We are likely to form friendships or to be in organizations in ways that nourish our values. We may spend money on a choice we value. We budget time or energy for our values. In short, for a value to be present, life itself must be affected. Nothing can be a value that does not, in fact, give direction to actual living. The person who talks about something but never does anything about it is dealing with something other than a value.

7. *Repeating.* Where something reaches the stage of a value, it is very likely to reappear on a number of occasions in the life of the person who holds it. It shows up in several different situations, at several different times. We would not think of something that appeared once in a life and never again as a value. Values tend to have a persistency, tend to make a pattern in a life.[6]

These processes, when taken as a group, define valuing; the results of the entire valuing process are called values. Raths and his colleagues also outline in detail activities and methods for helping children clarify their values. Although many of the activities listed in their book would not be appropriate to preschool and primary school children, the ideas contained in the activities could be adapted to these levels. As always, the important ingredient is the attitude of teachers and their willingness to provide appropriate settings for children to be free to choose, make decisions, explore alternatives, and clarify their beliefs.

Emphasis on Success

One of the characteristics often attributed to dehumanizing school or classroom is the emphasis on and preoccupation with failure. William Glasser, in his book, *Schools without Failure,* addresses himself to the task of making schools places where children can find success.

---

[6]Louis E. Raths, Merrill Harmin, and Sidney B. Simon, *Values and Teaching: Working with Values in the Classroom* (Columbus, Ohio: Charles E. Merrill Publishing Co., 1966), pp. 28–29.

We must develop schools where children succeed, not only in our wealthy suburbs, but in all parts of our cities, from upper-middle-class neighborhoods down through the poverty-stricken central city. It is the responsibility of each individual child to work to succeed in the world, to rise above the handicaps that surround him; equally it is the responsibility of the society to provide a school system in which success is not only possible, but probable. Too much of our present educational system emphasizes failure and too many children who attend school are failing. *Unless we can provide schools where children, through a reasonable use of their capacities, can succeed, we will do little to solve the major problems of our country.* We will have more social disturbances, more people who need to be kept in jails, prisons, and mental hospitals, more people who need social workers to take care of their lives because they feel they cannot succeed in this society and are no longer willing to try.[7]

Glasser feels that when we fail children, we are denying them the development of two basic needs of all humans, the need for love and self worth which, when taken together, lead to self-identity. Of failure, Glasser says,

Very few children come to school failures, none come labeled failures; *it is school and school alone which pins the label of failure on children.* Most of them have a success identity, regardless of their homes or environments. In school they expect to achieve recognition and, with the faith of the young, they hope also to gain the love and respect of their teachers and classmates. The shattering of this optimistic outlook is the most serious problem of the elementary schools. Whatever their background, children come to school highly receptive to learning. If they fail to continue to learn at their rapid preschool rate, we may if we wish blame it on their families, their environment, or their poverty, but we would be much wiser to blame it on their experience in school. Considering the great emphasis today upon school and education, and recognizing that for most small children school is the only part of their world that exists primarily for them, we can see that school must be and is an extremely important part of their lives. If school is failing to do the job that it should do, we should not look for environmental scapegoats, we should improve the school. Many educators who work with children from "disadvantaged backgrounds" believe that *the first years of school are critical for success or failure.* I agree *completely, not only for deprived children but for all children.*[8]

It is through the changing of current failure-promoting programs that schools and teachers can provide a setting in which children can find success. This setting would utilize such strategies as whole-group meetings and open-ended discussions. Whole-group meetings (all the children in the

---

[7]William Glasser, *Schools without Failure* (New York: Harper and Row Publishers, 1969), p. 6.

[8]*Ibid.,* p. 26.

classroom) provide an opportunity for children and teacher to come to-gether in an informal setting to discuss topics the teacher feels are impor-tant, and also topics of importance to the children. These whole-group meetings can incorporate open-ended discussions that encourage the explo-ration of different values and alternative points of view. Open-ended meet-ings should be conducted in such a way that children achieve success, recognition, and feelings of self worth. In addition, these meetings and discussions provide an excellent context for the development of *inter*per-sonal and *intra*personal skills such as communication, trusting relation-ships, creative and critical thinking, responsibility, and group interaction processes.

An excellent way to introduce preschool children and primary grade children to whole-group meetings and open-ended discussions is through planning times. For example, the school day can begin with the teacher and children discussing what activities they will engage in, and why. The day can end by meeting again and discussing what the children did and how they felt about it.

Glasser also proposes the use of heterogeneous grouping (where chil-dren of differing abilities are in the same class) and elimination of the traditional A, B, C, D, F grading system.

Emphasis on Communications

The Human Development Program is a process curriculum that uses com-munication as the process and emphasizes interpersonal relations as a means of promoting emotional health and growth. The program is preven-tive in nature in that it is designed to develop positive behavioral patterns and promote discussions of feelings, thoughts, and behavior. The setting for the communication process occurs in a Magic Circle, where seven to ten children gather with a leader who can be a teacher or a trained adult. The leader follows an activity guide, which specifies topics and procedures for a daily circle session throughout a thirty-six-week period. There are activity guides for preschool, kindergarten, and grades one through six. Topics for discussion cover three broad areas: "... *awareness* (knowing what your thoughts, feelings, and actions really are), *mastery* (knowing what your abilities are and how to use them), and *social interaction* (knowing other people)."[9] These three themes are incorporated into weekly topics so that the first eighteen weeks of the preschool and kindergarten programs are as follows:

---

[9]Harold Bessel and Uvaldo Palomares, *Methods in Human Development: Magic Circle Theory Manual*, rev. Harold Bessell (La Mesa, California: Human Development Training Institute, 1973), p. 1.

First Semester
  Unit 1—Six Weeks on Awareness
        Week 1—Feeling Good
        Week 2—Pleasant Thoughts
        Week 3—Positive Behavior
        Week 4—Feeling Good
        Week 5—Pleasant Thoughts
        Week 6—Positive Behavior
  Unit 2—Six Weeks on Mastery
        Week 7—Mastery in Personal Hygiene
        Week 8—Mastery in Motor Coordination
        Week 9—Mastery in Numerical Comparisons
        Week 10—Mastery in Performance Skills
        Week 11—Mastery in Counting
        Week 12—Mastery in Perceiving Colors
  Unit 3—Six Weeks on Social Interaction
        Week 13—How Other People's Behavior Affects Me
        Week 14—How My Behavior Affects Others
        Week 15—Learning about Cooperation
        Week 16—Acquiring Social Skills
        Week 17—Learning to Offer Kind Behavior
        Week 18—Learning to Ask for Kind Behavior[10]

These topics are explored by children and the adult leader in the Magic Circle, which is characterized as ". . . a sophisticated and efficient communication system"[11] in which children use verbal communication and can also observe nonverbal communication involved wherever interpersonal interactions occur. A Magic Circle begins in the preschool and kindergarten program by having the children join hands and sit on the floor. The teacher then says, "Today let's talk about . . ." Two important guidelines that are stressed for everyone in the circle are that everyone has a turn and everyone who takes a turn is listened to. Other features of the program include the use of open-ended questions by the teacher ("How do you feel when someone is nice to you?"), the use of active listening skills (for example, using all or part of a child's statement in responding to his statement), and the creation of an atmosphere of acceptance (the child feels free and secure to talk about his thoughts, feelings and behaviors). In this kind of setting, not only do children learn more about themselves ("I'm not the only person who feels the way I do") but teachers also learn more about children by increased communication.

---

[10]Harold Bessell and Geraldine Ball, *Human Development Program, Magic Circle Activity Guide for Pre-School and Kindergarten* (La Mesa, California: Human Development Training Institute, 1972), p. 2.

[11]Bessell and Palomares, *Magic Circle Theory Manual,* p. 11.

Emphasis on Self Understanding

Another program designed to provide activities for teaching in the affective domain is *Developing Understanding of Self and Others* (DUSO) which is published by American Guidance Services. The rationale of the program is based on the concept that children must understand themselves and others if the educational process is to be a meaningful one. Through an understanding of self and others, children gain the positive self concept they need in order to realize success.

> DUSO is designed to help the child become more aware of the relationship between himself, other people, and his needs and goals. Through DUSO the child is helped to develop a sensitivity to the causal, purposive, and consequential nature of his behavior. As the child comes to perceive the purposes and goals of his behavior, he is more likely to recognize the basis of his faulty relationships with others.[12]

The eight units in the program are built around eight developmental tasks or themes as identified by school personnel throughout the United States. A developmental task is identified as those tasks the majority of children must encounter and master through the process of growth. The eight units are as follows:

    I. Understanding and Accepting Self
    II. Understanding Feelings
   III. Understanding Others
   IV. Understanding Independence
    V. Understanding Goals and Purposeful Behavior
   VI. Understanding Mastery, Competence and Resourcefulness
  VII. Understanding Emotional Maturity
VIII. Understanding Choices and Consequences[13]

The program consists of two levels, one designed for kindergarten and primary grades and the other for the upper primary levels. Both programs are intended for use with children in all social, economic and cultural settings.

The program has three specific objectives which are:

---

[12]Don Dinkmeyer, *Developing Understanding of Self and Others,* Manual DUSO D-1 (Circle Pines, Minnesota: American Guidance Service, 1970), p. 10.
   [13]*Ibid.,* p. 11.

1. Learn more words for feelings.
2. Learn that feelings, goals, and behavior are dynamically related.
3. Learn to talk freely about feelings, goals, and behavior.[14]

Each of the eight units is divided into "cycles" with each cycle composed of the following activities:

1. A story to be followed by discussion.
2. A problem situation to be followed by discussion.
3. A role playing activity.
4. A puppet activity.
5. Several supplementary activities to be used as desired.
6. Recommended supplementary reading (stories to be read to the class by the teacher or read independently by individual pupils).[15]

Materials that accompany the program consist of hand puppets (DUSO the Dolphin is the central character of the program), two story books, records or cassette tapes, posters, puppet activity cards, role playing cards, group discussion cards and puppet props. The use of the materials is explained in sufficient detail in a teacher's manual which accompanies the program. All the materials are packaged in a metal carrying case.

Two student activities which receive emphasis in the program are group discussion and role playing. In the group discussion sessions, teachers are encouraged to: develop relationships of respect; make sure children understand the purpose of the discussions; be sensitive to the feelings of the group; allow the group to set its own limits; encourage silent members to participate when ready; promote student cooperation; point out similarities and differences between students' ideas; clarify implied feelings; emphasize positive feedback; help students express their ideas; and help students summarize and evaluate learnings.

Role playing, or the dramatization of a situation, is used as a means of encouraging a frank, open and honest exchange of ideas and emotions. In role playing situations, the teacher is the initiator of the setting for the dramatization and determines what roles will be dramatized.

Since the teacher is in control of the process, children generally feel free and secure to express themselves without fear of adult censure. Role playing is also an excellent context for children to become aware of other children's points of view through seeing, hearing, and experiencing how other children feel.

---

[14] *Ibid.*, p. 12.
[15] *Ibid.*, p. 13.

Strengths of Affective Development Programs

Particular strengths of the above programs and similar ones on the market would seem to be:

1. Children begin to realize that negative feelings are held (thought) by everyone. In many instances, children seem relieved when they find out that other children have the same or similar thoughts they have. I recently observed a Magic Circle in which a child was talking about his wanting to steal a particular item. When he was finished talking, another child exclaimed, "I've felt like doing that, too!"

2. Listening skills which are developed as a result of participation in the programs may be carried over into children's everyday lives. Children who participate in these programs tend to be more aware of what people are saying and consequently are more perceptive to how people feel.

In implementing the above programs and any program which deals with values and valuing, several points need close attention and consideration:

1. The teacher is the key to the program. While the importance of the way the teacher handles the circle and discussion sessions is stressed in the manuals, individual teachers need to guard against imposing their value system on the children.

2. The concepts contained in the programs tend to be cumulative. Topics in grade three may be based on an understanding of concepts presented in a lower grade or level of the materials. For example, a topic such as "Something I Did Wrong" should be discussed and explored only after students have had many opportunities to talk about the good things they have done. In addition, by talking about positive feelings, the children and the teacher gain the confidence and insights necessary to handle negative feelings.

   This does not necessarily mean that when implementing a program dealing with values that a school district must implement it a grade at a time beginning in first grade. What is important to remember, however, is that you as a teacher should determine what background of understanding you and your children need prior to involvement in a particular topic.

It is interesting to note that *The Human Development Program* and others like it are based on the assumption that if the mental health of children is enriched and expanded, then children may grow up to be better functioning adults. From this point of view, the programs can be perceived as preventive in nature in that the enrichment of the mental health of children may have a direct correlation to reduced adult problems. This preventive approach can in some respects be viewed as social engineering. Can societal problems such as drug usage and racism be ameliorated through the use of programs that have the potential for enriched mental health of young children? Only time will tell.

Issues

Should We Use Teaching Machines?

Critics who see the educational system as a dehumanizing process believe that certain techniques of instruction, methodologies, and procedures encourage dehumanization. While they acknowledge the need for providing for individual differences as a requisite of a humane setting, they object to certain procedures that have been designed to provide for individualization, such as programmed instruction and teaching machines. Critics substantiate this charge on the basis that if the child is "programmed" much like one would program a robot, then the result is a robotlike child who works through programmed material without ever being given the opportunity to think or inquire if what he is learning is of any importance or consequence. Certainly this could be the case if it were the only way the child could learn. However, there is no reason to believe that programmed instruction or teaching machines dehumanize education if used correctly. It is rather the way materials are used and how children are treated that dehumanizes the educative process. In actuality, teaching machines and programmed learning free teachers from a host of unnecessary classroom trivia so they can use their time and talents with children and their individual differences. In addition, critics feel that programmed materials and machines give children no opportunity for valuing. However, some material that is taught best by programming, such as math, may not be value laden at the preschool and primary levels.

Critics also believe that teaching machines tend to remove the student from direct interaction with the teacher. In this regard, the teacher is seen as an omnipresent ingredient in the teaching-learning process. However, we know that children can learn effectively from a wide variety of sources and that the teacher is only one source of information and processes. It might well be that some children might be better off if they had more opportunities for relief from an ever-present teacher. Children who are given opportunities for independent learning by any means benefit in the long run due to increased independence and enhanced self-image.

Is Structure Necessary?

Quite often, too, the enthusiasm of the educational critics leads them to advocate an entirely new kind of school, not just a reshaping or restructuring of schools as they currently exist. These new schools, often called *free schools,* are conceptualized as places where children can grow and become without undue adult supervision. The term *free* comes from two sources. First is the idea that the school itself should be free from many of the restraints and requirements that public school systems normally impose. Second is the belief that the child should be free from many of the restrictions of the public school, even to the point of freedom from required attendance. The urge to be unfettered from restraints has caused some of the schools to be located in out-of-the-way places and rural settings. One of the problems, however, with some free schools has been that in their advocacy of freedom they have created curricula without much substance. The result of settings without structure is a situation where everyone, including the children, are left to their own devices and little is achieved. Most people, including Pestalozzi who tried to rear his son in a context of absolute freedom patterned after *Emile,* come to realize sooner or later that the results of leaving children to their own devices leaves much to be desired.

Can We Allow Individual Values?

While we have always paid lip service to individual differences, we have probably been more willing to recognize individual differences at the cognitive level than at the affective level. Fortunately, schools are starting to pay more attention to the realization that children can and should have different values, one from the other. In addition, it is becoming increasingly apparent that values people hold should be talked about rather than repressed and hidden. Hopefully, teachers of young children will pay more attention to the needs and differences of all children, including their feelings, emotions and values. It is an extremely easy process for adults to impose their values on children, without really being aware that they are imposing. Children should be helped to develop their own value systems and in the process clarify the values that they have held and are developing. During this process adults should not impose values of right or wrong or belittle the responses that children make.

*Teachers who are aware of children's feelings realize
responsibility promotes a positive self-image. Knowing he has
successfully completed a clean-up task, this boy shows his
growth of self-esteem.*

A problem with classroom instruction that often occurs in the area of
valuing is that teachers think they must present right and wrong solutions
to problems of values. However, systems of clear-cut values exist only in
school classrooms. Although teachers are aware that such systems do not
occur in the real world, they persist in presenting such solutions.

Sometimes, too, teachers seem to have a felt need or moral obligation
to try to justify particular values. What can happen in such cases is that
teachers end up trying to convince students of the goodness or rightness of
a particular value instead of helping students clarify their values.

How Should We Deal with the Affective?

Another issue educators are faced with in the process of humanizing classrooms is the problem of teachers not knowing how to provide goals and
activities in the affective domain. It would seem that many of our training
programs for teachers have not been designed to help them deal effectively
with this area. In the preparation of preservice teachers, schools of education have acted exactly the way we find inservice teachers acting with
children. It is much easier to teach and work with subject matter than it
is to deal with values and the exploration of feelings and emotions. Thus
subject matter is emphasized by most classrooms, particularly after the
child enters first grade. There has, however, been a tendency on the part
of preschool teachers almost intuitively to recognize that the affective domain is as important as, if not more important than, the cognitive domain.

Therefore, many preschool programs have traditionally emphasized social and emotional development for young children. The whole spectrum of teacher education, including teacher training, needs to focus more attention on the affective domain so that children at all levels can benefit from an affective-based curriculum.

There is undoubtedly a great deal of interest in values and value clarification today. There is so much interest that it is possible to find people who call themselves experts literally behind every bush. It seems that people who call themselves experts in value clarification are rushing in where most of society, up till now, has feared to tread. There is a very real danger that in our rush to clarify values and to emphasize the development of value processes in children, we could end up with what I call a "messing-around-with-values" problem. I see a tendency on the part of some educators to "mess around" or "dabble" in the whole area of values and valuing. In this "messing-around" process, do we do more harm than good? Do we run a danger of being casual and careless about values and value processing? I think in some instances we have come dangerously close. Recently, I witnessed a teacher-training program in which the trainer, at the end of a half-day session, encouraged teachers to go back into the classrooms and use the techniques that had been used during the inservice training program. What the trainer failed to sensitize the teachers to was that many of the activities used with them were entirely inappropriate for use with children. Only through a process of modification and adjustment could some of the activities be implemented. Without this modification and adjustment process, children could almost be forced into situations that could potentially be emotionally and psychologically painful to them. I think two questions need to be raised for all teachers. "Do I know what I'm doing in clarifying values?" and "Is what I'm doing good for children?" It would seem to me that until these questions can be answered, then "messing around" with values and value clarification should not continue.

BIBLIOGRAPHY

Bessell, Harold, and Ball, Geraldine. *Human Development Program—Magic Circle Activity Guide for Pre-School and Kindergarten.* LaMesa, California: Human Development Training Institute, 1972.

Bessell, Harold, and Palomares, Uvaldo. *Methods in Human Development—Magic Circle Theory Manual.* Revised by Harold Bessell. LaMesa, California: Human Development Training Institute, 1973.

Dinkmeyer, Don. *Developing Understanding of Self and Others,* Manual DUSO D–1. Circle Pines, Minnesota: American Guidance Service, 1970.

Glasser, William. *Schools without Failure.* New York: Harper and Row Publishers, 1969.

Kohlberg, Lawrence. "The Claim to Moral Adequacy of a Highest State of Moral Judgment." *The Journal of Philosophy* 70, no. 18 (October, 1973): 630–646.

Piaget, Jean. *The Moral Judgment of the Child.* Translated by Marjorie Gabin. New York: The Free Press, 1965.

Raths, Louis E.; Harmin, Merrill; and Simon, Sidney B. *Values and Teaching: Working with Values in the Classroom.* Columbus, Ohio: Charles E. Merrill Publishing Co., 1966.

Shapp, Milton J. U.S. Department of Health, Education, and Welfare, Office of Education, Commonwealth of Pennsylvania. *The Report of The Citizens Commission on Basic Education,* Title IV, Section 402, and Title V-A, Section 503, E.S.E.A., November, 1973.

Silberman, Charles E. *Crisis in the Classroom.* New York: Vintage Books, 1971.

FOR FURTHER READING AND STUDY

Ashton-Warner, Sylvia. *Spearpoint.* New York: Alfred A. Knopf, Inc., 1972.
In describing her experiences with American school children, the concept of "organic teaching" (from the inner world, outward) is introduced. A good discussion of a humanistic approach to learning in an open setting along with some astonishing conclusions about American society.

Howe, Leland W.; Kirschenbaum, Howard; and Simon, Sidney B. *Values Clarification—A Handbook of Practical Strategies for Teachers and Students.* New York: Hart Publishing Co., Inc., 1972.
An excellent handbook of specific strategies for developing students' valuing processes. Each strategy is accompanied by a purpose, suggested procedure, suggestions to the teachers, and variations.

Johnson, David W. *Reaching Out.* Englewood Cliffs, New Jersey: Prentice-Hall, Inc., 1973.
Will help the reader develop and maintain effective interpersonal skills. These skills should result in a more humane teacher and a more humane classroom.

Kraft, Arthur. *The Living Classroom.* New York: Harper and Row, Publishers, 1975.
Subtitled *Putting Humanistic Education into Practice,* this book does exactly that, setting forth the skills necessary for teachers who want living, exciting classrooms. Selections from well-known authors who advocate humanistic approaches provide an even balance between theory and practice.

Moustakas, Clark E., and Perry, Cereta. *Learning to Be Free.* Englewood Cliffs, New Jersey: Prentice-Hall, Inc., 1972.
An account of the author's attempts to bring human resources into the classroom and restore human values and humanness to learning. Contains many practical ideas and suggestions for teacher and adult training.

For Further Study and Involvement

1. Observe a group of five-year-old children at classroom play and note evidences of their social development in their attitudes toward each other.

2. Observe the physical appearance of schools and classrooms. In what ways are they dehumanizing to children? How would you change some features if you could? What place did children's works, products, etc., have in the classroom? What does this tell you about classroom atmosphere and values?

3. Observe an early childhood setting to determine the different learning styles of children. Were children given an opportunity to use these learning styles? How can the different learning styles of children be used to humanize a classroom?

4. After observing an early childhood classroom can you find any evidence of the philosophies you read about in Chapter 2?

5. Do you think that educators today believe in the concept of natural depravity, i.e., that children are born "bad"? Can you find any evidence for this in classrooms you remember or have visited?

6. How important are the character and attitude of the classroom teacher to a child's mental growth and development during his primary years?

7. Recall your own elementary teachers and decide which of their characteristics you would imitate and which you would avoid imitating as a teacher. Why did you choose the way you did?

8. Do you feel that your teachers taught moral values? If so, cite specific examples. How do you feel about this?

9. Can you find evidence of values being taught in present-day early childhood education programs? How do you feel about the values that are being taught?

10. What one value above all others would you choose to teach to children? Explain why you made the choice you did.

11

Teaching and Beyond
Putting It All Together

American society is currently experiencing a fascination for the future. At no other time in our short history have we been so involved with projections about what life will be like in the twenty-first century and beyond. A general consensus of opinion on the part of the future forecasters is that regardless of what the features of everyday life will be like, learning will play a dominant role and will be considered a lifelong process. As learning is accepted and legitimized as a lifelong process, more money will be spent on educating and more people will be involved in the delivery system necessary to achieve this goal.

While any projection of the precise details of what education will be like in the future is a risky venture, it is possible, nevertheless, to have a broad picture of the educative process through an examination of current trends.

Current Trends in Education

Competency-based Education

Worth of CBTE. There is a cluster of trends that can be categorized as teacher-education trends. One of the major of these is competency-based teacher education (CBTE). Many educators and students are seriously questioning if the completion of courses in how to teach children results in competency to teach children. There is a growing realization that credits earned do not guarantee good teaching and the ability to regurgitate facts from a college lecture has little relationship to the ability to provide a meaningful learning environment for children. Specifically, competency-based education involves the demonstration of specified competencies by individuals as a prerequisite for being admitted to a profession or exited from a program. Competency is generally defined as the ability to perform or do a specific task. Instead of being asked to memorize the ingredients or factors in a learning environment, an inservice teacher would be asked to demonstrate, in a field setting, the ability to provide a learning environment for children. In a competency program, an individual would have an unspecified amount of time to demonstrate competencies considered necessary for entry into teaching as opposed to the four years that are usually required. (Refer back to the chapter on Head Start for a detailed discussion of the CDA competency-based program.) As with many trends, a great deal of heat has been generated by this approach to teacher training. Proponents view it as a realistic, relevant, and accountable method of training teachers. Opponents view it as a dehumanizing, inoperable fad. They see teaching reduced to a set of isolated skills which may or may not have any bearing on the process of learning and teaching.

What Competencies Are Necessary for Effective Teaching? While the educators of teachers have no difficulty specifying courses and number of credit hours believed necessary for teaching, they do have difficulty specifying competencies involved in effective teaching. Attempts at specifying competencies necessary for good teaching in general (known as generic competencies) lead quite naturally into the problem of role definition for teachers. For what role should a teacher be educated? It is not an easy question to answer and is one colleges and universities find perplexing. For example, should the role of the teacher be primarily one of working with parents, children, designing curriculum materials, or all three? In a competency-based program, the role conceptualized for a teacher is generally reflected in the competencies specified. The problem seems to be, however, that not enough colleges have thought specifically about the role for which it is training teachers. This is a critical topic especially since it involves professionals who will be teaching in the twenty-first century.

Additional Elements of CBTE. If CBTE continues to gain support, then it is likely that components of a teacher education program will include the demonstration of competencies, the preparation for and demonstration of these competencies in a field setting, a variable time frame for completion of the program, and the replacement of typical lecture courses with modules of instruction designed to help the student demonstrate competencies.

Field-based Education

Until recently, people agreed that the training of teachers should occur in colleges of education. However, since the 1960s, this assumption has been challenged with increasing frequency. Regardless of whether or not the CBTE movement becomes widespread, the trend toward teacher training in field settings (actual early childhood classrooms) will continue. Many colleges of education have entered into consortia relationships with public school districts whereby inservice teachers spend blocks of time in the schools (renamed clinical settings or teacher centers) under the supervision of college methods professors (renamed clinical professors).

Lack of Relevancy. Can training occur meaningfully in traditional college settings? The critics of the traditional college approaches include not only the romantic and avant-garde, but also taxpayers and students who fail to see a relationship between theoretical college teaching and the real world of public schools, day care centers and Head Start programs. The question is essentially one of relevancy and effectiveness. Students are saying that college classrooms are not relevant to the real world of teaching in good early childhood programs.

Many opportunities exist for volunteer service. By volunteering, this adult can decide whether or not she would like to teach.

This lack of relevancy is particularly true if students have experienced the exhilaration of helping or teaching in a classroom. To paraphrase the World

War I song, how are we going to keep them in college classrooms, once they have worked with children? Undoubtedly, more and more colleges will be forced to provide field-based settings for the education of teachers. More of a justification will also have to occur in demonstrating a relationship between required college courses and teaching children. Education courses are not the only ones whose legitimacy is being called into question. The courses that students have been told will provide them with "culture" are also seen by them as having little relation to teaching. Colleges and universities will change out of necessity to meet the changes demanded by students and society.

Providing Practical Experience. There is also a definite trend toward having inservice teachers gain practical experience early in their educational program. The past practice of having students experience teaching in the final semester of their senior year is no longer viewed as a sane or practical approach to the education of teachers. The number of teachers currently employed who completed four years of training only to discover in their final semester they didn't like children or teaching is greater than we care to admit.

Teacher Role

The role of the teacher will continue to be reconceptualized. Teachers will be trained for roles of working with parents, designing curriculum materials, and planning programs for other para-professional personnel, such as teacher aides, to implement. Many schools currently operate a system of differentiated staffing which utilizes staff members with differing role functions, levels of responsibility, training, and salary. Undoubtedly, this trend toward role specialization and differentiation will be encouraged through rapidly rising property taxes, which taxpayers are objecting to with increasing regularity. While higher salaries will continue to be paid for highly skilled, specialized and supervisory teaching, less specialized functions, which require less skill and training and therefore involving less pay, will be performed by other personnel.

The differentiated staffing trend will be accompanied by differentiated teaching. More attention will be paid to the different learning styles of students. Whereas in the past students were taught by telling and reading from textbooks, students are becoming involved in other modes of learning such as media, excursions into the community, and construction projects. The argument for this approach maintains that if students can learn best through hearing (the auditory mode) then they should be encouraged to learn through audio tape rather than given no alternative but the printed page. Increased attention to learning styles will also involve increased use of concrete learning materials, self-selection of activities and utilization of students as tutors.

Accountability

Accountability will assume a more important role in learning and teaching. As the cost of education continues to increase and the taxpayer finds himself burdened with the high cost of education, more demands will be made for accountability from teachers and schools. Curricula appearing frivolous and unrelated to discipline, the three R's, and the world of work will probably find themselves on the short end of the money supply. Efforts by teachers to blame children and their backgrounds for failure to learn will be rejected and teachers will be challenged to develop programs which will provide children the help they need for success.

Humanization

Humanizing the classroom will not only continue, but will gain in acceptance and application. More attention will be given to strategies and procedures designed to make the classroom a more conducive place to live and learn. Transactional analysis (TA) with its emphasis on enhancing communication between teacher and student will be an increasingly popular topic in college classrooms and inservice programs. Techniques and methods of value clarification for increased teacher and pupil awareness will also become more popular.

The rights of children as individuals and groups will be clarified and redefined. These rights and responsibilities of children before the law will be extended into the classroom and will be contained in student bills of rights. More people will recognize that many of the artibrary rules of schools have not benefited nor promoted the mental health of students. Most of the benefits associated with the increased emphasis on the rights of students will probably accrue to students in high schools. The extent to which young children will benefit will depend upon the maturity and understanding of the adults who design and operate early childhood programs.

Utilization of Parents

The late 70s and early 80s will see a renewed effort to involve parents in educational processes, such as Home Start. More ways will be explored for utilizing parents as teachers of their own children in light of the effect the environment and early experiences have on later learning. Efforts will also be made to increase and strengthen linkages between the home and the school by involving parents as advisors and volunteers. Many parents are willing and able to give of their time and talent to the educational process, and the public schools will finally recognize this pool of untapped talent. Teachers will consequently devote more time to explaining to parents instructional processes and educational goals. Reporting to parents via the personal conference will increase in frequency and effectiveness. Teachers will use these parental conferences as one means of helping parents and themselves understand the unique characteristics and needs of each child. Parents will be encouraged to help in the implementation and extension of educational strategies designed by teachers to meet the unique needs of their children.

Demand for Alternative Education

As incomes and educational levels of the population continue to rise, there will be an increased demand for alternative types of education. These demands will be met by the private sector, causing an increase in the number and kind of private preschool programs. While the issue surrounding the propriety of making a profit on young children's education will continue to be hotly debated, large corporations who manufacture learning materials will nevertheless view the operation of learning centers as one means of utilizing their products.

Occupational Awareness

While parents have always been concerned about the employment for their children following their graduation or exit from school, educators have not always responded to this concern. The current interest in occupational awareness and career orientation reflects the growing demand of the public for increased accountability in this area. Discussion of the world of work and programs of occupational awareness and occupational skills through related activities will occur in most early childhood programs.

Packaged Curricula

There will be a continued emphasis on packaging units of curricular materials for use as complete programs in early childhood education classrooms. This emphasis will necessitate a more articulate, critical teacher willing to examine these materials on the basis of goals and objectives locally developed.

The Future Outlook

Given the above trends, it is possible to hypothesize what the early childhood education classroom of the near future might be like. It will take place in an architecturally open space characterized by multiage grouping, and a curriculum personalized and individualized to the needs and interests of children. There will be a higher ratio of paid assistants and parent volunteers to students than is present in today's classrooms. These assistants and volunteers will perform many of the instructional tasks now assumed by the classroom teacher.

Learning experiences for the child, while based upon his interests, will also be controlled by specified goals and objectives personalized to the child and the needs of society. These goals will stress the subject matter of reading, writing, and arithmetic. The teacher will be more of a specialist, and this role will be revealed through the designing of individual learning programs, planning with parents and volunteers, and creating an environment that facilitates learning. The learning atmospheres will be emotionally healthy places, and the mental health of children as individuals and as learners will have priority in the learning environment.

While the above scenario represents what I conceive the classroom of the near future might be like, many of you will recognize it as possessing the qualities and characteristics of some existing classrooms. While this is true, it is nevertheless a questionable matter as to the number of classrooms in America that will have these characteristics. There will continue to be, whether we as educators personally like it or not, traditional classrooms where traditional teachers, in spite of their good intentions, will fall short of their highest potential and prevent the fullest development of the children they teach.

You and Early Childhood Education

It seems appropriate as we conclude our discussion of early childhood education that I share with you some thoughts about the profession of teaching, and what you can do to make your career happy and productive for both you and the children you will teach.

I make no claim for originality or universality. Many of the ideas listed below have probably been said in one form or another at some other time and there are other ideas that some professors may think are worthy of inclusion. I encourage addition or subtraction from what I say as you and your professor see fit. Most of what I believe is based on optimism and enthusiasm for teaching. Teaching can be a great and rewarding career for those who want it to be so. With this in mind, then, I encourage you to do the following:

1. *Go where the jobs are to find employment.* It is only natural for you to be concerned about finding a job, for, after all, your hopes and dreams about teaching cannot be fulfilled unless you get employed! The two factors most responsible for the declining demand for teachers are colleges training too many teachers, and the trend toward zero population growth. However, I firmly believe there will always be a teaching job for the individual who is willing to look for a job and go where the jobs are. Most problems of teacher oversupply are usually geographical. Too many students limit themselves by thinking they have to live at home after they graduate or that the only place for them to teach is the elementary school they attended.

2. *Seek every opportunity for experiences, with all kinds of children, in all kinds of settings.* Too often individuals limit themselves to experiences in public school settings. Opportunities exist through church schools, day care, babysitting, and children's clothing stores to broaden and expand your knowledge of children. These experiences can often be work related and can be doubly rewarding. Sometimes these positions may pay little or not at all. However, be willing to volunteer your services, for volunteer positions have a way of leading to paid positions. Many career possibilities and opportunities can become available through the volunteer route.

Good teachers have made learning a happy experience for these children.

3. *Honestly analyze your attitudes and feelings toward children.* Do
   you really want to teach, or would you be happier and more suited
   to another field or profession? During your experiences with children, you should constantly test your attitude toward teaching;
   too many decisions about teaching have been based on romantic
   memories of childhood, which certainly is not a safe basis for
   decision making. If you decide that teaching isn't for you because
   of how you feel about children, then by all means don't teach. In
   the long run you will be doing yourself and children a big favor.

4. *Explore the possibilities that exist for educational service in areas
   and fields other than the public school.* Don't limit your career
   choices and alternatives because of your limited conception of the
   teacher's role. Too often students think the only thing teacher
   education prepares an individual for is to teach. Other opportunities for service include religious organizations, federal, state and
   local agencies, private educational enterprises, hospitals, libraries,
   and social work. Don't ignore opportunities that exist for graduate study through assistantships.

   I would suspect some of you will find employment in jobs you
   currently don't know about and which may not exist at the present
   time. One of my advisees in early childhood education was recently hired by a private corporation to help gather data for an
   analysis of jobs performed in day care programs. When this student entered college, the job for which she was hired didn't exist
   and she was able to gain the job, in part, because of her willingness
   to rethink her role as a participant in the educational process.

5. *Employ every educational opportunity to enhance your training
   program and career.* Through wise course selection, weaknesses
   can be strengthened and new alternatives explored. For example,
   if your program of studies requires the selection of a fixed number
   of social science credits, use these to explore such areas as sociol-
   ogy and anthropology which have fascinating relationships to
   education. If there is an opportunity for field work and field
   experiences in lieu of courses, by all means select the field work.
   Independent studies can often be designed to include experiences
   for enhancing your educational background. Many service agencies such as Goodwill Industries will work cooperatively with
   colleges of education to provide work experiences, under supervision, for college credit. Music requirements might be used to learn
   to play the piano.

   One of the implications for exploring alternatives is that you
   meet regularly and often with your educational advisor to plan

your program of studies to fit your needs. Too many students plan their own program or follow a predetermined one in a catalogue, much to their sorrow as they approach graduation.

6. *Start now to develop a philosophy of education and teaching.* You may feel it is trite of me to encourage you to do this and you may be saying to yourself, "Oh, no! Not another person telling me to write a philosophy." I realize you may have been asked to write a philosophy and you probably did so to satisfy an assignment. I'm not asking you to write one. I'm encouraging you to develop one, and therein lies the difference. Your philosophy should be based upon what you believe about children and the learning process, how you think children should be taught, and should summarize and explain your beliefs at the present time. A philosophy of teaching serves as a guide for classroom practice.

So many teachers fill the school day and the lives of children with unrelated activities found in teacher magazines. They say to themselves while looking through a magazine, "Wouldn't this be a nice activity for children to do?" without ever asking themselves questions such as, "Does it fit in with my objectives?" and, most importantly of all, "Is it good for children?" So much of teaching is not based on any philosophy at all.

I hope that you take what we have talked about in this book and ideas from readings and other people, and on that basis begin to develop your philosophy. This philosophy can then be incorporated with and adjusted to the school where you will teach. It is on this basis that goals and objectives are developed that provide the guidance and the context in which teaching occurs. Your philosophy may be the only guide to help you teach, for as surprising as it may seem, many schools operate without a written philosophy. Basing your teaching on a philosophy will make the difference between whether or not you are going to fill up children's school days with unrelated activities or whether activities and experiences will be directed toward helping children learn and develop to their fullest potential. As you develop your philosophy during preservice training, seek every opportunity to discuss it with friends, professors and inservice teachers. Be willing to revise your philosophy constantly as you gain new knowledge and insights. What I believe today is very different from the beliefs I held as a beginning teacher.

I don't mean to imply that the development of a philosophy will automatically solve your problems and make you a good teacher. This is not the case, but it will provide you a foundation on which to build a good teaching career and will also help protect you from what I call the "Alice-in-Wonderland Approach" to teaching. Alice asked the Cheshire Cat:

"Would you tell me, please, which way I ought to go from here?"
"That depends a good deal on where you want to get to," said the Cat.
"I don't much care where _____," said Alice.
"Then it doesn't matter which way you go," said the Cat.[1]

Unfortunately, some teachers behave like Alice.

An added benefit of developing a philosophy is that it will enable you to respond in a meaningful way during a job interview. Invariably your philosophy of education is a topic of discussion during the interview, and it is surprising the number of interviewees who are ill prepared to respond.

7. *Examine in detail your willingness to dedicate yourself to teaching.* Acquaint yourself thoroughly and constantly with what teaching involves. This examination cannot be done by remembering what you thought or think teaching is like. Visit many different kinds of schools. Is the school atmosphere one in which you want to spend the rest of your life? Talk with many different teachers and determine from them what is involved in teaching. Ask yourself such questions as: "Am I willing to work hard?" "Am I willing to give more time to teaching than a teaching contract may specify?" "Are teachers the kind of people with whom I want to work?" "Do I have the physical energy required for teaching?" "Do I have the enthusiasm necessary for good teaching?"

While these questions by no means exhaust the ones available for asking, they will, if honestly examined, make you more sensitive to the demands and conditions of teaching. Teaching is often undertaken without the necessary introspection for what might properly be called fitness for teaching. The result, of course, is unhappy people who view themselves as stuck with and in the profession.

These seven things, if done with any amount of effort and sincerity, will help you in a self-analysis and evaluation for teaching. Should you ignore them, it is not unreasonable to expect your career in teaching to resemble Alice's journey through Wonderland.

---

[1]Lewis Carroll, *Alice in Wonderland,* ed. Donald J. Gray (New York: W. W. Norton and Company, Inc., 1971), p. 51.

As you enter your chosen profession of teaching, there are several other suggestions which may help you to a career which is more productive and rewarding.

1. *Adjust to the ever-emerging new careers of teaching and society.* Careers of any kind are a product of society molded out of the needs of society and the resources which society has available. Many teachers and schools waste potential and miss opportunities because of their unwillingness to adjust to changing circumstances and conditions.

2. *Be willing to improve skills and increase knowledge.* The obvious way many teachers choose to do this is by returning to school. This is usually encouraged by state certification requirements that specify minimum number of credits for a permanent or continuing certification, and many teachers fulfill these requirements through a master's degree. A trend in teacher certification, however, seems to be the completion of certification requirements through the accumulation of a specified number of "points." Points may be gained through college credits, inservice programs, attendance at professional meetings and conferences, and other professional involvements. Too often, however, these miniumum requirements are viewed as maximum requirements or as hurdles to be jumped and once requirements are met, little, if any, effort at self-improvement is undertaken.

These children have the benefit of a teacher who is dealing with the topics presented in this chapter.

Another method of self-improvement is through reading. Although we frequently overlook this approach, we can still keep current by reading. The self-discipline we need to read can often be encouraged by joining an educational book club and participating in a discussion group.

A not-so-obvious method of self-improvement, but one that works quite well, is to force change by periodically teaching at different grade levels. Personally, I never thought there was any particular merit in being able to say you taught your entire career at the same grade level. Also, by always teaching at the same grade level, there is the very real danger of having the same teaching experience repeated year after year. By changing grade levels, teachers can gain new insights and perspectives on children and teaching.

Whatever the method you choose for self-improvement, you should recognize the need for constant retraining. While some school districts do provide opportunities for retraining, the majority of the responsibility will be yours.

3. *Be willing to try new things.* It is surprising how deep a rut some teachers can make for themselves and when this happens, teaching becomes a drudgery. Surprisingly, a teacher can get in a rut immediately upon entering the profession, for some new teachers feel that their college education has provided them with the one right, only, and true way to teach children. This attitude often results in new teachers trying to teach with a preconceived, fixed notion of what teaching is. The result of this, of course, is they become so preoccupied fulfilling this image of good teaching they seldom relax enough to try new ideas.

In spite of new ideas and methods that are available for consideration, it is surprising how few are tried or implemented by the rank-and-file teacher. Many innovations and good ideas die simply because they were never tried. It is my opinion that this may well happen with open education. It may never realize its potential because too many teachers are fearful, for one reason or another, of even trying to implement some of its concepts.

Attempts to try something new may have to occur in the face of colleague pressure in opposition to change. Recently I had an opportunity to interact with a group of teachers from school districts where it is customary to use corporal punishment with kindergarten children. Several teachers expressed their personal concern about this but felt corporal punishment was expected of them by other teachers. They also expressed feelings of guilt from not using corporal punishment. In other words, they, in a very real sense, had withdrawal pains of guilt feelings, uncertainty, and lack of confidence by attempting something new!

4. *Be enthusiastic for teaching and in your teaching.* Time and again the one attribute that seems to separate the good teacher from the mediocre teacher is enthusiasm. I don't wish to become embroiled in the argument whether you believe that one must be born with enthusiasm or that one can learn to be enthusiastic, *trying* to be enthusiastic will help a great deal.

5. *Maintain an open-door policy in teaching.* This policy means that as a teacher, you welcome into your classroom, parents, colleagues, interested lay personnel, college students, and all who want to know what schools are doing. It is often remarked that teaching is a lonely profession, and indeed it can be, as we discussed. But it need not be that way. Too often, teachers are so busy keeping people out of their classrooms that they fail to see the advantages resulting from an open-door policy. First, parents want to know what the schools are doing. Research indicates that when parents are aware of the policies, philosophy and procedures of the school, there is support for these programs. Where knowledge is vague or nonexistent, fear, suspicion, and nonsupport are the result. Second, parents and other people in the community are eager to help in and with school programs. We should utilize their talents and capitalize on their willingness to serve. Third, there are many talents that exist in a community that can enhance a school's program. We have wasted much of this talent by ignoring it and denying it access to the classroom. The educational setting should be viewed as a community of scholars—which includes teachers, students, parents, and anyone else who can contribute meaningfully.

Since this book has been concerned with the education of young children, it is only appropriate as it concludes for us to reflect on some thoughts about this topic. First, I would hope that you care enough about children to face squarely the issue of becoming a good teacher. If you have read this text, then you undoubtedly realize by now my concern that this issue is frequently avoided and only half-heartedly addressed. Second, you as prospective teachers must be committed to improving the quality of school life and, by extension, the quality of student life. Students and teachers spend an incredible amount of time in a school setting. Why shouldn't this environment be of the highest quality? The best environment many students have an opportunity to enjoy is the school. For this reason alone, they deserve better than what we have often been willing to provide.

BIBLIOGRAPHY

Gray, Donald J., ed. *Lewis Carroll's Alice in Wonderland.* New York: W. W. Norton and Company, Inc., 1971.

FOR FURTHER READING AND STUDY

Greer, Mary, and Rubinstein, Bonnie. *Will the Real Teacher Please Stand Up?* Pacific Palisades, California: Goodyear Publishing Co., Inc., 1972.
A delightful and extremely readable collection of stories, poems, ideas, games, activities, philosophies in a handbook format. Stresses an individualized humanistic approach to education. Good reading for preservice teachers which will help them keep their enthusiasm for teaching.

Gross, Beatrice, and Gross, Ronald, eds. *Will It Grow in a Classroom?* New York: Dell Publishing Co., Inc., 1974.
A collection of incidents and experiences written by teachers for teachers on the assumption that only teachers themselves can be responsible for their own self-renewal and school reform.

Milgram, Joel I., and Sciarra, Dorothy June. *Childhood Revisited.* New York: Macmillan Publishing Co., Inc., 1974.
A collection of autobiographical statements by such people as Joan Baez and Chet Huntley about their early childhood experiences and education. A good way for the preservice teacher to reflect upon values and issues in education.

For Further Study and Involvement

1. How important are the character and attitude of the classroom teacher to a child's healthy growth during his primary years?

2. Recall the elementary teachers who taught you. Decide which of their characteristics you would imitate and which you would avoid imitating as a teacher.

3. Some educators believe that teachers are born, not made. Interview public school teachers and college professors to determine their views about this idea.

4. Do you think teachers must be trained specifically in early childhood education in order to teach young children?

5. For what specific role or roles do you think early childhood teachers should be educated?

6. Reflecting back over your school years in the primary grades, what experiences do you consider most meaningful? Why? Would these experiences be valid learning experiences for children today?

7. As a class, brainstorm and compile a list of competencies for early childhood teachers that are: (1) generic, i.e., applicable to all teaching; (2) specific for early childhood education. Have professors of education and inservice teachers respond to these competencies.

8. Develop a list of questions you could ask a school principal when being interviewed for a job.

Index